EXPONEN[illegible] N

Exponential Emirates

Tom Hudson

ISBN: 978-1-80068-770-7

UAE NMC Approval Number: MC-02-01-3849940

DEDICATION

To my wife Jess, for introducing me to the UAE for the first time, to my daughters who were all born here, to my parents for putting up with me moving for "only 6 months", and my parents-in-law for taking me under their wing.

EXPONENTIAL EMIRATES - TOM HUDSON

CONTENTS

Economy

Trade

Tourism & Hospitality

Tech & Innovation

ACKNOWLEDGMENTS

I want to thank the 50 people that I have interviewed for this book. They are some of the busiest people in the UAE and they generously gave their time to share their experiences, insights and perspectives. My path has crossed with all of them in some shape or form over the last 15 years and they have made the UAE what it is today and will be in the future. Aside from the 50 interviewed, there are a few people behind the scenes who have also helped enormously, so a huge thank you to:

HH Sheikh Zayed bin Suroor al Nahyan, who was one of the first people I shared the idea with and who encouraged me along the way.

HE Saif Ghobash who kindly steered me in Abu Dhabi, and, along with Rebecca Sageman and Hkmat Basmok in the Abu Dhabi Media Office, generously supported the project.

Abdulla al Rumaithi in The Executive Office of HH Sheikh Mohammed bin Rashid al Maktoum, who likewise guided. When I said I wanted to write the book in three months, he said, "if you can do it anywhere, it is in the UAE".

Mohammad al Hashimy, a great friend and old colleague, who also gave his time and was a sounding board for some of the ideas that culminated in this book.

Finally, a thank you to all friends, colleagues and clients who have been on the journey with me in the UAE over the years. You have all been part of the exponential growth story of the Emirates, and I have loved every step of the journey.

BRIEF HISTORY OF THE UAE

"He who does not know his past cannot make the best of his present and future, for it is from the past that we learn"
HH Sheikh Zayed bin Sultan Al Nahyan

The land that is now the UAE, and the surrounding region, was historically simply referred to as the Arabian Peninsula. Archaeological excavations reveal that ancient civilisations flourished in the area from as early as 6000 BC. In this period, Bedouin communities lived simply in an extremely harsh environment.

Islam came to the region in AD 630. The geographical location between Europe and the Far East attracted merchants from India and China and was prized by Europeans, particularly the Portuguese, Dutch and British. The period was dominated by trade. While Europeans sought control of the coasts, inland, the Bedouin made the sandy deserts of Abu Dhabi and Dubai their home. In the 19th century, the British signed a series of agreements with individual Emirates that led to a truce, hence the area became known as "The Trucial States." The Emirates agreed to partner with the British, and the British promised to protect the coast from all aggression by sea and to provide assistance in the event of an attack by land.

The pearling industry thrived in the 19th and early 20th centuries, providing income and employment to the people of the Gulf. Many inhabitants were semi-nomadic, pearling in the summer and tending date gardens in the winter. However, the economic depression of the late 1920s and early 1930s, coupled with the Japanese invention of the cultured pearl, irreparably damaged the pearling industry.

In the early 1930s the first oil companies conducted geological surveys in the area. Thirty years later, in 1962, the first cargo of crude oil was exported from Abu Dhabi. With the economy steadily progressing, HH Sheikh Zayed bin Sultan Al Nahyan was chosen as the Ruler of Abu Dhabi in 1966. Under Sheikh Zayed, the steady oil revenues resulted in an infrastructure overhaul with the construction of schools, housing, hospitals and roads throughout Abu Dhabi. Soon after assuming power, Sheikh Zayed underscored the importance of a united country and remarked, "In harmony, in some sort of federation, we could follow the example of other developing countries."

One of Sheikh Zayed's early actions was to increase contributions to the Trucial States Development Fund, with Abu Dhabi becoming the Fund's largest donor. Meanwhile HH Sheikh Rashid bin Saeed Al Maktoum, de facto Ruler of Dubai since 1939, replaced pearling revenues by converting Dubai's creek into a thriving port. In 1969 as the Emirate of Dubai began exporting oil, Sheikh Rashid too focused his attention on development.

In early 1968, the British declared their intention to withdraw from the Gulf by the end of 1971, having decided to withdraw from "East of the Suez", and Sheikh Zayed acted rapidly to establish closer ties with the other Emirates. Sheikh Zayed, along with Sheikh Rashid met on 18 February 1968, at Al Samha in today's Abu Dhabi near the south-western boundary of Dubai. They agreed to merge their respective Emirates into a union that others would be invited to join. This agreement came to be known as the Union Accord and is considered the first step toward uniting the Trucial Coast as a whole. In order to strengthen the federation further, Sheikh Zayed and Sheikh Rashid invited the Rulers of the other five Emirates that formed the Trucial States to join the negotiations for the formation of a union. An agreement was reached between the rulers of six of the Emirates (Abu Dhabi, Dubai, Sharjah, Umm al-Quwain, Fujairah and Ajman), and the federation to be known as the United Arab Emirates was formally established on 2 December 1971. The seventh Emirate, Ras al-Khaimah, acceded to the new federation on 10 February 1972.

Since the formation of the Union, the seven Emirates have forged a distinct national identity. The UAE's political system has been designed to ensure the country's heritage is maintained, adapted and preserved by combining tradition with a modern administrative structure. This has been the foundation for the exponential growth in the UAE.

INTRODUCTION

exponential *adjective* (of a rate of increase) becoming faster and faster

The first 50 years of the United Arab Emirates have seen extraordinary growth in all sectors and by all metrics at a rate that seems to be getting faster and faster. 2nd December 2021 marked the Golden Jubilee for the UAE, and this book is published to celebrate the occasion and to look at the UAE's past, present and future.

Over the summer of 2021, I was asked to write an Op-Ed for the *Khaleej Times* in the lead up to the Golden Jubilee. The brief was to answer a simple question: what do the Emirates mean to me? I had recently read Salim Ismail's brilliant book "Exponential Organisations" which identified a new breed of company, with characteristics ideally suited to ride the wave of the 4th Industrial Revolution. These companies typically have a "Massive Transformational Purpose" and are structured in a way that can eliminate the incremental, linear way traditional companies get bigger, leveraging assets like community, big data and new technology into achieving growth ten times better than their peers. This "10X" mentality has been enshrined with the likes of Google's X-Lab which was set up with the goal of having a 10X impact on the world's most intractable problems, and not just a 10% improvement. At the same time, I had also read "Start-up Nation", the Story of Israel's economic miracle, which describes how, in the first 60 years of its existence, Israel had developed such an innovative economy. I believed that elements of both these books resonated with the UAE's story.

The thesis of my Op-Ed, therefore, became that the UAE is an "Exponential Country for the Exponential Age", with Expo 2020 Dubai showcasing this to the world, and that the Golden Jubilee marks the beginning of a Golden Era for the Emirates. This is not a "Start-up Nation" but a "Scale-up Nation" where people and companies can come and scale-up their ideas and enterprises by plugging into the magic mix that exists here, creating network effects and catapulting the country into the future.

After publishing the piece, and during the opening of Expo 2020 Dubai and the Golden Jubilee celebrations, the thesis triggered a range of fascinating discussions with a range of people. Those discussions became the basis of this book. I have always been inspired when listening to the individual stories of how this country became established and grew. I therefore decided to interview 50 of the people who have been part of, and continue to be part of, this country's extraordinary growth story. I wanted to interview Sheikhs, Sheikhas, Emiratis, Expatriates, male, female, young, old, government officials, business leaders, economists, futurists, founders, astronauts and everyone who represents the rich tapestry of this country.

However, before I launch into their stories, I believe it is first important to get a sense of the rate of growth in the UAE over the last 50 years. I have looked at 10 different areas, all of which are expanded upon later in the book.

Water

For millennia, fresh water was very scarce in the region. Sir Wilfred Thesiger, the great explorer, when he arrived in Abu Dhabi in 1946, 25 years before the Union, described local inhabitants either having to travel to find an oasis in the desert, or being forced to dig holes in the sand, where the groundwater would be brackish and barely safe to drink.

The Dubai Water Department ("DWD") was only established in 1959, and piped water only began to flow in Dubai in 1965 when a pipeline was completed, linking the well at Al Aweer to the city. Abu Dhabi only installed its first desalination plant in 1961. Fast forward 60 years and there is more than enough water to meet the growing needs of the country with, for example, the Emirates Water and Electricity Company having built the world's largest reverse osmosis seawater desalination plant in Taweelah which is almost double the size of any other.

Energy

In 1955, Mr. Nasser bin Abdullatif Alserkal, was the first citizen to build an electrical generator in his house in Dubai. He then assisted in the establishment of the Dubai Electricity Company ("DEC") in 1959. The DEC built its first two generating stations which depended on diesel to run and had a total capacity of 60 MW. If you look at where we are today, DWD and DEC have long since merged into the Dubai Electricity and Water Authority ("DEWA") which floated in 2022 with a valuation of more than $30bn. DEWA has built The Mohammed bin Rashid Al Maktoum Solar Park which is the largest single site solar park in the world. Abu Dhabi Power Corporation also announced a new 2 GW project in Al Dhafra, which is said to have secured the world's lowest tariff for a solar power plant.

The UAE is well-known for its proven oil and natural gas reserves (ranking 7th in the world). What is less well known is its move into Nuclear Power. The Barakah nuclear power plant opened in 2020 and is the first nuclear power station in the Arabian Peninsula. It will deliver up to 25% of the UAE's electricity with zero emissions. The combined solar and nuclear plans all feed into the "UAE Net Zero by 2050" strategy announced at COP 26.

Economy

In 1971, the population of the UAE was approximately 250,000, with around 85% Emirati. In 2021 it touched 10m. Of this, approximately 85% are now expatriates, representing more than 200 nationalities that call the UAE home. Taking Dubai, as an example, it has roughly doubled in size of population every decade over the last 50 years and is now 3.5m and by some predictions set to double again in the next 10-20 years.

In 1971, the GDP was less than $2bn. In 2021, it was more than $400bn, and more than each of Singapore, Hong Kong and Israel. HE Abdulla bin Touq Al Marri, Minister of the Economy for the UAE, and interviewed later in the book, believes that it can double again over the next decade.

Environment

The UAE went from having virtually no trees in 1971, to a

programme of "greening the desert" with the result that there are now more than 100m trees. The Emirates is already home to 60 million mangroves, but in 2021, the UAE committed to planting 100 million mangroves by 2030, which will increase the coverage to 483 square kilometres, with the mangrove forests able to capture about 115,000 tonnes of carbon dioxide a year. There are now more than 30,000 farms in the UAE - an exponential increase from around 4,000 farms in the early 1970s. The UAE has recently announced an "AgTech Park" in Abu Dhabi and "Food Tech Valley" in Dubai, and is making investments into vertical farming, cellular agriculture and aquaculture such that one day the UAE even may become a net-exporter of food.

After the Arabian Oryx was declared extinct in the wild in 1972, HH Sheikh Zayed launched a successful conservation programme that is now applauded globally. The UAE is now home to the largest population of Arabian Oryx in the world, and the species has gone from 'endangered' to 'vulnerable' being the first species in the world to have achieved this after having been declared extinct. The work has continued with, for example, the Mohammed bin Zayed Species Conservation Fund having made more than 2,300 grants to aid a diverse range of species across the world.

Transport

For centuries, trade and transport centered around Dubai's creek. Having been dredged in 1961 by HH Sheikh Rashid, it permitted 7-foot draft vessels to cross through at all times. However, this was too small for Dubai's ambitions. Now, the UAE boasts the world's largest man-made harbour at Jebel Ali which is DP World's flagship port, hosting the world's largest container ships. DP World itself manages more than 70 port terminals in over 40 countries across 6 continents.

Roads were only built in the 1960s. In early 1966, Abu Dhabi had about 30 vehicles. The first paved road, other than the city streets of Dubai, was between Dubai and Ras al-Khaimah which was built between 1966 and 1967. What is now Sheikh Zayed Road, then called the Dubai – Abu Dhabi Road, was built between 1970 and 1973. Although it was two simple lanes of tarmac, it nevertheless enabled travel time between Dubai and Abu Dhabi to be cut down from several days to about four hours. Now, of course, you can make the journey in about an hour and a half on a 14-lane highway. Soon that will become 50 minutes with Etihad Rail which, by 2030, will connect 11 cities in the UAE. The UAE is also at the cutting edge of experimenting with autonomous vehicles and electric vertical take-off and landing aircraft.

In 1962 the British Political Agent noted that "the Ruler is determined, against advice [from the British authorities] to press on with the construction of a jet airport." However, press on he did, completing construction of a sand compacted runway over the following years. Now, Dubai International Airport is the world's busiest airport for international flights, accommodating 80-90 million passengers annually. At the same time, Al Maktoum International Airport, when completed, will become the world's largest airport with an ultimate capacity exceeding 160 million passengers.

In 1971, the UAE had no airline of its own. Now, it has two of the world's best-known in Emirates and Etihad. Emirates went from two rented planes in 1985 to more than 250 planes; Etihad has grown to 100 planes in half the time. Emirates flies to 161 destinations in 85 countries, with Etihad flying to 120 destinations. Approximately one-third of the world's population is within a 4-hour flight of the UAE, and two-thirds within an 8-hour flight.

Towers

HH Sheikh Mohammed recalls, "In the 1960s, a dream started when my father and I ascended the world's tallest building - the Empire State in New York. We returned to Dubai fired with the dream that one day our city could be filled with such wonders as the world's tallest building." In 1979, Her Majesty the Queen inaugurated the Dubai World Trade Centre, a 38-storey, 184m high skyscraper in Dubai, which was the first skyscraper in the Middle East. In 2021, the UAE was ranked 3rd globally in terms of the number of skyscrapers with 300 towers reaching 150m or greater in height. Although this is behind the USA and China, the UAE has more skyscrapers than Manhattan. Of course, the UAE is also known for having the World's tallest building, the Burj Khalifa, standing at 830m high. As HH Sheikh Mohammed noted, "now our dream is alive with the Burj Khalifa and the Dubai Holding/Emaar tower. New heights are in our road ahead".

Tourism & Entertainment

In 1971, the Hilton Al Ain opened as the first international chain hotel in UAE. Now there are more than 1000 hotels including, of course, the world's first "7-star hotel" with the Burj al Arab Hotel. The UAE in a normal year welcomes more than 20m visitors, which is double its population. Dubai has recently been named the "World's Most Popular Destination" of 2022 in TripAdvisor's Travelers' Choice Awards.

On the formation of the Union, if you had wanted to go to a restaurant, you would probably have had to go to Beit al Wakeel, Dubai's oldest, which still serves great fresh fish down by the creek. However, you would not have had the choice of what is now 20,000 restaurants in the UAE, which include those run by 11 Michelin Starred Chefs, and indeed the Michelin Guide to Dubai is being published in 2022.

Fifty years ago, if you had wanted to go shopping, you would have to go to the old souqs down by Dubai creek. Now, you need to look no further than the Dubai Mall which has over 1,300 retail outlets. At over 12 million square feet (equivalent in size to more than 50 football fields), the Dubai Mall is the largest shopping mall in the world based on total area. It is the most-visited retail and entertainment destination in the world, welcoming more than 100 million visitors annually (Walt Disney World has approximately 20m visitors annually).

Now the UAE boasts the Louvre Abu Dhabi, Dubai Opera, "Ain Dubai" (the Dubai Wheel) and a host of theme parks: Bollywood Parks; Legoland Dubai, Ferrari World, IMG World of Adventure. Culturally, there are archeological sites, mountain walks, and everything in between for tourists. On 22 February 2022, the Museum of the Future opened, showcasing what the world might look like in 2071, when the UAE will celebrate its centenary.

Abu Dhabi has also built one of the most impressive F1 circuits in the world, hosting the season's climax which in 2021 broke records in terms of a global audience. The UAE also hosted the Special Olympics World Games in 2019, as well as the FIFA Club World Cup in 2009, 2010, 2017, 2018 and 2022, with Barcelona, Inter Milan, Real Madrid and Chelsea all crowned World Champions there.

As a young man HH Sheikh Mohammed bin Rashid al Maktoum, Ruler of Dubai rode bareback races with his friends on the sands of Jumeirah Beach. During his studies at Cambridge, Sheikh Mohammed attended his first horse race at Newmarket in May 1967. Ten years later, Sheikh Mohammed's own involvement with international racing began with the filly Hatta, who gave him his first success in Brighton, on 20

June 1977, and went on to win the Group Three Molecomb Stakes at Goodwood the following month. Sheikh Mohammed's passion for horses grew into a major investment in bloodstock and has resulted in the growth of the world's largest and most global racing team, Godolphin, as well as the successful stallion operation, Darley. In 2010, Meydan Racecourse opened in Dubai, with the largest grandstand in the world, stretching to 1.6kms and hosting the Dubai World Cup, which is the world's richest race day. HH Sheikh Mohammed's daughter, HH Sheikha Maitha and her UAE Polo Team also won the Cartier Queen's Cup 2021, and the UAE now boasts some of the best polo fields and developments in the world.

Technology

In 1971, if you wanted to make a telephone call, there was a phone directory that listed all the 30,000 phone numbers in the UAE, including those of the Rulers' palaces. Etisalat, one of the national Telcos was established in 1976. Now, for example, Etisalat has 150m subscribers in 15 different countries, and in 2019, the UAE achieved first place amongst the Arab countries and fourth position globally in launching and deploying 5G networks.

In 1969, the USA had put a man on the moon. On 25 September 2019, Hazza Al Mansoori became the first Emirati astronaut to travel to space and in February 2021 the UAE's "Hope" probe orbited Mars. The UAE joined an elite club of countries that have had Mars Missions, alongside the USA, Russia, India, China and Japan. However, not stopping there, the government has also established a programme with the aim of building a habitable settlement on Mars by 2117.

HH Sheikh Mohammed summed up the technological advancement well when he said in 2019: "In 1999, many people questioned our idea to establish Dubai Internet City in the desert. Two years ago, Amazon acquired the multi-billion dirham Souq.com and [in 2019] Uber acquired Careem for Dh11 billion. These giant companies have flourished from the "desert" of Dubai." More recently, three more unicorns have flourished: Swvl, Kitopi and EMPG. The UAE aims to become home to 20 unicorns by 2031 as part of a programme it launched in October 2021 to attract and expand small- and medium-sized enterprises.

On 12th December 2021, Dubai became the "World's First

Paperless Government" with all entities moving to digital. The UAE also appointed the world's first Minister of Artificial Intelligence, who is interviewed later in the book. He aims to double the size of the digital economy in the next 10 years.

Healthcare and Education

In 1971, there were only 7 hospitals across the whole UAE, all having been built in the previous decade. Now there are more than 100 and more than 2.5 physicians per 100 people, one of the best ratios in the world. In July 2021, the UAE became the world's most vaccinated country according to the Bloomberg Vaccine Tracker.

In 1971, there were just a handful of schools across the UAE, now there are more than 1000. The International Schools Market in the Mena Region 2021 Report, produced by ISC Research, found that the UAE has 725 international schools with a total of 696,600 pupils. In terms of pupil enrolment at international schools, China is in second place behind the UAE, with 419,000 children, while India is in third place, with 316,000 pupils. In 1975, the adult literacy rate of the UAE was 53.5 % but now stands at more than 97.6%.

International Relations

In February 2019, the Pope visited the UAE for the first time, which was also the first by a leader of the Roman Catholic Church to the Arabian Peninsula. He signed a document on "Human Fraternity" with Grand Imam Ahmed Al-Tayeb. Out of that visit sprung the vision for "The Abrahamic Family House" which will comprise a mosque, church, synagogue, and educational center to be built on Saadiyat Island in Abu Dhabi. Through its design, it captures the values shared between Judaism, Christianity, and Islam – the "Abrahamic" faiths, and a symbol of the ongoing commitment to tolerance in the UAE, and relations between faiths. Following that declaration, on 13th August 2020, the UAE signed the "Abraham Accords Peace Agreement" a "Treaty of Peace, Diplomatic Relations and Full Normalization Between the United Arab Emirates and the State of Israel". On signing, HH Sheikh Abdullah bin Zayed, the UAE Minister for Foreign Affairs and International Co-operation said, "I stand here today to extend a hand of peace and receive a hand of peace… Today, we are already witnessing a change in the heart of the Middle East, a change that will send hope around the world." Many Israelis now call the UAE home, with many Israeli businesses setting up here, with a reported $1bn boost to the economy in the last 18 months.

In June 2021, the UAE was elected to the United Nations Security Council for the 2022-2023 term, chairing it in 2022. The UAE can rightly claim to have a seat at the table and have an impact on global affairs.

Since its establishment in 1971, the Abu Dhabi Fund for Development has been helping to strengthen the economies of developing countries, as well as supporting the national economy and enhancing its global competitiveness. The Mohammed bin Rashid Global Initiatives was established in 2015, combining under its umbrella over 30 humanitarian and developmental initiatives and entities and in 2020, for example, spent $325m in more than 80 different countries. In 2018, the UAE was named the world's largest donor of development assistance in proportion to its gross national income for the fifth year running, according to the Development Assistance Committee of the Organisation of Economic Cooperation and Development. In 2022, HH Sheikh Mohammed bin Rashid announced the launch of the "One Billion Meals" campaign to secure food aid for vulnerable communities in 50 countries, the campaign was 10 times bigger than the UAE's previous "100 Million Meals" launched in 2021.

These are all remarkable changes for any country to achieve. However, the aim of the book is also to explore some of the cultural elements that have perhaps stayed the same and indeed underpinned the change. Sir Wilfred Thesiger said of the people he met when he first came to the region, "some people maintain that they will be better off when they have exchanged the hardship and poverty of the desert for the security of a materialistic world. This I do not believe. I shall always remember how often I was humbled by those… who possessed, in so much greater measure than I, generosity and courage, endurance, patience and lighthearted gallantry. Among no other people have I ever felt the same sense of personal inferiority."

As Sheikh Zayed said, "No matter how many buildings, foundations, schools and hospitals we build, or how many bridges we raise, all these are material entities. The real spirit behind the progress is the human spirit…. thanks to God, our nation has a flourishing civilization, deep-rooted in this land for many centuries." On the 31st UAE National Day, HH Sheikh Zayed said "What has come about did not happen all of a sudden, and nor did it just take place over the course of the last three or four decades. It is the result of the cultural and social heritage that we inherited from our fathers and our forefathers, who faced difficulties that are today beyond our capacity to imagine."

It is against this background of exponential change and cultural heritage that I conducted the interviews. Given the range of people interviewed, I also wanted to provide a simple framework for each to tell their stories and give their views, so I decided to centre the interviews around the following 10 themes and questions:

1. **Earliest Memories**: What are your earliest memories of the UAE?

2. **Journey**: Please tell us about your professional journey and the part you have played in the UAE's growth?

3. **HH Sheikh Zayed**: What did HH Sheikh Zayed and his legacy mean to you and the nation?

4. **Exponential Growth**: What for you signifies the UAE's extraordinary growth story?

5. **Secret of Success**: What is the secret to the UAE's success?

6. **Challenges**: What are the biggest challenges that you or the UAE have overcome?

7. **Opportunities**: What business opportunities excite you?

8. **Lessons**: What lessons are there for other countries?

9. **Expo**: What opportunities has Expo provided?

10. **Future**: What are your predictions for the UAE for the next 50 years? What is your vision for the UAE in 2071?

For ease, I have not repeated each question 50 times, but have arranged the answers around the various sub-headings. All interviews were conducted between 1 October 2021 and 31 March 2022, over the 6 months of Expo, and serve a snapshot of the country as it celebrates its Golden Jubilee year, but I hope will remain relevant for many years to come.

1. INTERPRETING THE VISION

HE Zaki Nusseibeh, Cultural Advisor to HH the President of the UAE

"The message of the UAE is that the impossible is possible, that being small is no obstacle to great impact, and that whatever the problem, whatever the menace to mankind, it is possible to do something about it"

HE Zaki Nusseibeh became the translator and interpreter for HH Sheikh Zayed bin Sultan Al Nahyan, Founding Father of the UAE, three years before the federation was established in 1971. As a result, he had a ringside view of the formation and growth of the UAE, and became part of that growth himself, leading on many of the cultural initiatives that the young nation took.

For this interview, I traveled to Al Ain where he kindly hosted me in his house. His home is an Aladdin's cave of art, books and photos. The photos in particular tell the story of the UAE, from the picture of HH Sheikh Zayed taken by Sir Wilfred Thesiger in 1947, all the way through to portraits with the heads of state who ultimately visited the UAE. In every photo, often in-between HH Sheikh Zayed and the dignitary is HE Zaki, translating and, perhaps more importantly, witnessing the incredible growth of the UAE and interpreting the vision of HH Sheikh Zayed to the rest of the world.

Earliest Memories

I first came to Abu Dhabi as a tourist in the winter of 1964, a time of great excitement about new opportunities following the discovery of oil. I arrived from my sister's house in Kuwait where I had been passing my UK school's winter holidays. She had suggested I go to see where my family had just started a contracting company and she persuaded me that the sea was good for swimming.

I flew into Dubai, and we took a Jeep. We passed the Clock Tower and Jebel Ali, and then all roads and tracks ended. We crossed the sabkha and sands to arrive at a makeshift crossing to the island of Abu Dhabi that was assembled in a combination of tarmac, gravel, stone, and rock. Arriving or departing vehicles had to take turns on its single track.

It turned out there was very little to see except for the 18th Century Qasr Al Hosn that imposed itself over the island. The seat of the Al Nahyan family, it was still functioning as the center of government and the Diwan. It had an open view of the sea because there was nothing around it except a couple of stone buildings, a well, and a guest house. Apart from that, there was the British Agency in a white stone building and one large mosque. Yet my sister was right, there was an abundance of sandy beaches, and I could swim anywhere I wanted.

Today's Abu Dhabi provides contrast and continuity with these first memories. The wider urban environment has expanded in all directions. Yet a few of the 1960s and 70s developments survive, to demonstrate the unique architectural imprint of Sheikh Zayed, who took an immense personal interest in the city's design and planning. These older buildings have many arches and large windows that open onto courtyards, gardens, large outside enclosures, and have views of the sea. The sea itself remains a prominent feature of the experience of Abu Dhabi and we are fortunate today that the reclaimed and newly opened islands of Abu Dhabi preserve and extend our access to the water.

The Qasr Al Hosn is now an iconic cultural site, restored in full to its original stature. The preservation of historic buildings was one of Sheikh Zayed's priorities. Indeed, in recalling my first crossing to the island in 1964, my thoughts also turn to the 1969 restoration of the Maqta Tower that had been built at the same time as the Hosn, as a sentinel guarding the entrance to the island from the mainland.

Journey

My personal and professional journey in the history of the UAE has a single point of origin - a chance meeting with Sheikh Zayed in the

Jordanian Embassy in London in the summer of 1966. I was there as a Cambridge student with my father, who was then Jordanian Ambassador to the UK. At this point I had no idea though that my life and career would become closely interwoven with that of the Emirates. However, the six-day war of 1967 changed my life course forever.

I left for Abu Dhabi to work with the family contracting company I visited in 1964. However, I did not enjoy this field and I soon became a stringer to several Arab and Western newspapers and news agencies. I translated for Sheikh Zayed for a British documentary in 1968, and it was after this that I was recruited as his translator. I worked out of the nascent Government media office, and this linked me to the emerging communications and information industries and the development of their national infrastructure.

This began a lifelong career of public service, during which time I worked on national cultural and educational strategies and infrastructure, including cultural and public diplomacy, schools, the UAE University, the Sorbonne, museums, and galleries.

So I am proud to have played a small part in the immense project of nation building, an incredible journey it was my fortune to witness at close hand, at the side of our inspirational founding father.

HH Sheikh Zayed

As Sheikh Zayed's personal translator and advisor, and through my role in the press and media, I served as my master's voice, transmitting his message to the world. It was through this relationship that my career took shape.

Sheikh Zayed's humanitarian values underpinned his vision for the country. The UAE was purposed to serve the wellbeing of its people, and to provide stability, tolerance, and peace in the region. This was the message that it was my role to convey. He had long commanded respect as a loyal, determined, and indomitable tribal leader and as President he developed an international reputation as a visionary national leader, able to motivate the self-belief and ambition of others to work for the impossible and achieve it. Every moment with him that I recall is imbued with this strength of character, spirit, and values.

We are privileged that his successors, our present wise leadership, continue Sheikh Zayed's legacy. They extend the horizons of the nation's development and purpose. The UAE's future role is to serve global wellbeing and sustainability. Our endeavours in advancing space science, renewable energies, artificial intelligence, and creating a knowledge-based society represent Sheikh Zayed's ethics - this sense of responsibility for mankind, both at home and in all parts of the world.

Exponential Growth

To find a significant story to tell we must think back to the 1960s. Then, the whole idea of creating a stable and prosperous society here was thought fanciful. The region was turbulent and ridden with conflict. The new Federal Union lacked every infrastructure necessary for statehood. And yet the UAE has succeeded and continues to do so even as regional turmoil continues and other states fail, and global economic environments are unstable and challenging.

So the message of the UAE is that the impossible is possible, that being small is no obstacle to great impact, and that whatever the problem, whatever the menace to mankind, it is possible to do something about it. We are a 'can-do' nation.

As an example, from my field, think back to the 1960s when there were few elementary schools. And now we are a major education hub, and a world center for the cultural and creative industries. The UAE is enriched with a quality of life that attracts tourists and professionals from all around the world.

Secret of Success

There are a few threads that intertwine to suggest that the essence of our success lies in people.

First, we rely on good governance. Just like enterprises, countries collapse without good governance. We require a leadership with both vision and the sense of responsibility to society, the region, mankind, and the world. It is not good enough just to have vast ambitions; it is essential that leaders have humanitarian values and virtuous ethics.

Second, the UAE is fortunate always to have been an open, tolerant society that has had global horizons throughout history. Over 5000 years ago the people of the region were trading with the Indus and Mesopotamian civilizations. A nation's success is not achieved unilaterally, resilience and growth depend on playing an active, positive role in a global network.

Third, we are fortunate that Sheikh Zayed imparted a moral and ethical framework that guides all our actions today. Education – the development of human potential – is a large part of this. My message for young people is that they must aim to learn throughout their life. Finishing school or completing a degree are not endpoints, they are the starting points for future achievements. Sheikh Zayed taught us that each day is an opportunity to learn something new to help meet a new challenge. It is my personal conviction that if we want to grow in wisdom and understanding we must continuously engage with diverse peoples and their cultures, languages, arts, and sciences.

Challenges

In the years leading up to the Union and thereafter the UAE has been a rapidly developing society. In such a fast-moving environment it was necessary to learn, develop, and align myself rapidly. The UAE has had to develop agility, resilience and flexibility to respond to challenges that are ever-present and often unexpected. Even today the UAE sits within a very troubled region, where conflict is rife. The world is disordered, powers are transitioning, and societies are afflicted by poverty in many forms – lack of education, health, food, employment, environmental security and peace. In my view the major challenge faced by the UAE is what lies ahead. But this is what the leadership is readying itself for, as expressed in the ten principles developed to guide us in the next fifty years.

Opportunities

Within my field of educational and cultural development, there are rich and open-ended opportunities for innovation. We need diverse, creative minds to work together to invent educational methodologies and tools that will prepare us for lifelong learning and the challenges of tomorrow. We need to increase our capacity for sustainable development – the combined well-being of economy, society, and environment. We need creative communities, leaders, and entrepreneurs who are all dedicated to building peace and social harmony.

We need to continue with the process of institutionalization – building physical, social, governance, and economic infrastructure. Just as interdisciplinarity lies at the heart of the Fourth Industrial Revolution, networking is essential for institutional development. I am sure that digitalization and communications technology will enable this. There is an opportunity there. But we must also find ways to stabilize our institutions; during development institutions must develop a root system, an institutional memory.

Lessons

Sustainable, stable, and meaningful economic, social, and political development is hard work. The UAE is a lesson in the essentials of leadership vision, leadership capacity to motivate and enable people and to develop a collective consciousness that is committed to making effort, continuous progress, and serving the good of others.

Expo

The message of the Expo is that by connecting minds we can create a future that is happier for mankind. It tells us that we can do something about the challenges we face, but that we must do it together.

My hope is that first time visitors to the UAE reflect on the country's relative youth. Yet I would like them to think not so much about the magnitude of the UAE's achievements in fifty years and more about the manner of these accomplishments – the humanitarian values that have led us to this point. I hope that our guests experience those values, as expressed in a multicultural, tolerant, welcoming, and safe society.

Future

Guided by the ten principles for future development, I am optimistic that we will achieve the goals of becoming world leaders in the fields of education, culture, space, and artificial intelligence whilst making a positive contribution to the well-being of mankind, and not only our own nation.

2. A CULTURE OF CREATIVITY

HH Sheikha Latifa bint Mohammed bin Rashid al Maktoum, Chairperson of the Dubai Culture and Arts Authority

"To build the UAE out of nothing is just a huge symbol of hope that anything is possible."

HH Sheikha Latifa bint Mohammed bin Rashid al Maktoum is daughter of HH Sheikh Mohammed bin Rashid Al Maktoum, Vice President and Prime Minister of the UAE and Ruler of Dubai. Her Highness, through hard work and dedication, has been shaping Dubai's creative ecosystem, which has also spread throughout the UAE and the wider region. When we meet, she is just 48 hours from giving birth to her third child, when many people would have long since left work, but she is still in her office, meeting people at Expo and packing in as much as she can to drive forward with her mission. Her passion is contagious, and her insights into the culture that underpins the nation are unparalleled.

Earliest Memories

One of the first things I remember growing up in my family were stories about my grandmother Sheikha Latifa bint Hamdan Al Nahyan, who was the daughter of Sheikh Hamdan bin Zayed Al Nahyan, the former Ruler of Abu Dhabi. I was born a month after she passed, but I was aware of the role she had and the guidance and support she gave my grandfather, HH Sheikh Rashid bin Saeed al Maktoum, former Ruler of Dubai. She was also symbolic of the strong bond between Dubai and Abu Dhabi, even before the Union. My grandparents were committed that every Emirate was successful. I grew up in the Palace with our wider family, so I witnessed firsthand my grandfather in action. I remember waking up at dawn before school, and already seeing him getting into his car and doing the rounds. What was fascinating is that he would not just concentrate on Dubai, he would go to all the other Emirates too. He built a lot of villages around the UAE and would often visit them and closely monitor their progress. I'd also see my dad, at that time the youngest Minister of Defence in the world along with my grandfather both dedicating their lives to the UAE. They did it through their majlises that anyone could walk into, and still can, and listen to their concerns and ideas. The whole community celebrated and mourned together.

For me, growing up the bar was very high, but it was a very natural transition for me to want to work in the public sector. Living in service for the country and our people was just our everyday life. We didn't know any different. Growing up I was always surrounded by really strong women in my family and I remember how much they were respected and how much they contributed towards the country and the city. My aunt and older sister also brought me closer to the arts. One of my first memories of holding a paintbrush was sitting at my aunt's easel. I was around five years old, and whenever I sketched something, I would run to my dad to show him my work, he always encouraged me – even though I'm sure at that young age my drawings weren't any good at all!

Life was slower and simpler then, but I remember this feeling of hope and opportunity. There was this energy, an excitement about what Dubai could become. We could feel the potential. Everything my dad was launching and doing was exciting and full of purpose. He didn't wait for anyone to give him new responsibilities, he actually grabbed opportunities. This rippled throughout the family and is a notion that inspires me in everything I do today. Everything we do now is for Dubai and its success will contribute to the UAE's success. We don't mind who takes credit.

One of my other earliest memories is at my dad's stable in Zabeel. Now it looks totally different, but then it was surrounded by desert dunes. I am lucky that I grew up in a family with a lot of interests and many passions – the love of sports and animals. I still go there now, it's my childhood 'happy place', and you see Dubai has grown around it and it's surrounded by the most amazing skyline. The energy of riding there is like the energy of Dubai.

Journey

I may have taken it for granted back then, but I'm so grateful that I went to school with kids from so many different countries and cultures. The minority at the school I went to was the Emiratis, but it just felt normal. All my classmates spoke different languages and celebrated different things. I thought that this was normal around the world, for this mix of cultures to coexist and thrive together, but I realise it's not and this is what is so special about living in Dubai. You appreciate it more when you travel and you see that this diversity is not universal. I was in the Christmas choir and we had Santa coming to the school – admittedly via a helicopter that my family had arranged! My first school was actually run by nuns. We have an assimilation of cultures within the city where everyone celebrates Christmas, Divali and Eid, all while retaining their own culture and religious values and celebrating who they are and where they come from.

I went to Zayed University, and upon graduation, my dad asked me what I wanted to do, and I said I wanted to work. He asked me "where?" and I said that actually they had a marketing job open at the university and I signed a contract and started working there. He thought for a bit and said "aren't you going to learn more with us at Dubai Holding"? I said "yes!" I still had to go for an interview with HE Mohammed al Gergawi and I started at the bottom with an internship there and rotated around each of the companies for 7 months. I was front of house and back of house with Jumeirah in the hotels which was fascinating. However, after the internship I heard about the new Dubai Culture and Arts Authority and I really wanted to work there as I had always loved creativity and art ever since I could remember.

When I came on board I was on the lowest grade of the government's scale, but the authority was essentially a "start-up" so everyone did everything. There was no marketing department, and as I had a marketing degree, I helped set that up. I then stepped back and worked in a supervisory role so I could give someone else the opportunity to have a governmental job. To me this wasn't a job, it was my mission and purpose. I was appointed vice chairman in 2014 and in 2019 my father appointed me Chairperson. I actually found out about my promotion via Twitter when my dad tweeted it! He likes surprising people. I know I wasn't given the position until he was sure I could handle it. I had his support from day one. He has never micromanaged, he just let me learn and evolve myself. I am given complete autonomy to prioritise the direction we will take. On the other hand, I get calls from my brothers, Sheikh Hamdan bin Mohammed bin Rashid Al Maktoum, Crown Prince of Dubai and Chairman of the Executive Council, and Sheikh Maktoum bin Mohammed bin Rashid Al Maktoum, Deputy Ruler of Dubai and Deputy Prime Minister and Minister of Finance saying "Do you need anything? How can we support you"? Our leadership are extremely diligent and vigilant when it comes to Dubai's progress in every industry, whenever I'm working on a new strategy or direction for the creative industry I never have to chase them for approvals, instead I'm held accountable for delivering and we all work at a fast pace. At the same time all the other government entities lean in and want to support. This is how the government of Dubai works. It is an organic way of operating, with just a guiding light of service to the people.

I feel lucky and humbled to be part of the creative economy and industry and working with a leadership that recognizes the importance of these sectors on the success of a country, and indeed not just regionally but internationally. We're now focusing really heavily on highlighting the contribution of the creative economy to the progress and economic standing of the nation. My dad launched the Dubai Creative Economy Strategy which aims to transform the emirate of Dubai into an international destination for creativity and the capital of the creative economy by 2025. We aim to double the contribution of the creative industries to the GDP of Dubai from 2.6 percent in 2020 to 5 percent by 2025 and double the number of Dubai-based creative companies from 8,300 in 2020 to 15,000 by 2025, and more than double the number of creators based in the Emirate, from 70,000 in 2020 to 140,000 by 2025. This doubling is itself a sign of our exponential mindset!

Over the years, our leadership has strategically focused on developing different industries at different times, as a result we now have a very strong digital and physical infrastructure. Dubai is ready to be a global creative city. We're working on launching different creative zones. We don't want to be overly prescriptive, culture needs to grow organically, but we want to make it easier for people and companies to operate within the industry. Our job is to look at the legislation, rules and regulations and be the voice of the industry on a governmental level, help creatives succeed and really support on laying down the foundation of the industry. We want creatives and creative entities to not only exist, but to thrive and be sustainable.

What's different here is that we can easily point out issues in the current legislation within the creative industry. We are lucky to have such a flexible government that listens and takes swift measures to change what isn't working. It now takes 7 minutes online to get a creative license in Dubai. My dad says that laws are in place to make people's life easier, not to create hurdles.

To me, the reason this is happening is that we have a top-down vision. It's very simple: the reason we come to work every day is for the happiness of the people of Dubai. I learned this from my dad. Once you understand this concept, it helps decision-making at all levels. It gives you a sense of urgency. Everything needs to happen now. The energy comes from our leadership. We want our people to be happy now. Why wait? We are just getting started.

HH Sheikh Zayed

I've heard so much about Sheikh Zayed through my dad. He stands for unity and bringing people together for a greater good. He and Sheikh Rashid for me epitomize selfless dedication to the people and to the country. My dad once said that if it wasn't for the relationship between them both, he's not sure the union would have happened. My dad was actually at the meeting where it was all decided on 18 February 1968 when the two rulers met in a simple Bedouin tent between Dubai and Abu Dhabi on top of a dune. As the youngest member of the party, he was serving them coffee, and he heard part of the conversation. Sheikh Zayed said "So Rashid, what do you think? Shall we create a union?" Sheikh Rashid replied: "Give me your hand Zayed, let us shake upon the agreement. With the blessing of God, you will be President." Sheikh Zayed said "with the blessings of God we have laid the foundation stone." It happened in a very simple place in a simple way, but it was such a noble pursuit. Back then, they had nothing. To build the UAE out of nothing is just a huge symbol of hope that anything is possible.

The Founding Fathers came from nothing and they invested everything they had in the country, the infrastructure and people. Everything they received was re-invested. Sheikh Zayed believed that the real treasure of the country is the people who will build the country long after we're gone, which is why there's a real focus on people and the youth.

Exponential Growth

To think that 50 years after unification, we have sent a probe to Mars and are now exploring colonizing Mars is extraordinary. In the

UAE things actually happen. Dreamers who Do. We actually follow through. Twenty years ago my dad started talking about e-government, and "mobile government" and now we are the first paperless government in the world. That's exponential change in front of our eyes.

Secret of Success

There is a spirit that has cascaded down from our grandfather, to our father and our leadership and to, hopefully, every single person in Dubai, where there is selflessness in success, where it truly doesn't matter who takes credit, but what is important is just that it's done for Dubai and the UAE. This is the spirit we all carry within us. Whatever we do, we do for the country and the future, for our children and the youth. It is a selfless way to work but it also gives you so much purpose, drive and energy.

You also just get things done. You just do it. Recently I heard a story from one of my colleagues in the government of Dubai about how my dad set out to build the Endurance Village in Dubai, he just got in his car, drove out in the middle of the desert and marked out a route. This is how organically things happen in Dubai and the UAE. I remember when I first became Chairman I said to my dad that I wanted my team to feel free to take risks and make mistakes, so that they are able to innovate. In order to pioneer, teams must be able to take on a certain amount of risk. He totally supported that and I believe having the freedom to take risks is part of the success of Dubai and the UAE.

The Arabian culture of a majlis evidences the collaboration and discussion that takes place in government. Our leadership is used to consulting with and listening to people with expertise, so decision making is not really centralized. This is a very successful model. The majlis model provides a framework for feedback from the community. There is a time when a leader takes onboard everyone's opinions, but there are also times when you have to make the decision yourself.

What has also struck me about the assimilation of cultures that you find in the UAE is that normally when one moves to a country, one has to speak the national language to get by, but even from the early days, the Emiratis were very quick to learn English, Urdu, Farsi and speak the languages of our guests. It was normal to speak two to three different languages. I realized that this was a symbol of our people's acceptance and tolerance. They went out of their way to communicate and to make guests feel welcome and at home. When people choose to come and live here, they can retain their culture, their language and their religion. They are accepted and celebrated for it.

Our success doesn't happen by accident, it happens with sheer determination and inner belief in yourself and your people. We have a leadership that believes in the potential of our country and invested in industries systematically to be in the position we are in today and the country is ready to thrive in so many directions. This passion and dedication comes from the top down. I see my dad and my brothers work so hard and you can't help but be inspired.

Challenges

We're in a very turbulent region. However, we have created a safe-haven. This should not be underestimated and is a constant challenge. For me personally, I need to understand what is going on in the cultural and creative world and ensure that I do the best for Dubai and its creatives. Data was a challenge when we first started putting together our new direction for the authority and the industry, and without that it's hard to make strategic decisions.

Another challenge is actually the perceptions of some internationally as to how they think women from the region are treated. We are not weak, but they perceive us to be. I grew up in a family of very powerful women. They were and still are well respected and revered by the men in my family and by all of Dubai. They served their country with passion and pride and it was inspiring to see them pursue their different passions. To me my dad was always very understanding, compassionate and empowering. Growing up, I heard so much about my grandmother, and her deep knowledge of traditional medicine. People came to her for treatment and advice: she ruled alongside my grandfather. Growing up in this environment and then hearing from some people about how "oppressed" they think we are sounds extremely ignorant to me, all it takes is a little bit of research and an unbiased outlook to dispel those perceptions. Growing up I never felt there was any difference between me and my brothers. What they learned to do, we learned to do. They went riding, we went riding; they did martial arts, we did martial arts. My sister, HH Sheikha Maitha bint Mohammed represented the UAE in the Olympics in 2008, where she competed in martial arts. I don't remember ever not being allowed to do something because I was a girl. My dad backed me 100% when I decided I wanted to work in the public sector. My experience is that our men respect our women and they don't feel intimidated by them. When our men used to go away for months on end on pearl diving trips, it was the women who took care of everything. You would see women selling in markets, raising their children, taking care of their families and running businesses here, it's in our culture.

Opportunities

In the creative and cultural industry, we are laying the foundations for a sustainable ecosystem, so that the opportunities for our creatives and those who chose to call Dubai home are endless. This is the same across many industries here. I am thankful that when my children grow up they will have limitless opportunities in the UAE. One example of this is the way Dubai is working towards new industries, for example the Dubai World Trade Centre becoming a hub for cryptocurrencies, is extraordinary.

Lessons

For me this is two-fold. First, as a country, we're not afraid to take risks, fail, and correct course. We know we're not perfect in everything, but we strive every day to get better and do better. Second, a collaborative spirit means that what everyone does is for the success of the country and the people, not just the success of individuals or individual entities. It enables everyone to work towards one vision, with one direction and one strategy. This way success is attained quicker, and the rewards are more gratifying.

Expo

It gives me so much pride to know that one of the world's biggest events is happening here in Dubai. The opportunities it presents are endless too. It's the biggest cultural gathering in the world, and countries get the chance to showcase the best of what they have achieved and what they want to achieve. It is an honour for us to provide this platform and to be the first Arab country to do so. If you go to Expo, you can visit 192 countries in one location. It's hard to wrap your mind around. It's wonderful connecting to each culture and collaborating. We have to grasp this opportunity and build on it.

Future

I believe the UAE will be a place that provides endless opportunities for its people, a place where our people, and everyone who calls the UAE home thrives. I believe there's one thing that sets this country apart, and it's the fact that the leadership is genuinely happy to see people succeed, and that they do everything they can to help them succeed. We don't believe that resource or success is finite. We believe that success is contagious and there is enough success to go around and for the whole world to share.

3. COEXISTENCE

HE Sheikha Lubna al Qasimi

"When I think of our country's growth, I think of the amazing partnership of Emiratis and Expats. We built the UAE together. This coexistence, at heart, is the soul of the UAE"

In November 2004, HE Sheikha Lubna became the first woman to hold a ministerial post in the UAE, when she was appointed to manage the UAE's newly merged economy and planning portfolio as Minister for Economy. HE Sheikha Lubna subsequently became Minister of Tolerance, and was named the most powerful Arab Woman on the Forbes Power List in 2017. Added to this over the years have been many accolades, including becoming Honorary Dame Commander of The Most Excellent Order of the British Empire.

Having met with the Pope and Her Majesty the Queen, Sheikha Lubna has represented the UAE at the highest levels, but equally she has been an ambassador for everything the UAE stands for with everyone she meets. I first met her a decade ago, and I was struck then by just how down to earth she was, and that she took time to speak with everyone. As we meet to conduct this interview in one of her favourite cafes in Abu Dhabi, a Californian-style boho chic, beach-side restaurant, again I can see that many of the staff have warmed to her as just a regular customer, without knowing her extraordinary pathfinding, pioneering story.

Earliest Memories

I'm 63 years old. Growing up in Sharjah in the 1960s, even as a member of the Ruling Family, we had a modest home. My mum did everything from cooking to sewing our clothes. It was a very simple life. Life was based around our immediate neighbourhood and the local community. I remember traveling to the other Emirates would take forever, even though we were one of the first families to have a car. For us, there was only one secondary school in Sharjah for girls. My breakthrough was upon finishing high school in 1975 and my first request was to go to the UK to study. It was a challenge for my parents as they were very protective of me as a girl. However, my brother said "I'll take her" and so I went to study for my A Levels, and then I followed my brothers to California. My parents insisted I lived with families, from their eyes, for protection, but for me it offered much more, as living with these families, I really understood the culture. I learned much more from the people themselves than from the establishments I studied. This really helped me when I became a Minister. I encourage our students to travel and live with other nationalities.

Despite the isolation of people living a simplistic life up until the 1960's, it's amazing how quickly and foretelling it was that we traveled when we could, after unification, and welcomed so many nationalities here. In Sharjah, there was the only Hospital which was staffed by midwives who were nuns – Christian missionaries. It was where my mum gave birth to my youngest sister and I remember visiting and the nuns spoke Arabic and would read the bible, and I would recognise a lot of the stories from the Qu'ran. Even I heard the story of Jesus, Issa bin Miriam, and this intrigued me. They had tolerance and co-existence even then, pre-unification. When you look at the core and soul of the UAE this is at its heart. It's not something that the UAE just woke up one day and said we should embrace others, it is ingrained in our culture.

Journey

I graduated in 1981 and I'm a computer engineer by training. When I came back, there weren't many computer jobs, but I landed a role as a programmer for the Indian software company Datamation. I then acted as the Dubai branch manager for the General Information Authority, the organization responsible for automating the federal government of the United Arab Emirates. After this posting, I took up the position of senior manager of the Information Systems Department at the Dubai Ports Authority (DPA) which was a game-changer. The DPA was business orientated. Focused on performance. The learning and understanding at that time, integrating technology into the process was tremendously exciting. There was a direct correlation between tech and performance and profitability. It wasn't your normal government job. Some of the applications we developed were considered the first worldwide. The work was creative and original.

My work there actually got me recognized by HH Sheikh Mohammed, Ruler of Dubai when I won the "Distinguished Government Employee Award" in 1999, the first woman to receive it. He then appointed me as the head of www.Tejari.com, the online marketplace upon its launch in 2000. However it was not easy: within four months, the dot.com bubble burst. However, I actually used this to our advantage and I got on the plane and flew to see Larry Ellison's team at Oracle and used the market disruption to negotiate with them to prioritise the Arabic language on their platform.

In 2001 I was also appointed to the Dubai e-government executive team responsible for instituting e-government initiatives throughout the public sector and if you think about it, "e-government" as a concept was way ahead of its time – the fact we would have a paperless platform as a Government.

In 2004 I was then asked to join the UAE Government as the first female Minister. I had anxieties about being the first woman, however I thought the government put me here in this post, and I know they don't want me to fail, and that gave me peace, focus and energy. Now there are 9 female Ministers, I felt I did my job. My training as a software engineer was actually very fitting to the switch to Politician as my training was about efficiencies and process which I also applied to the Ministerial brief.

HH Sheikh Zayed

I sadly never met HH Sheikh Zayed in person. We were due to meet upon my Ministerial appointment, but he sadly passed away a couple of days later – but I will always be the only female Minister who ever served under him. I have a picture of him in my office though taken by Sir Wilfred Thesiger which is for me the traditional Bedouin image of him with a Falcon on his hand. To me he's a true Bedouin with solid character, thriving the way that he did on the principles that the Bedouin had. Things haven't changed. We are Bedouins. I'm reminded of his quote: "He who does not know his past cannot make the best of his present and future, for it is from the past that we learn".

Exponential Growth

When I think of our country's growth, I think of the amazing partnership between Emiratis and Expats. We built the UAE together. The UAE is a small country with a lot of wealth. We could have closed our minds to the world and remained small, relying on Social Welfare and survived. That was not the intent of our leaders. We wanted to build our country and thrive. We could never claim we built this by ourselves. Every nationality contributed. This isn't about having hired consultants, people came to help build, and they became partners. Everyone played their part, security guards, construction workers etc. This co-existence at heart is the soul of the UAE. I love that every workers' name is etched in stone on the wall of Expo. For years to come they and their families can take pride in what they built. People used to go to the US for the American Dream, we call it here the UAE Dream.

Secret of Success

We had to build a country that was safe. A foundation. That infrastructure from the outside looks like a graceful swan, but under the water, people are paddling furiously to keep that infrastructure solid. Because of this safety, people can build a life: we have great schools, amazing health system, and a family-orientated space. You can maybe cut and paste the infrastructure, the towers, but you can't build the soul of the UAE, it is the combined soul of everyone who calls the UAE home. I feel so proud on UAE National Day when I see children like yours with blonde hair and blue eyes waving the UAE flag. That is a reflection of what we have all built.

The real secret of the UAE's success is the leadership. I'll give you an example: HH Sheikh Mohammed likes to bet on the right horse. When I worked in Dubai, and I met him at that time, he would always say "you've done a great job, I'm going to give you another job, you will work a lot harder!" Rewarding with a new job was like getting a medal. There was a trust in your capabilities. He's a natural leader but he builds an army of leaders. People have authority. When you arrive at border control, the Emiratis on the border who welcome you have the power to make decisions. Even if by the letter of the law they should do one thing, if something makes common sense or there is a chance to show compassion, they can take personal responsibility and show their leadership.

Challenges

For me being "the first woman" in many of my roles has been a challenge, but you can either be anxious, or you can say "if I do a good job, they will bring other women on board". The main challenge for the UAE is maybe regionally. There are countries that have instability in the Middle East and we also want them to develop their own peace and security. We want the region to thrive.

Opportunities

It doesn't matter what your business is, we have the infrastructure for you to thrive. We have established the basics. The hard infrastructure like the telecoms network, the highway and the metro, and then the soft infrastructure, the regulation and the laws. We also have the manpower, not just in the UAE, but the ability to recruit from the region within a 5 hour flight. Transparency too has a track record of eliminating corruption. And the Lifestyle. These are the basics. In addition, the flexibility of the Government and the leadership is critical – look at COVID: the UAE has been acknowledged as having had one of the best responses. And not just the response, the fairness of the response. The vaccine wasn't just for Emiratis first, Expats were treated the same. When we needed people to stay here longer regardless of job, we issued the Golden Visas, we changed the Companies Law to allow 100% foreign ownership. HH Sheikh Mohammed says "if you build it, they will come". And I believe we have built the foundations for anyone to come here and succeed, and we have a leadership that can adapt to a changing environment. I believe that is the greatest opportunity.

Lessons

For me it is simply co-existence. If you look at other countries, they really struggle with immigration and integration. They don't seem to give the new nationalities a chance or afford them the same opportunities and security.

We also have a government that leads by approaching our customer base: the children of the Future. We want to hand over a great legacy.

Expo

Whenever I visited previous Expo's abroad, I used to just look at the UAE pavilion and that was really it. However, for this year's Expo, I think the design and layout is incredible, with Al Wasl, the "meeting place" cleverly connecting all the pavilions. I love the thematic pavilions and specifically the Women's Pavilion, which is the first time in history that there is such a thing. I think all of this shows that Dubai and the UAE didn't just want to replicate Expos as they were in other countries, but really re-think the whole concept of what an Expo can be, and infuse it with some of the soul of our country. I can't wait for everyone to see it and experience it.

Future

This is like a science fiction question! What's great is that the UAE thinks this far ahead and plans. Importantly though we are not afraid to tweak the plan over the years as the external factors change. I think the main difference is that as well as being UAE citizens and residents, we will consider ourselves Universal citizens. Every problem we see today, seems to affect everyone around the world, given the interconnected way that we operate now. We all have to shift our thinking, not just from local to global, but Universal. There is a limit to what you can plan now, so the focus should be on leaders for the future, our children.

4. BUILDING A NATION

HE Saeed al Eter, Director-General of the Executive Office of His Highness Sheikh Mohammed bin Rashid Al Maktoum

"We have a passion for the future, and are on a quest to establish the UAE's part in that future"

His Excellency Saeed Mohammad Al Eter serves as the Chair of the UAE Government Media Office, which is responsible for proactively sharing The Emirates' strategy, vision and outreach to local, regional and global audiences.

Al Eter also serves as Director-General of the Executive Office of His Highness Sheikh Mohammed bin Rashid Al Maktoum, conducting specialized studies in vital areas to facilitate the process of strategic and development decision-making. In addition, he conducts the continuous follow-up of plans, programs, projects and decisions issued by His Highness's platform for incubating and launching many innovative ideas. He is also the Assistant Secretary-General of the charitable foundation, the Mohammed bin Rashid Al Maktoum Global Initiatives; which served 83 million beneficiaries across 82 countries in 2020 alone.

He has deep experience in driving strategic government communications initiatives, including the establishment and management of the Office of Government Communication at the General Secretariat of the UAE Cabinet. During this time, he developed the Federal Government Communication Strategy, designed the organizational structures of several government communications departments at federal entities, and championed the development of strategic government communications guidelines within the UAE government.

He has led several strategic national media campaigns, ranging from the launch of the Emirates Mars Mission through regional initiatives such as the Arab Reading Challenge and Hope Makers to a range of government strategy launches, including UAE Vision 2021. He was responsible for leading the media and communications management of the World Government Summit, the UAE Year of Reading and National Reading Strategy, and the UAE Year of Giving and National Giving Strategy.

Earliest Memories

My earliest memory of the UAE nation itself was sitting in our family room every day watching HH Sheikh Zayed on TV. That was my first recollection and understanding of what a country was, what a nation is. He wasn't the kind of leader you see sitting on a chair or sofa, he was hands-on. Driving his Mercedes in the desert, checking on all sorts of projects: from houses and farms to roads and infrastructure. He'd be visiting other Emirates, speaking to people of all ages, going to universities, talking to students. He once said, "whatever I'm doing now, is for you to continue". People questioned that at the time: "why is he saying the baton will be handed over?", but now I understand: it is the way he empowered young people. An integral part of the reason that the UAE has seen exponential growth is this emphasis on youth and the youthful spirit of the nation that was engraved by Sheikh Zayed early on. We are a young nation, most of our decision-makers are also young. The Founding Fathers were young, and so were the leaders. When people come up with exceptionally innovative and inspiring ideas, as a young ambitious person, you get excited. When your leader says, "we are going to space", you want to go! It's the case when approximately $200m of the budget was handed over to a 29-year-old to take a probe to Mars! It's this mindset of our leadership that fueled the success of our nation. Extreme empowering of young people. That's unprecedented and unparalleled. For the young people to believe in themselves, take responsibility and deliver with high standards is also remarkable.

I go back to Sheikh Zayed in the field. I don't remember him ever lecturing us or making long speeches. He'd be on the farms and construction sites. The message is that we should work, not just talk. It was about delivering projects. A "let success make the noise" type of mentality.

Journey

I'm an engineer by background. I went to Khalifa University (formerly the Etisalat College of Engineering). After which I joined the team at Etisalat for six years. Those years had a huge impact on my professional journey, considering the high standards that Etisalat operates with. I also finished my MBA from the American University of Sharjah. In 2006, when HH Sheikh Mohammed bin Rashid became Prime Minister of the UAE, I joined the Prime Minister's Office. I was really lucky to join his government from the early days and I'm really blessed to have seen it all, and been part of the amazing, beautiful, exceptional, exciting journey. I have lots of stories to tell my grandchildren in the future!

I have worked with most ministries on their first ever strategic plans. They were not used to having a 3-5 year strategy, so I was involved in that cycle of work. I saw each Ministry's mandate and the reasons they exist and how they all work together and complement each other. I also worked on drafting the first ever strategy for the Federal Government which was announced at the end of 2007. In 2008 I established the Government Communications Office. I made sure we had the right modus operandi for communications, learning from all the other countries. We have also trained all the Government spokespeople. I established the "Special Project Office" reporting to HE Mohammed Al Gergawi, Minister of Cabinet Affairs.

The idea for the Emirates Nation Brand is that we are a global country and we talk to everyone all around the world. To talk to them you need a brand. With all globalization, countries are like corporations. You want to sell the opportunities, the lifestyle, the investment opportunities. You want to sell the story of your nation. If you are a good salesperson with a good marketing strategy, the impact on your economy and global status will be much stronger. Also, each Emirate had its own brand, but we wanted to talk to the world as one nation.

When we developed the idea, we didn't just want to go to a consultant to design the brand, we went to every Emirate, and each Emirate nominated seven of their painters, sculptors, authors, researchers and graphic designers, so we had 49 Emirati artists in total to design a logo that represents the UAE globally. They generated multiple designs, among which three logos were shortlisted. People across the world were invited to vote for one of the shortlisted logos and we had over 10 million votes. It was such an interesting process and great to have both

Emiratis and expats voting.

HH Sheikh Zayed

Wisdom. Education and knowledge are different from wisdom. There is a saying in English that I like which is "common sense is not common". HH Sheikh Zayed made sense not only in his own time, but beyond his passing and into the future. He also made sense to all people, regardless of their background and education. His messages are simultaneously simple and deep. He also conducted himself with real focus. He was genuine. He was philanthropic. He loved other nations and he loved his own nation and he wanted the best for all. He walked the talk. That was something unique. HH Sheikh Zayed's impact will last for a very, very long time.

Exponential Growth

We went from no roads to space roads… That is something truly unique.

Secret of Success

We have a passion for the future and are on a quest to establish the UAE's part in that future. We are all constantly thinking about what the future holds. That's why we can be ahead of the game. We are also fast. We deliver projects, change laws, we strategize, we restructure. Being fast is an integral part of your intelligence as a nation. You don't have to be perfect, but you have to be fast, and able to pivot.

Every hour that passes in the UAE is 10 million human hours of our nation. If we waste one hour, we are wasting 10 million hours. If we galvanize every citizen and resident in our country, we have 10 million hours to grow the nation.

We also have a healthy competition between the Emirates. Our governance model is smart and has helped us grow fast over the years. If Dubai Municipality does something very well, the other municipalities try and better it. That drives innovation. We have varieties of mindsets and thinking. The leadership encourages this.

Challenges

When we began the UAE, there were only 40 university graduates. Most of our people were illiterate. Now we are number one in the world in terms of women's involvement in education. That is quite something. We are very proud of this. This was a huge challenge. However, if you solve the education challenge, you can overcome every challenge. Going through that journey of building up our people over two or three generations is fantastic.

Opportunities

We invite investors to be part of our success across all sectors. The UAE is known for future technology and we want to be flexible to make that work. Take, for example, the RegLab where we can specifically sandbox new laws and regulations to enable new sectors and companies to test and grow.

Lessons

The ASDA'A BCW Arab Youth Survey has regularly asked young Arabs the following questions: If you could live anywhere in the world, where would you live? And which country in the world, if any, would you like your country to be like? For the tenth year in a row, the answers were the same this year: the United Arab Emirates. I believe in every aspect of life in the UAE, you find good models that other countries can learn from.

Expo

Expo represents the essence of the UAE. Expo answers an eternal question that humanity has dreamt of for many, many years, which is "can people from different cultures, religions and backgrounds come together in one place and live in harmony and achieve their dreams?" It has been a philosophical question for thousands of years for humanity. Expo is just here for six months, but it is the essence of the UAE. This is a dream for humanity, that we can live together and dream together.

Future

Where will we be in 2071? That is an impossible question! I can't predict the UAE's future for the next month, it is full of surprises…. And this is the secret of the UAE.

5. FROM RAGS TO RICHES

HE Mohammed al Fahim, Chairman of Al Fahim Family Council

"Money is worthless if you lose your dignity and responsibilities."

The Al Fahim Group is one of the UAE's most successful family businesses. The company was founded by the late Abdul Jalil Al Fahim in 1958, a visionary entrepreneur who led the company until his passing in 1996. Since then, the Al Fahim Group has continued to evolve and grow to become one of the region's leading commercial groups.

HE Mohammed Abdul Jalil Al Fahim, Chairman of Al Fahim Family Council & Al Fahim Supervisory Board Member, joined the family business in 1968 and helped in diversifying the business by adding Real Estate, Automotive, Industrial Projects, Travel and Tourism, Agriculture interests. Amongst his numerous business achievements, Mohammed Al Fahim has occupied several honorable positions that allowed him to contribute in the development of the UAE: he was a Board Member at the Telephone Company, the Council for Water and Electricity as well as Chairman of the National Investment and Securities Corporation (Niscorp) and 1st Vice President of the Abu Dhabi Chamber of Commerce and Industry. His book: "From Rags to Riches - A Story of Abu Dhabi" is a best-seller and has been published in English, Arabic, French Japanese, German, Italian, Russian, Spanish, Urdu and now in Malayalam versions.

Earliest Memories

It's important to understand the harsh climate and conditions that we grew up in. Most people were illiterate, but my father was lucky as he

ught by a Mulla. He was born in 1910. My father and uncles
t and parcel of Sheikh Zayed's domain. My Grandfather had
d for Sheikh Zayed's uncle in the 1920's and 30's. My father and
ikh Zayed were similar ages and were friends from those days.

For me, when I was born at the end of 1948, it meant that I used to see Sheikh Zayed all the time in our house. My father built a shed facing the sand dunes that became a majlis. In the evening they'd sit on the sand dunes. Sheikh Zayed was in my father's house almost every day. I actually lived with his son Sheikh Khalifa in his house from 1 to 6 years old. I am the same age as Sheikh Khalifa.

Life still was very difficult. There was no comfort, no electricity, no lights, running water. We were like a local Bedouin encampment. The only transportation was camels, horses and donkeys. Sheikh Zayed got his first car in 1953 with petrol provided from Sharjah that took 3 days to come to Al Ain. It was an ex-military truck used in WW2. It was better than riding a camel, as Sheikh Zayed wanted to get around quickly to visit the tribes. He drove this truck until 1955 when he got his first Land Rover, the first one in the country. I remember as a 7-year-old, being driven by Sheikh Zayed, with my father and Sheikh Khalifa, all being in the front, and 6 guards in the back! I have a similar Land Rover today and I always look at it and wonder how we used to travel with 10 people in…

However, I remember in 1959, people were still on camels and it took 6-7 days to go from Al Ain to Abu Dhabi. My grandfather and grandmother passed away on such trips. The sun, the lack of water, no healthcare. Anyone who got flu or anything just died.

Journey

At that time, my family would send me to Abu Dhabi for school in the winter, and then back to Al Ain for the summer. For my initial schooling, I attended the "Qur'an Religious School" and then joined the "Al Falahiya School" for further studies in 1959. This was more of a concrete shed that had about 6 classrooms and a canopy in the front. It took until 1961 though to get textbooks. We were about 65 children in total. Life was still pretty primitive. Although oil was first exported in 1961, it took a while to be reinvested.

I travelled to England for higher studies in 1963. I didn't know another world existed. I was a Bedouin from my shed all the way to

London! Mind boggling. It took 3 months to get used to seeing cars, planes, life, restaurants, coffee shops… We stayed for 3 years. We came back in 1966 and saw that not much had changed in Abu Dhabi. In August 1966, HH Sheikh Zayed became the new ruler and that's when the real change happened. I came back from England in the summer of '68 and I found Abu Dhabi like a construction site. It was amazing to see the work and developments. Cranes, trucks, cars everywhere.

For three generations and with the personal contribution of every family member, the group has successfully achieved key milestones over these years. As a close-knit family venture, we ensure that every member adds consistent value to our operations. We are all intrinsically motivated to persevere and enhance the business seeds sown by our father. The Group is proud to be continuously acknowledged by our stakeholders through multiple awards reinstating the solidarity and persistence of the family to contribute to the development of the company and Abu Dhabi's community as a whole.

I'm most proud of serving my country when they needed me, from '68-'90. I was in the government, lots of committees, promoting the emirate. I was working for the country. When I retired, I wrote from Rags to Riches, and I found a new horizon, speaking about our country's achievements about how we created a country in such a short time. That has been my best achievement.

HH Sheikh Zayed

It was like I had two fathers – we called him uncle. He was very striking looking. Very manly. He had a belt around his chest. He was always presentable.

Sheikh Zayed had always had a plan in his mind. That plan was to build Abu Dhabi and unify the Emirates. When he became ruler, he already had a goal and a vision. He was thinking about it and working towards it. While building Abu Dhabi he was visiting the other rulers and talking to them about unification. People may have thought they were casual, friendly visits, but he was testing the appetite. Thank God he succeeded.

Exponential Growth

Before Sheikh Zayed came to power, we didn't have a road or telephone to connect the Emirates. We didn't even go to the other Emirates. There was no means to travel. When Sheikh Zayed opened the road and the infrastructure, suddenly the UAE became smaller and easier to travel and communicate.

This period from 1966 to 1976 was the biggest change for me. We went from small Bedouin villages in different emirates to a unified nation that was recognised by the United Nations in 1976. We had to create a government, infrastructure, rules and regulations. We were a start-up Nation.

Secret of Success

First the leadership had faith. Then they had driving ambition for change to catch up with countries ahead of them. Secondly, they were sincere in administration and leadership. They could have enriched themselves, however they put the country and people as their priority. Sheikh Zayed set an example for everyone that to become a leader, you have to take responsibility. You must promise to the people and to God that you will not let them down. He literally instilled that feeling in all of us. With all the money flowing in, there was no corruption. Sheikh Zayed was a mentor and example. Money is worthless if you lose your dignity and responsibility.

Challenges

When Sheikh Zayed started developing the country, we didn't know what we had. People wrote us off as small, weak and couldn't exist on our own. Sheikh Zayed knew this and created the government infrastructure, diplomatic relations, an army and a police force so that we were a force to be reckoned with.

They were disruptive years in the region in the early years: we had the Iran Revolution, the Iran-Iraq war. Thankfully Sheikh Zayed kept us focused on developing our own country and catching up with the rest of the world.

Opportunities

I see a lot of joint ventures with international companies. We started with roads, schools and hospitals, now we are going to space, all through partnerships. Technology and innovation are not new to us. We are part and parcel of the future world and can work hand in hand with these companies. We have a shared language and ambition with companies in the future.

Lessons

Western societies are old. What they have created in infrastructure has taken them far in the twentieth century. I think the 21st century requires a different mindset. We have to change our attitude towards people and technology. We are all on this earth to work together. A lot of the advancement in the world has come from all over the world. We must treat everyone equally. Embrace change and people regardless of race, nationality and background.

Expo

I want them to see that we are a peaceful, tolerant country. We are hardworking and not selfish. We want to share what we have. We are not a backward country. We have tradition and culture of our own, but that doesn't impinge on any visitor's experience. We are open to all religions and sects. I was invited to HH Mohammed bin Zayed's majlis yesterday, half of the attendees were female representing their departments and ministries.

Future

In 1971 we couldn't even think about envisaging in 2021, let alone 2071. We as a community back then lacked the education and insights into other countries to have that foresight. Luckily Sheikh Zayed had that foresight, as well as the other leadership that we are blessed with.

I remember meeting with HH Sheikh Mohammed bin Rashid in 2010, when the financial crash happened. We were about 15 of us businesspeople, gathering on an island, and some expressed concerns that we were growing too quickly. I remember HH Sheikh Mohammed said "What I'm doing today is only 10% of what I intend to do tomorrow. Catch up today or be left behind tomorrow." A decade later, here we have Expo, with the world coming here. Today I must admit it, he was right, and we were wrong. He had the foresight not to slow down and continue the race for constant improvement and betterment. That all happened within the last decade, who knows where we will be in 50 years' time!

6. BEDOUIN TO BUSINESS

Nick Cochrane-Dyet MBE, Chairman of the British Business Group Abu Dhabi

"HH Sheikh Zayed always used to say, 'you pick up one stick it's easy to break, you pick up ten sticks, they're harder to break'. It summed up the Bedouin mentality that we're stronger together"

Nick first came to the UAE when his father served with the Trucial Oman Scouts in 1965. He began his working life reporting directly to HH Sheikh Zayed where he managed the President of the UAE's Royal Stud Farm. He subsequently became a Captain in the British Army in the Brigade of Gurkhas. He returned to the UAE in 1985, working as the Representative of Citicorp Investment Bank in Abu Dhabi before joining BP in 1989. He is Chairman of the British Business Group Abu Dhabi and Chairs the Middle East Advisory Board of the Energy Industry Council and is the UK Co-chair of the Energy Working Group of the UAE-UK Business Council. He was awarded an MBE in the 2013 New Year's Honours by Her Majesty The Queen.

Nick has seen and been a big part of the UAE's journey from Bedouin roots pre-1971, through to the business hub the UAE is today.

Earliest Memories

I came here as a child in 1965. My father was with the Trucial Oman Scouts. He was based in the Jahili Fort in Al Ain. I'm reminded of it every time I open a bottle of Al Ain water as it's on the label, in the foreground of the mountain Jebel Hafeet. The local Emiratis wore Kanduras but not the bright white ones you see nowadays, more sandy. My earliest memories were just of the sands and only later, upon my return as a teenager would I come to understand, what a simple life it had been at the time – but it was happy. What little they had they had huge gratitude for. There was no materialism. They literally thanked God for everything - "Alhamdullilah" – genuinely grateful from the heart.

There was the one hospital in Al Ain, the Oasis Hospital, which was a missionary hospital. There was no school, no running water, no electricity and no waste! We also didn't have garbage or plastic - we used up or recycled everything.

Journey

In 1975 I returned to the UAE and got a job looking after HH Sheikh Zayed's horses at his royal stables in the Al Ain village of Mezyad. I lived with a Bedouin family in a barasti dwelling. I liked being with the Bedouin. I was like a village doctor, although not trained, I could spot malaria and other ailments. Generally, I could see a huge need for education. One of the things I have been most proud about is helping establish the secondary part of the British School in Abu Dhabi – Al Khubairat. Then the Petroleum institute, now part of Khalifa University. They are both proper homegrown Abu Dhabi institutions and rank internationally.

For 30 years I worked for British Petroleum. While other countries looked for ways to kick out the big oil producers by nationalization, HH Sheikh Zayed wanted to keep BP and develop the partnership. He had the Bedouin mentality of "we're in this together" and that we were stronger working in partnership.

Ultimately, I became Chairman of the British Chamber of Commerce, Abu Dhabi. I believe that countries that do business together don't have soldiers on their borders, and that was something that HH Sheikh Zayed recognized.

HH Sheikh Zayed

HH Sheikh Zayed was my direct line manager. He was a subject matter expert on horses. He was hugely passionate. I was very lucky that I got to witness his leadership style. He'd be dealing with matters of state and I would wait, and I'd see other heads of state come and go. I could see his wisdom in action. You could see people inspired.

I think the most important thing was respect. He respected everything and everyone. He was a very humble gentleman. He could see that everyone had something to offer. He looked for the good in people. It went beyond simple tolerance; it was much more than that. He didn't just tolerate everyone, he respected everyone. He didn't tell people to respect him, he just earned it.

It wasn't just tolerance for people, he had a real, genuine, respect for nature. I personally witnessed this in the oil and gas sector when there was flaring going on in the 50s and 60s. People didn't want gas at the time, so it was being burned off. Sometimes Abu Dhabi smelt awful when the wind was blowing the wrong way. He knew it was wrong. He called in the BP engineers and said we have to stop. BP said it will cost more money but HH Sheikh Zayed said it was worth it. We developed a method to store it. This was actually the start of Liquified Natural Gas. He started it not to make money, but to stop flaring and stop the environment being destroyed. The country was rewarded decades later when LNG had a real value. Instead of burnt gas, we had sweet-smelling grass, vibrant hibiscus, tantalizing bougainvillea and ample amounts of other colourful shrubs were the result of Zayed's determination.

I last saw Sheikh Zayed in London in 2004. It was only a few months before he died but even from his hospital bed, Sheikh Zayed was watching footage of a venture in Al Ain through live satellite feed while he was in the hospital. He loved this country and its growth and remained forever in touch with the whole population and its progress.

Exponential Growth

For me, I witnessed the exponential growth of the UAE literally from nothing. Look at the photos: literally just sand. Now the country has sent a probe to Mars. Who would have imagined looking at the stars and planets in 1971 and imagined sending something up there. The probe is fittingly called Hope. I don't think anyone could have dreamt that.

Secret of Success

It has to be HH Sheikh Zayed and his long-term vision. However, it was not just a single vision. He had introspection and flexibility. This means he has left a legacy that gets continuously upgraded. We've had a 2021 plan, a vision 2030 plan and a Centennial 2071 plan.

He had the Bedouin mentality that if you are in this country, he had a responsibility to look after you. And even then, beyond the country, as the region impacts the country. Everyone was included: we're in it together, a team effort. I want to stress that this is not an autocracy – this is a consultative system. The majlis is informal, we debate. We have a Federal National Council. The leadership listens. Yes, they make decisions, but it is with input. As a Bedouin, you give your enemy food. They take it very seriously. Prime Ministers and Presidents come and go. Sheikhs are here for life. There is that mentality that you're on my territory you're my responsibility. This was so obvious during the pandemic when we were all looked after so well.

Challenges

When I first joined the British Business Group and tried to persuade British businesses to do work in Abu Dhabi they thought Abu Dhabi was a place in the north of Wales! Convincing people that it was a great place to live work and grow a family in a region that has its issues was hard then, it's not hard now. Abu Dhabi and the UAE are firmly on the world map.

I was honoured to be invited to 10 Downing Street in September 2021 with HH The Crown Prince and the British Prime Minister to announce Emirati investment into the UK of $10bn. What an incredible development from the mere millions half a century before.

Specifically, to overcome the business challenges and become successful, I believe firms need to overcome three main challenges. First, there has to be a degree of cooperation and coming together as one package to win the attention of UAE decision-makers; a genuine long-term partnership. Second, once they are able to unify their intent, firms need to make the right connections and find the right people who can make these networks work ensuring efficient in-country value. Third, companies must be price competitive and recognize that the UAE is becoming an increasingly price sensitive market

Opportunities

With 30 years at BP, I have most experience in the energy sector. One of the latest big opportunities has been between BP and Masdar with energy transition. Not just about stopping burning hydrocarbons and switching to solar, it is about all elements of the transition that can involve R&D, education, integration of AI.

The UAE's passion for innovation and can-do attitude influences every aspect of life here, as the country keeps walking down the journey of continuous improvement. This dynamic environment means companies and businesspeople see the UAE as a place where dreams can become reality. For the UK, as an example, this place is attractive not only because there are fewer barriers, less bureaucracy, and more action, but also because there is a great deal of compatibility and history between the two countries. Today, the UAE is one of the UK's largest trading partners, and the UK is one of the UAE's leading sources of FDI. This compatibility is vital, though it might lead to a degree of complacency. There is a need to reinvent ourselves with vigor and creativity to continue to bring value to the country. As for the business channels of cooperation, there is great potential for UK firms to supply the UAE with the latest and greatest technologies, as well as for UK academic institutions to conduct research, develop new capacities, and fill in the gap left by the shying away of R&D.

Lessons

Long term planning. The other lesson is that this country sets clear boundaries. If you respect the country and the boundaries you will be fine. It has left us with a very safe country.

Expo

Seeing all the country pavilions side by side is amazing. It demonstrates we can all live happily together: no one is fighting. I've seen lots of happiness, talking, discussing. It tells me the world can unite and we can learn from each other. The takeaway is that there is hope for the future. We all need hope. There is still hope. Expo can demonstrate how and why we have hope. Better to smile and the world smiles with you: we can have a bright future.

Future

I don't know where we'll be with all of the innovation – probably a hyperloop to Venus! All of that innovation will be part of the next 50 years, but I think the UAE will be an international role model. It will be a country that the world looks at and who knows even other planets may come to admire! We're living and practicing the United Nations in this country already. People are seeing how this country works both for people and for the planet. It will be a truly sustainable nation.

7. DREAMERS WHO DO

HE Noura al Kaabi, Minister of Culture and Youth

"Yesterday's dreams became today's reality"

Her Excellency Noura bint Mohammed Al Kaabi was named UAE Minister of Culture and Youth in July 2020. Al Kaabi's professional career really took off when she joined twofour54 as employee number one in 2007. Twofour54 is a government entity named after the geographic coordinates of Abu Dhabi that is at forefront of UAE's fast-growing media industry. The company's vision was to grow the Arab media industry by creating world class content through its work with local television, radio, film, publishing, online, mobile, music, gaming and animation businesses. Her Excellency also currently also serves as President of Zayed University and Chair of the National Commission for Education, Culture and Science

Her Excellency has most recently been appointed commissioner general of the UAE Pavilion at Expo, which is where we meet for the interview. It looks like a James Bond lair, shaped like a falcon in flight, with the wings slowly flapping ("wings not feathers!" she warns). The carbon fiber "wings" can be closed to shelter the roof solar panels, and each wing pivots around a single point and the entire roof can be opened in three minutes. Inside, the light slowly ebbs and flows like a Falcon's breath, which is wonderfully calming. Before our meeting I walk through the exhibition and it is a journey through the UAE's story. On the ground floor are sand dunes, with early pictures projected on to them, including ones that Sir Wilfred Thesiger took of a young Sheikh Zayed. It is the perfect setting for our discussions.

Earliest Memories

My earliest childhood memory is of growing up in Abu Dhabi on our compound. My father served in the army, and we lived in a camp of military personnel. I remember playing there outdoors on my bicycle, alongside Emiratis, Egyptians, Pakistanis and Sudanese. Those neighbours were my first friends, my first community. This memory reflects the story of this UAE Pavilion where we sit today, one of international unity and the community found here.

Journey

After graduating in IT, I worked in the IT Health sphere in a military hospital, following in my father's footsteps. In 2005, it was the start of Clean Energy, and a new world since the traditional professions of banking and oil. I joined Dolphin Energy in Mubadala, and it opened the horizon for clean energy. I became very interested in the plan of diversification and joined twofour54 and then began to focus on gaming, content creation and culture.

I was the first employee of twofour54, having started in our partner support services division. Witnessing the growth of twofour54 has been the highlight since the beginning. Growing with twofour54 and becoming its CEO has been a great gift because I was part of paving the way to establishing a leading media hub in the UAE and the region's driving force behind media and entertainment entrepreneurs.

We have been committed to creating a thriving entrepreneurship ecosystem at twofour54 and through a variety of initiatives, we have supported local talent and helped startups fulfil their creative potential, which is vital to building and sustaining our media and entertainment industries.

As Minister, I have been working extensively to meet the UAE's cultural agenda as part of the country's Vision 2021 program. This will determine our competitive knowledge economy through entrepreneurship and emerging talent by unlocking the potential of youth and enabling them to be a driving force of the country's economic development.

A key part of this strategy is to start with education right from the very beginning; instilling an entrepreneurial culture in schools and universities to foster generations endowed with values of leadership, creativity, responsibility and ambition. This is supported by a curated and targeted support of the arts in school curricula. The challenges are ever evolving, and we are committed to listening carefully and working on identifying them as foundational steps towards providing a solution.

The UAE pavilion here at Expo 2020 is a culmination and testament of a dream and vision.

HH Sheikh Zayed

HH Sheikh Zayed saw the future, in the desert. He was a true leader, delivering a message rooted in our values and which continuously evolves, bringing us to where we are today. When you see the heritage film of him in the Pavilion, sitting in the desert under a ghaf tree, he was looking at the dunes, but like he was wearing a VR headset, he saw a factory, he saw a hospital. Everyone said, "are you crazy?" "What are you seeing?" He saw the future that we live today rising out of the desert.

In the same way, his legacy lives through his son, HH Sheikh Mohammed bin Zayed who said, "I want to celebrate the last barrel of oil". The idea that oil production was not essential, that we can still sustain the future of this country and make sustainable diversified investment. We're in a place where we see hope, we dream and we want the majority of our population, which is the youth, to live in a better place than today. We want to live a very sustainable life. It's about exploring and empowering the youth... and embedding that future agenda in everything we do.

Exponential Growth

Yesterday's dreams became today's reality. For example, in 1976, the UAE was just five years old but HH Sheikh Zayed met Apollo 17 astronauts and was gifted a model rocket. I know then he even envisaged the recent Hope mission to Mars with his dreams of space from that meeting.

Secret of Success

My family is the reason for my success. They support every step I take but never force any choice on me. It is a wonderful mix of support and freedom that I enjoy.

I have served the UAE on both a local and federal level. While each entity operates individually to develop different parts of the chain, they also help each other to grow the overall culture.

The youth are very much a part of the nation's onward march to the future. Our national vision is very futuristic, and the role of the youth is integral to that vision. Their involvement in nation-building actually starts before they graduate.

Challenges

The way we handled the pandemic. I am so proud in the way it's been handled, the progression of the vaccines, hosting Expo at this time.

My challenge as a Minister was to run a Ministry which is integrally linked to the UAE's identity in a way that does justice to both our past and present. The role has been a multilayered one. When you deal with the cultural scene, you are interacting with multiple aspects – the historical, the ancient, the modern. To digest that entire complexity was not easy in the beginning. I remember my first meeting as Minister of Culture with HH Sheikh Mohammed Bin Rashid Al Maktoum to discuss the plans for the first hundred days. He was very specific that the Ministry should function as an enabler of the whole sector and not as a mere operator.

Opportunities

What is most important is to be ahead of the game and invent the way forward. When you look into the arts, look into music, look at all the multi-genres that we are working on here in the UAE…we have amazing UAE talent, we also have great residents that are part of the scene, and that makes it a richer scene. There are many opportunities to be part of it.

Digital is definitely the future... but not the only future as there will always be a place for traditional media such as broadcast television. Digital media is a fast-growing industry in the Middle East, with consumers now spending more than a quarter of their total media and entertainment time on digital platforms

I think the UAE works best when we join forces with one another and have a clear roadmap to guide our vision. Building a healthy ecosystem to support this cultural renaissance that the Middle East is in need of, requires the collaboration of all the sectors from governmental bodies to private institutions.

The Creative Economy has become an important part of our global economy. Not just as a narrative, but also as an implementation model. Many countries have realised the importance of knowledge-based industries, and the UAE in particular believes that these cultural and creative industries are key assets in order to create sustainability for the economy. The UAE is a major player in the growth of CCI in the Middle East and North Africa region. The UAE's preeminent position as an innovation hub is central to the growth of CCI in the wider region.

Lessons

Investing in human development and human connections. Embrace diversity, embrace everyone.

The UAE is a product of the collective effort of the people from different countries and different nationalities.

The UAE was founded on strong values – tolerance, respect for other cultures and people, and peaceful coexistence. Look at the way multiple nationalities and cultures live together in this country in absolute peace. The UAE has embraced different cultures with open arms and allocated places of worship for various faiths.

We believe we are living out the true principles of Islam through our embrace of different cultures, respect for all faiths and acceptance of difference. Professionals, businessmen, teachers and so on from across the globe are not only making their living, but also helping in the process of nation-building shoulder to shoulder with the Emiratis. That is what we all grew up seeing, and we knew that it's the natural and the right thing to do.

Expo

You have to see the UAE Pavilion to understand our country. It is such an immersive experience that takes you on our journey and invites you to be part of it going forward. We are celebrating our 50th year and this is an opportunity to know the country and connect with its people.

Future

Venus! We joke but just this morning a new interplanetary mission was announced by the UAE Space Agency that will launch in 2028. The spacecraft will go on a five-year expedition, orbiting Venus and Earth before reaching the main asteroid belt located between Mars and Jupiter in 2030.

We are in a race, and every day there is a new announcement about us pushing the frontiers.

My hope is that we'll be seen as a responsible country for the challenges we are going to see face our children, that we lay the tracks for a world and country that is future-proof. If we continue with such consistent steps we will thrive.

We are the land of dreamers who do.

8. BRIDGING CULTURES

HE Mansoor Abulhoul, UAE Ambassador to the UK

"The UAE works tirelessly to build bridges and forge links to create stability and prosperity across the region and beyond"

Ambassador Mansoor Abulhoul is the UAE's Ambassador to the UK, having been appointed to the post in June 2019. Ambassador Abulhoul aims to enhance bilateral relations with the UK. While serving as Ambassador, he developed a personal 'cycle diplomacy' programme. The Ambassador is cycling from John o' Groats to Land's End, using his passion for cycling to foster cultural understanding on a cross-country tour of the UK. The cycle tour will also raise funds for Great Ormond Street Hospital. Ambassador Abulhoul brings experience in business and international relations to his post, as well as a history of engagement across the UAE and UK. With both British and Emirati parents, Ambassador Abulhoul is part of a family with deep connections in both the UK and UAE.

Earliest Memories

Growing up as the son of the Commander-in-Chief of Dubai Police, in the 1970s, I recall family life at the Officer's housing compound at Dubai Police HQ, including the nursery school, central playground and relishing the opportunity to mimic my father's actions by saluting Dubai Policemen.

When I was around six years old, my father surprised me with a miniature Dubai Police uniform, which I was so proud of, and I would wear during visits with my father to majlis' for Eid celebrations!

Journey

My mother is from Cambridge and my father is from Dubai, and I attended schools in both countries, and went to university in the UK.

At the start of my career, I worked in the private sector in Dubai for a British bank, then the family business, Magrudy's before I eventually transitioned into the government sector and had the honour and privilege of becoming the UAE Ambassador to the UK. Looking back, I am proud of the journey I have made so far – it almost feels full circle.

HH Sheikh Zayed

I vividly remember meeting His Highness Sheikh Zayed at Kempton Park Racecourse in Surrey with my father when I was a teenager. I remember His Highness telling my father about the etymology of his name and its connection with the different tribes in the Emirates; His Highness had such an astounding knowledge of ancestry and tribal history and could easily see connections that others may not have seen as swiftly.

I remember being struck by his charm and how he made everyone feel welcome and part of the group. And that was something he did on a large scale, he succeeded in bringing people together, which ultimately resulted in the founding of our nation. This ideal of inclusion and respect for all is a value I try to live by every day.

Exponential Growth

Our ground-breaking space exploration efforts - the UAE was the first Arab country to have launched an interplanetary space mission when it sent the Hope Probe into orbit on the Mars Mission, and the fifth player to reach Mars overall, alongside the US, the then Soviet Union, the European Space Agency and India.

The Hope Probe represents the great ambitions of our nation, and I hope that our commitment and success in this field will continue to educate and inspire younger generations in the Emirates and across the world.

Secret of Success

It is less a secret to the UAE's success, and more our

commitment to growth, acquiring knowledge and building trusted friendships, that has contributed to our success over the past 50 years. An example of this is our historic partnership with the UK, which spans from joint initiatives in trade and investment, health, and energy, to education, culture and tourism, boosted by various landmark agreements, including most recently the UAE-UK Partnership for the Future.

Challenges

Over the past 50 years, the UAE has transitioned from being a newly founded nation, to a trusted partner for countries across the world. In a consequential region, the UAE works tirelessly to build bridges and forge links to create stability and prosperity across the region and beyond.

Opportunities

In the past few years, the UAE Government has implemented a variety of economic and societal reforms that have further opened up our society, making it extremely attractive for foreign companies and talent to choose the UAE as their next business destination.

Recent reforms for example include new visa schemes allowing for greater options for expats to live and work in the UAE, and changes to the commercial companies' law allowing for full foreign ownership of mainland companies. Advancing the UAE's economy further, we recently announced the 'Projects of the 50' programme to celebrate our Golden Jubilee. The series of development, economic and legislative projects include the launch of ground-breaking economic initiatives, such as a 10% increase in exports to 10 key markets, including the UK, by 2030.

Lessons

Governments across the world should remain open to dialogue and discussion with their counterparts, as society will never cease to evolve and we need each other to navigate associated common challenges. One point that stands out with regards to the UAE in this context, is our drive and ambition. Whether it's with our fast and remarkable venture into space exploration, our launch of the Projects of the 50, or our push for a more sustainable society, the UAE is at the forefront of innovation, and working with our friends across the world to realise these ground-breaking projects.

Expo

Expo 2020 Dubai is a global experience dedicated to bringing together people, communities, and nations. The six-month event – one of the first of this size and scale to take place since the start of the pandemic – really is a beacon of hope for many.

I have been impressed by the UK Pavilion, which, focused on 'Innovating for a Shared Future', highlights British expertise in sectors including artificial intelligence and space. It also provides a platform for an ongoing six-month programme of business, cultural, educational and tourism activity.

Future

As the current UAE Ambassador to the UK, I foresee that the bilateral relationship between the UAE and the UK will continue to go from strength to strength, expanding into new areas of innovation, collaboration, and entrepreneurship to future-proof our economies and societies.

The UAE has thrived over the past 50 years, and it will continue to do so for the next 50. The possibilities are truly endless, and it is exciting to think about the position we will hold in the future, alongside our friends and partners.

9. AN AVENUE FOR ARTS

Abdelmonem Bin Eisa Alserkal, Founder of Alserkal

"In the UAE, we are fortunate to have founding fathers and leaders who are visionaries. Their pioneering spirit, collaborative and forward-thinking approach, commitment to progress, and deep dedication to our people is inspiring"

Abdelmonem Bin Eisa Alserkal is the founder of Alserkal, a socially responsible cultural enterprise that has helped transform the cultural landscape of the UAE and wider region. Through his vision, Alserkal Avenue, which was established in 2007, has become a thriving community of more than 70 contemporary art galleries, visual and performing arts organisations, designers and entrepreneur-led businesses, providing an essential platform for the development of creative industries in the UAE.

Alserkal is renowned for its experimental approach, ground-breaking artistic productions, and for the creation of culturally meaningful spaces that inspire and shape communities. The enterprise comprises three major initiatives: Alserkal Avenue, a renowned cultural district based in Al Quoz, the industrial area of Dubai; Alserkal Advisory, which consults public and private entities on their engagement with the arts and culture sector; and Alserkal Arts Foundation, which supports cultural practitioners, scholarship and research through public artist commissions, residencies, research grants and educational programmes. Abdelmonem commissioned Rem Koolhaas' Office of Metropolitan Architecture (OMA) to design Concrete, a multi-disciplinary space that was the first building in the UAE to be completed by the practice. Concrete was shortlisted for the 2019 Aga Khan Award for Architecture.

Abdelmonem is also the managing director of Nasser Bin Abdullatif Alserkal Est., a Dubai-based family business with diversified interests in the UAE and abroad and serves as a member of the board of the Alserkal Group. Abdelmonem sits on the boards of some of the UAE's foundational businesses, including Emirates Telecommunications Group Company PJSC (Etisalat) and contributes in an advisory capacity to numerous other concerns such as the Tharawat Family Business Forum.

Abdelmonem serves on the boards of numerous art institutions around the world, including: the British Museum's Contemporary and Modern Middle Eastern Art Acquisition Group; the Tate's Middle East and North Africa Acquisition Committee; and the Guggenheim's Middle Eastern Circle. He is also a Supporter of the Centre Pompidou International Circle - Middle East, a patron of the Peggy Guggenheim Collection, a member of Art Dubai's Board of Patrons, and an honorary member of the Thinkers & Doers Forum, Paris.

Abdelmonem and the Alserkal family have long been supporters of the arts and have been awarded the UAE Patron of the Arts award twice.

Earliest Memories

From a very early age, it was clear to me that Dubai was a progressive city, a city full of pioneers with the determination and ambition to build infrastructure, cities and economies that would be seen as exemplary on the world stage. I remember the UAE was seen as a country of possibilities. Today, I see this pioneering value reflected in the homegrown entrepreneurs that call Alserkal Avenue their home and that work collectively to build our creative economy and ecosystem. Taking stock, it gives me great pride to see the successes that the UAE has charted, and it is that drive to take a risk on the risk-takers that we have steadfastly championed throughout the growth of Alserkal, Alserkal Avenue and Alserkal Arts Foundation, and now also with Alserkal Advisory.

Journey

A thriving cultural scene is the backbone of integrated societies, engendering a sense of belonging and prosperity. My vision has always been not only to help create the infrastructure within which the arts and culture sector can thrive, but to ensure that, as we make strides in growing the impact of arts and culture, we remain mindful of our relationship with the environment and the legacy that we are building for generations to come.

From the very beginning, I was drawn to the idea of cultural enterprise. I was privileged to see the emergence of cultural districts the world over and to witness their positive impact on the social and economic fabric of the societies in which they existed.

I wanted to see such a space brought to life in Dubai, to encourage discourse and dialogue, to allow the creative spirit of the city's multicultural communities to excel, promoting a sense of belonging and identity amongst those who call Dubai home. My goal was to create a space where those willing to reimagine their industries could come together; where we could support the risk-takers and enable them to make a success of their ideas. Over a decade later, it's now clear that Alserkal Avenue was just the beginning. The Avenue has given rise to our commissions programme, to Concrete, and more recently to Alserkal Arts Foundation and Alserkal Advisory.

HH Sheikh Zayed

His Highness Sheikh Zayed was a visionary leader with a long-term vision who valued sustainability across all paradigms. He embodied the essence and the principles that form the cornerstone of the United Arab Emirates' values and culture—tolerance, unity and vision. Long-term thinking and legacy-building for our future generations is a key pillar that I strive to instill in everything that we do at Alserkal.

Exponential Growth

For me, the UAE's story isn't just about exponential growth, but the value that has been created through that growth, and the ecosystem and support structures that now exist as a result. The UAE's art scene may be young, but it has been a privilege to bear witness to and contribute to its growth. Artists such as the late Hassan Sharif, a prolific artist who is regarded as the father of conceptual art in the Gulf, alongside Mohamed Ahmed Ibrahim and Mohammed Kazem and the Flying House collective built this scene alongside the gallerists and patrons who supported them. They paved the way for more emerging artists including Shaikha Al Mazrou and Afra Al Dhaheri, who today have showcased their works not only within the art galleries in Alserkal

Avenue but also on an international stage.

Secret of Success

I hold strong to the principles on which the UAE has been founded. They have been fundamental to our success as a nation. I carry those values with me in all aspects of my life. I believe that resilience and the ability to adapt and mutate through a tolerant and inclusive society allows us to collectively tackle complex issues such as sustainability.

Challenges

For many of us, COVID has reinforced the vital importance of community and coming together for meaningful cultural experiences. I expect we will continue to learn from our experiences during the pandemic in years to come. The Alserkal family, together with the community, created the 'Alserkal Pay It Forward Programme' during COVID, inviting our community members to apply for a subsidy for their lease commitment for three months, in return for giving back to their neighbours. More than 50 Alserkal Avenue organisations joined forces to support each other (and the wider Dubai community) in the face of the unprecedented challenges posed by the COVID-19 pandemic. This powerful community collaboration saw the businesses in Alserkal Avenue generate a barter economy to the value of more than AED2 million in just two months. As a forward-thinking socially responsible cultural enterprise, we are committed to considering sustainability in all its forms in everything that we do.

Opportunities

At Alserkal, supporting and spearheading new projects with our artists, galleries, creative pioneers and global cultural partners remains at the core of what we do. Collectively, we form a civic network and commercial nerve centre for the arts sector, for the region and internationally.

Alserkal was built on the premise of community, solidarity and collaboration, and it was through this that Alserkal Advisory was recently established to work with public and private sector entities to develop cultural production projects, inspire and shape communities through heritage creation initiatives, and advise on through Alserkal Advisory policymaking for the creative sectors. We look forward to more collaborative practices and projects regionally and beyond.

Through Alserkal Arts Foundation, we will continue to support artists and practitioners who are engaged in unconventional modes of research and cultural production in our region.

Lessons

In the UAE, we are fortunate to have founding fathers and leaders who are visionaries. Their pioneering spirit, collaborative and forward-thinking approach, commitment to progress, and deep dedication to our people is inspiring.

Expo

Expo 2020 Dubai is a milestone for the UAE, being the first Expo in the history of the Arab, Africa and South Asia region. This presents a unique opportunity for cross-cultural collaborations, and so it is fitting that Alserkal will play its role in this momentous occasion by programming Cultures in Conversation, commissioned by Expo 2020. We see our role in programming this series as an opportunity for diverse people from around the world to unite, take ownership of the programme, and re-think global issues that have become critically urgent.

I would hope that visitors to Expo 2020 will take the time to explore the city of Dubai, to immerse themselves in our arts and culture scene, and to meet the change-makers and risk-takers who are helping build our creative economy, and the artists and practitioners who are challenging the status quo. In my view, no visit to UAE is complete without a visit to the galleries, foundations and creative businesses in Alserkal Avenue, as well as our friends and collaborators in Jameel Arts Centre, Sharjah Art Foundation, NYUAD, Warehouse421 and the Louvre Abu Dhabi.

Future

Through arts and culture we can find common ground, shared ideas and philosophies. It encourages dialogue, curiosity, critical thinking, and the evolution of our societies. It enables us to build bridges, at home and around the world. To the Alserkal family, and Alserkal as an organisation, making a contribution and creating positive social impact are values that we've always held dear. It has particularly been a privilege for us to work together with incredible artists, cultural producers and institutions to grow the cultural landscape of this region.

This comes with a responsibility to put sustainability at the core of everything we do, in order to ensure that we have a future for the generations to come.

In 2071, I hope that as a nation we will have nurtured a generation that embraces arts and culture as an intrinsic part of our social fabric, and that sees the importance of patronage in sustaining our arts ecosystem and supporting our future artists and creative communities. I also hope that by 2071, we can look back and see the exponential growth of the creative businesses that started out with their homes in Alserkal Avenue.

10. COMBATING CLIMATE CHANGE

HE Mariam bint Mohammed Saeed Hareb Almheiri, Minister of Climate Change and Environment

"As the land of opportunities and collaboration, we look forward to bringing the world together to explore effective solutions to the most pressing challenges our planet faces"

HE Mariam Almheiri leads the Ministry of Climate Change and Environment's mission of spearheading the UAE's drive to mitigate and adapt to the impacts of climate change, protect the country's ecosystems, and enhance its food and water security. Prior to her current role, HE Mariam was Minister of State for Food and Water Security. Her responsibilities included monitoring national food stocks and water supply, channeling investments in food and water technology innovation, and building international partnerships in this area.

Although most people think of the UAE as a barren desert, in fact, it is an area of ecological abundance with a history of conservation and protection. Abu Dhabi means "Father of the Gazelle" and as such there is an ancient connection between the land and the animals on it. After the Arabian Oryx was officially declared extinct in the 1970s, HH Sheikh Zayed launched a successful conservation programme which is now applauded globally. As he used to say, "On land and in the sea, our fore-fathers lived and survived in this environment. They were able to do so because they recognised the need to conserve it, to take from it only what they needed to live, and to preserve it for succeeding generations." HE Mariam continues his mission to balance the country's extraordinary growth with this need to protect its natural riches.

Earliest Memories

I loved the area of Nad al Sheeba where my school was and where the racetrack was. We used to go on hacks with the horses there and see all the Camel Farms. There was a lot of desert, but they had also taken care in greening the area, and riding on the grass and between the trees was always special. My interests as a kid were with animals: we had rescue dogs, cats, parrots, hamsters and horses. You could even go riding on Jumeirah Beach in those days. That was beautiful taking the horses out swimming in the sea.

Journey

I have had no idea where this journey was going to take me! Sometimes things happen in a very surprising way. However, I believe that having passion for something is very important. My parents were adamant on me having a good education and giving me the freedom to go abroad to study. I was finishing my A levels and had a choice between the US or Europe. Most of my contemporaries went to the US, however I wanted to do something a bit different. I spoke some German so looked closer at Germany. I loved animals but actually airplanes fascinated me the most – and I remember thinking at a young age how amazing it was that humans had created a "metal bird". I'd always go to the cockpit and it was such a treat as a little girl, seeing all the buttons and the crew. As a result, I decided to apply for Aeronautical Engineering at the Rheinisch-Westfälische Technische Hochschule (RWTH) in Aachen, Germany. I luckily got a scholarship and started there. The nature of the university really encouraged independence. This really shaped me. The course itself was actually very theoretical so I switched to Mechanical Engineering and decided to get my own private pilot licence. I started the course there, however I knew my dad wasn't a fan of small planes, so would not fund it so I had to get a student job to start. I didn't get to finish the course but the passion for flight is still there! The engineering mindset is crucial to how I think: you learn to solve problems and work under pressure. For four years I worked in a high-tech engineering company that was a spin-out from the University.

I then came back to the UAE and actually set up a few personal businesses in sport, real estate, medical – a true entrepreneur! I also started a new hobby: diving. This actually began my climate journey, appreciating the beauties of the treasure under water. I started working with the Emirates Marine Environmental Group, as I saw that they were doing a lot in this space. I always made sure I went to Abu Dhabi

Sustainability Week, which is where I met HE Dr Rashid bin Fahad, when he was Minister of Environment and Water. I saw him go into his booth and I just thought I'd go and say hello – I wasn't looking for a job, but through the conversation he explained that he needed passionate people like me. Three months later I became an Expert Advisor in the Minister's Office and the first project they gave me was concerned with the marine environment in Umm al Quwain, breeding fingerlings and putting them into the sea for restocking purposes. I was a project manager with my helmet and boots and got very involved. I then set up the Project Management Office, then the Education and Awareness programme. I started getting more and more responsibilities. My first project has actually become what is now going to be the Sheikh Khalifa Marine Research Centre. I was proud of this aquaculture initiative and I ultimately became Assistant Undersecretary for the Marine Sector. From here I became Minister of State for Food Security in October 2017. The Water security mandate was added to my responsibilities in 2019 and then in 2021 I became a Cabinet Member and Minister of Climate Change and the Environment.

If I think of this journey, it actually all started by me being born into a family that loves and respects animals, and the environment.

HH Sheikh Zayed

HH Sheikh Zayed was always on television in my youth and was always giving. He always put the people first. He had a heart for the environment. He was a real advocate, and he created a number of laws and policies in the early days of the federation to conserve the environment, green the desert and protect the animals. I also remember his humanitarian efforts, helping other countries. He invested in schools and water wells globally. He had such a sweet smile. My dad received a horse racing trophy from him once. Sheikh Zayed was always promoting horse racing, falconry and other cultural events. You always see people's faces soften when they remember him and speak of him. You see these traits living on with his sons as well.

Exponential Growth

Regarding the environment, HH Sheikh Zayed learned that 15,000 years ago, the Arabian Peninsula was covered in dense forests and full of greenery. The land became desert only after a long drought. Over time, the forests were buried in sand and gradually transformed into the region's oil. HH Sheikh Zayed however was determined to "green the desert" again. The "experts" advised HH Sheikh Zayed in the early days that you couldn't do agriculture here – but that did not deter him. They said it was impossible, but he was adamant. He got the local geologists who discovered water and invested in a tree-planting project that began at the end of the 1960s and continues to prosper even today, with more than a 100 million trees currently existing within the borders of the UAE. The city of Al Ain alone has more than 75 modern forests, each with an average area ranging between two to three square kilometres. The variety of trees planted were chosen carefully and assessed for their ability to survive in the harsh summer climate of the region, with greater emphasis on local breeds. It is why Al Ain is known as the "Garden City" of the UAE. This green growth has been exponential from the harsh desert environment that Sheikh Zayed was born into, but he saw what was possible, and would not accept "impossible".

Look also at what we did with solar energy. Yes, we have oil and gas, but we also need to ramp up our renewables to diversify our energy mix. If we look at the solar journey in the last 16 years, we are now building the world's largest solar power plant in Abu Dhabi. The new plant will eliminate more than 2.4 million metric tonnes of CO_2 emissions per year, equivalent to removing 470,000 cars from roads. We also built the first zero carbon emission nuclear power plant in the Arab world and are the first in the region to have an industrial scale green hydrogen production plant.

Secret of Success

There is a real consistency of leadership. This is why we've been able to build so quickly. This is one of the keys as to why the UAE has developed so fast. We are nurturing the seeds that HH Sheikh Zayed has sown.

Challenges

We are a water-scarce country. We don't have arable land. We have to think out of the box. We are dependent on technology and innovation. We have always had to be innovative for water and food. However, this is also an opportunity, especially as other countries are only just beginning to realise their own water and food needs.

Opportunities

We're so blessed that the leadership is open to any good idea.

The leadership has an open-door policy. They are open to game changing initiatives. For example, we created Food Tech Valley. It is a Playground for Agtech. The Agtech sector is a real opportunity.

Lessons

Swings between left and right in politics I believe hinder progress. In the UAE we are all pulling in the same direction and have been doing so consistently in the last 50 years. There is full trust between the leadership and the people.

Expo

Coming out of the pandemic and having a world stage where we can see everyone face to face, the energy is electric. Sustainability is at its core - it is fantastic.

Future

In the near future we are very proud that the UAE will host COP28 in 2023. We are ready to deliver a productive, accessible and inclusive COP that builds a strong economic case for climate action and mobilizes countries to increase the scale and pace of their efforts to address climate change Net Zero by 2050. As the land of opportunities and collaboration, we look forward to bringing the world together to explore effective solutions to the most pressing challenges our planet faces. Hosting this global gathering will also provide us with a prime opportunity to involve our most dynamic segment of society - our youth - in the meetings and negotiations that will ultimately ensure a sustainable future for generations to come.

By 2071, I see us continuing our sustainable economic trajectory. We want to attract people that want to join us on this path, to live in a country that not only speaks about sustainability but acts. As well as announcing Net Zero by 2050, the UAE has also allocated over $163 billion to meet our goal. We have political will and ambition.

We're not perfect, but the good thing is that we have forward thinking leadership, we have the targets and the funding to make this a reality. We're on this amazing sustainable trajectory to 2050 and beyond to our Centennial Plan.

11. UNITED IN CONSERVATION

HE Razan al Mubarak, President of the IUCN

"The conservation of nature can only be successful when we work together to tackle the challenges we face."

HE Razan Al Mubarak became President of the IUCN in 2021. She is the second woman to lead the organization in its 72-year history and the first female president from Asia. She is also the first IUCN president from the Arab world since 1978. Razan Al Mubarak is also the Managing Director of the Environment Agency Abu Dhabi (EAD). In 2018, the World Economic Forum selected her as one of the top 100 Young Global Leaders for her contribution to building a more sustainable future for humankind. Razan Al Mubarak is also the Managing Director of the Mohamed bin Zayed Species Conservation Fund – a philanthropy providing grants for the protection of endangered species worldwide. Since its inception the MBZ Fund has supported thousands of projects in more than 160 different countries benefiting more than 1,300 different species and subspecies across all taxa. Through the work of its grant recipients, numerous species have been discovered or rediscovered, and others pulled back from the brink of extinction.

Razan also helped establish Emirates Nature WWF (EN-WWF) in 2001 and is currently its Managing Director. Under her stewardship, EN-WWF has undertaken the most comprehensive coral reef mapping in West Asia, pioneered research and conservation efforts to protect marine turtles and was crucial to the establishment of the first national park in the UAE (Wadi Wurayah National Park), as well as a number of leading sustainable education and stakeholder engagement initiatives.

Earliest Memories

My strongest memories of this time were formed in my grandmother's majilis where her endless curiosity was on display; listening to the women's age-old wisdom; learning the traditions of generosity and welcoming guests from both near and far. My grandmother together with my aunts and mother would host daily exchanges and collectively we would learn about cultures, beliefs, customs, values, and experiences. It was a place where our own sense of self, family, national identity, and place in the world were formed and defined. The women of this majilis, and other majilis, played such an important role in helping to shape and define the Emirates today.

I also remember fondly our Fareej – literally our neighborhood. It was our playground where my siblings and cousins could explore and take risks – unchaperoned because we were in the safety of our Fareej. From these childhood experiences, I learned about the centrality of Al Balad Al Tayeb or "Dar Al Khair" 'the land of blessing' to the UAE's identity. The UAE welcomed people from all over the world who shared a common dream of making the Emirates a land of blessing; committed to forming a society based on similar values, one that is very much a multicultural melting pot with a shared concern for one another's welfare. It is through embracing the whole, commitment to the weakest amongst us that gives the UAE its strength to realize its destiny.

Journey

Since before the establishment of the UAE, our forefathers and foremothers instilled within all of us a passion for nature. Protecting Arabian Oryx, Houbara bustard, falcons and wild places has always been a priority in the UAE. At about the same time I graduated from university, Abu Dhabi had organized several wildlife conservation initiatives into a government agency called the "Environmental Research and Wildlife Development Agency (ERWDA)." I remember walking into the offices of this entity, which was to become the Environment Agency Abu Dhabi, to ask for a job. Fifteen years after that fateful visit to the original ERWDA offices, I found myself as the Secretary General of the Environment Agency - Abu Dhabi. Of course, none of my success would have been possible without Emiratis' innate passion for nature or our leaderships' foresight to formally protect it.

Throughout this I began to realize that nature is central to our cultural identity as a nation. When a country develops as quickly as the

UAE, we witness the loss of nature firsthand and there is a personal sense of loss. Nature conservation becomes central and important. It is because of this that the UAE has been a game changer in nature conservation efforts both at home and around the world. Because of the successful conservation efforts in the UAE, the Arabian oryx has been brought back from the brink of extinction. The Mohamed bin Zayed Species Conservation Fund is a great global example. To date, the Fund has supported thousands of species conservation projects across more than 160 countries benefiting more than 1,500 highly endangered species and subspecies. And this is something for which we can all be proud.

HH Sheikh Zayed

HH Sheikh Zayed loved nature, particularly the desert. The desert and its wide-open spaces were in his soul. He was an avid horseman and falconer. He instilled this same respect for wildlife and passion for nature in all of us. For his efforts to protect the last remaining Arabian oryx, he was awarded the "Golden Panda" in 1997 by the World Wide Fund for Nature (WWF). He was also recognized in 2005 by UN Environment (UNEP) as a "Champion of the Earth." His example of nature conservation continues to inspire me today. His legacy is our legacy. The support for the reintroduction of the Arabian Oryx here in the UAE and the Scimitar-horned oryx in Chad, as well as the International Fund for Conservation of Houbara are largely attributable to his legacy and the desire of our leadership to continue to honor his legacy with these world-renowned conservation programmes.

Exponential Growth

Mangrove National Park on the northeast side of the island of Abu Dhabi signifies the UAE's extraordinary growth. As the city grew from its roots, so too did this mangrove forest. It was originally planted more than 40 years ago at the direction of Sheikh Zayed. Today, along the coast of our capital city, there are 20 square kilometers of wetlands where 20 million trees provide an extensive ecosystem for migrating and resident birds, nursery grounds for fish and other animals, and recreational opportunities for residents. This mangrove forest, because it absorbs and stores carbon dioxide in its leaves and the soil below, provides a nature-based solution to climate change. Mangrove National Park is a great example of people living in harmony with nature. Every time I visit or even pass by, I am reminded that we are part of nature, and it is part of us.

Secret of Success

There is no 'secret' to success. Success is realized through consistent, disciplined, goal-oriented hard work and a little luck.

Challenges

Fifty years is not long to establish and grow a community into a successful country. We can see with our own eyes the exponential growth in the physical infrastructure of the UAE. One doesn't have to live here long to witness impressive changes, but what many of us don't consider is the same growth occurring in the UAE's structure of governance. For example, thirty years ago, there was no official government regulator of the environment. In less than 25 years, the Environment Agency – Abu Dhabi has established itself as the largest environmental regulator in the Middle East. In addition, the UAE has established the Ministry of Climate Change and Environment to help regulate the environment on a national level and to oversee regional and global environmental agreements. Greenhouse gas inventories, water and air quality measures, protected areas, fisheries regulations, species conservation programmes, all of these needed to be built from the ground up. The Environment Agency Abu Dhabi has established and currently manages many globally recognized initiatives to protect the environment. These are the challenges and success stories that many of us don't see as we marvel at the breakneck speed at which the UAE's infrastructure has risen from the desert.

Opportunities

Business opportunities that target climate change excite me. In October 2021, the UAE announced the launch of the UAE Net Zero by 2050 Strategic Initiative that builds on the country's three decades of climate efforts and the UAE was selected to host the climate talks, COP28, in 2023. These visionary actions reinforce the UAE's leading role in the global drive to combat climate change and represent a new step in the country's approach to sustainable development. Sustainable energy, agriculture technology, water efficiency, green-tech will all play a significant role in the continued success of the UAE's business environment.

Lessons

I believe the success of the UAE is based in its common sense of optimism. The leadership and the people of the UAE see a bright future and we all work together to help realize it. There is a common sense of hope, opportunity, and optimism that helps lead to our success. It's a winning formula that can benefit others, as well.

Expo

Expo highlights what's possible through its sustainability, mobility, and opportunity pavilions. Expo is at once inspirational and aspirational. It draws attention to what humanity is on the cusp of achieving. It is this spirit of optimism, sense of purpose, and view toward the future that the UAE exemplifies to the world.

More importantly, Expo demonstrated to the world the importance of building convergence and celebrating multiculturalism in a world that has been trending toward polarization. While every country's pavilion showcased their progress and innovation, every pavilion also showcased their culture. To me, this was the greatest value of Expo. Its strength was showcasing the beauty of every country's culture. Its way of life.

Future

Along with its many other achievements by 2071, the UAE will be living in full harmony with nature. This will be realized through the UAE's commitment to be Net Zero by 2050 and its progress toward protecting more than 30% of marine and terrestrial territory. These are visionary goals that will help nature and the people of the UAE to continue to thrive for generations where both nature and people thrive.

12. EVOLVING ENVIRONMENT

HE Dr. Shaikha Salem Al Dhaheri, the Secretary General of the Environment Agency

"The last 50 years was about internal infrastructure, building the foundations of the nation. The next 50 is about outward focus, on how we can help humanity, specifically about how we can combat climate change."

HE Dr. Shaikha Salem Al Dhaheri is the Secretary General of the Environment Agency - Abu Dhabi (EAD), the largest environmental regulator in the Middle East, responsible for protecting and preserving the Emirate's natural resources and promoting sustainable development.

Dr. Al Dhaheri holds a PhD degree in Wildlife Conservation and Protection from the University of Aberdeen, the first Emirati woman to earn the accolade. She also holds two Masters degrees: in Environmental Science from UAE University (UAEU) in Al Ain, and another in Biological Conservation From the University of Kent. She earned her Bachelor's degree in Environmental Species from UAEU.

Dr. Al Dhaheri began her career at EAD as a Researcher Assistant in the Agency's Terrestrial Environment Research in 2000 and was later appointed as Executive Director of the Terrestrial and Marine Biodiversity Sector in 2012. In this role, she spearheaded initiatives to promote a comprehensive understanding of the state of biodiversity in Abu Dhabi and ensured that the sector's goals were in line with Abu Dhabi Environment Vision 2030 and the Abu Dhabi Plan, among other national and emirate-level directives. She has played a defining role in establishing a clear vision for the sector to facilitate a sustainable environment and future for Abu Dhabi.

Earliest Memories

From my earliest memories, of more than three decades ago that are still etched in my mind, much of the country was largely desert with few buildings near the main townships of Abu Dhabi and Al Ain. High rise buildings were even fewer at that time.

I come from a family tribe in Al Ain. My parents moved to Abu Dhabi in early 70s following the discovery of oil. I still remember visiting my parents' home every weekend from Abu Dhabi to Al Ain and we could travel for kilometers and kilometers across the empty landscapes on a single carriageway through vast stretches of desert. Roads were not as busy with fewer cars and much less people. It is totally transformed now. The cities have extended further, grown bigger, roads wider and more and more traffic.

Simplistic design and low-rise buildings characterised Abu Dhabi. Though schools were basic, they were good enough and provided a solid platform for all of us to receive good education. I lived in a very social community in a neighbourhood of around 30 houses. We knew practically everyone and had very strong social bonds.

Inspired by the vision of the leadership, my father always asked me to dream big and focus on a goal. This is the way I have been raised. My father always called me a "doctor" or "dentist" and I think like any other parent, he wanted me to be in the medical profession. Also, possibly he was mirroring the vision and the wish of late sheikh Zayed for his nation to become doctors, engineers and teachers. I am now a "Doctor". A different kind of doctor, not in the field of medicine but environment.

Journey

Soon after graduating from Al Ain University, I joined EAD in 2000 and started my professional journey. In this period, I also completed my two masters' degrees from the UAE University and the University of Kent respectively. I fell in love with my job with EAD, however while working in the field, I realised, I needed to further equip myself with knowledge and skills and understanding of how things function in nature and how creatures, from small insects to large Oryx play an important role in maintaining the balance of the ecosystem. This led me to go for my PhD on Butterflies from the University of Edinburgh in Scotland.

If my early days exposed me to the UAE and its desert biodiversity, my PhD gave me a new perspective in understanding ecological inter-relations. This was vital, as I returned to EAD in 2009 as the first Emirati with a PhD in Biological sciences. It gave me a sense of pride as well as responsibility as I started working within the Biodiversity Sector. I continued to make professional progress from Manager of Biodiversity Assessment and Monitoring to the Executive Director of the Sector until 2019. During this period, we undertook initiatives and programmes which have not only been successful but also satisfying. There are many which I can mention, but I will highlight just a few of the most important ones which I am immensely proud of.

The now successful reintroduction of the Scimitar-horned Oryx; establishment of the Sheikh Zayed network of 19 protected areas and turning our fisheries to sustainable levels within three years from a collapse stage are the highlights of my professional journey, directly under my watch.

Today, as one of the first Emirati women to work in the field of environment and biodiversity, my professional journey from an aspiring researcher to the Secretary General of the largest environmental regulator in the Middle East has been, both very satisfying and fulfilling. Hopefully it has also inspired other young Emiratis along the way.

HH Sheikh Zayed

Sheikh Zayed our father of the nation is a father-figure to all of us. He inspired all of us, those who met him and those who didn't. He left behind a rich legacy, a legacy of tolerance, generosity, commitment, resilience, and care. His work and ethics positively influenced all those living here; however, his human values and concerns went beyond the UAE boundaries. He touched our lives and he touched others as well, outside the UAE.

One of the biggest legacies he left behind is the environmental conservation. He was truly a champion conservationist, but for him the UAE and its environment would have been poorer. He believed in remaining connected with nature and much ahead of time as this quote sums up:

"On land and in the sea, our fore-fathers lived and survived in this environment. They were able to do so because they recognised the need to conserve it, to take from it only what they needed to live, and to preserve it for succeeding generations."

His work on the Arabian Oryx and its reintroduction, not only helped us in reintroducing the Arabian Oryx into the UAE but also inspired regional conservation efforts, ultimately leading to the down-listing of the species from endangered to vulnerable. His collection of the Scimitar-horned Oryx helped us create the world herd for reintroduction in Chad, which is now called one of the most ambitious and successful large mammal reintroductions in the world. His efforts to breed Houbara, not only helped protect and release the threatened Houbara, but was fundamental to the establishment of the National Avian Research Centre in 1989 which gave birth to ERWDA (now EAD) in 1996.

Exponential Growth

It was the vision of the leadership which has been largely responsible for the extraordinary growth that we have seen in the last 50 years. Of course, the discovery of oil in the 70's was a major catalyst and created the kind of wealth needed for development, however wealth alone is not enough as many countries far richer than the UAE have not been able to develop the way the UAE has done in 50 years. It was about nation building. Leaders were committed to the nation and nation building. They laid the foundation and concrete plans for overall development- from infrastructure to educational institutions. While doing so, they ensured that we remain connected to our culture and established centres to do so – investment in falconry, pearling and traditional fishing received special attention. More than the world class infrastructure, it's the UAE's soft power that has been fundamental to the UAE's unprecedented growth.

Secret of Success

There are possibly three key reasons for the UAE's success, in my view. Strong courageous leadership, commitment, and development of an inclusive society with human development at the core it. By inclusive, I mean a society that was welcoming of people from all walks of life, caste, creed, and religion and that also helped the UAE in attracting talented individuals who contributed to the country's growth and development. This allowed everyone to take part in nation building, without making distinction between men and women. Leaders had a grand vision and were inspirational. They inspired a whole new generation of Emiratis, men, and women alike. It allowed us to dream.

To dream big and to be the best. Our journey, from the emptiness of the Rub-al-Khali to the rarefied Martian atmosphere has been truly astronomical.

We are also a very optimistic nation. In the darkest of times, in our past, the leadership were always sending messages of hope and positivity to the communities. When I think of my grandparents living in the desert with almost no resources, they would all gather with the leaders and share their hopes for the future. I think this is part of our DNA.

Challenges

I personally won't term them as challenges. These were cultural and generational changes. Transitional changes. When I chose conservation as a discipline, more than two decades ago, I was one of the first Emirati women to do so. It involved going out with the team of mixed nationalities and genders in remote deserts to collect scientific data. Our society and families were not used to this, and it took some convincing and understanding on their part. I was lucky to have all the support from my parents; however it took some time for the society to accept this. Today, I am glad to see more and more women taking to this field and proving themselves.

At the country level, we don't see challenges as challenges anymore. When in the 1970's the British offered to end the Trucial states, the late Sheikh Zayed took this as an opportunity, more than the challenge. This is the belief that has been passed on from Sheikh Zayed to our leadership and to all of us. To build a country from a sandy desert to one of the world's most modern countries in five decades is remarkable. The next challenging opportunity is how do we transition from oil to a non-oil economy and how do we sustain and maintain, what we have created in 50 years and further build on the successes.

Opportunities

We have created adequate investment in all the key sectors, from social to economic and environment, over the last fifty years. These will be further boosted and will create opportunities for everyone. Opportunities for investment, opportunities for innovation and opportunities for socio-cultural development. We may run out of oil, but by then we will have diversified our economy to the extent, that the transition from an oil-based to non-oil-based economy will be smooth.

The Net-Zero pledge will present enormous business opportunities for public and private sector companies in energy, transport and infrastructure sectors and will stimulate a new era of growth. Companies need to repurpose themselves to the new reality, to be smart and innovative and invest in waste, ecotourism, sustainable transport, sustainable food, and clean energy solutions. There will be huge investments in human health and particularly in understanding the connect between human health and environment. Pandemic, disease prevention will get special attention and investment decisions will be more and more based on environmental, social and governance (ESG) credentials of companies.

Lessons

So many. To be tolerant, welcoming, resilient, and relentless. We as a nation have shown all this over the last fifty years. We have been a tolerant country and welcomed all nationalities with open arms, no wonder we have nearly 200 nationalities peacefully living in the UAE. Our development story shows that we have been resilient and relentless in the pursuit of excellence. Another important thing that countries can learn from the UAE is to dream big and realise them and it's not the size of the country, but the power of your vision and ability to take bold decisions that take you forward. Our success in outer space, the Hope Probe to Mars sums up our ability to dream big and realise our dreams as well.

Expo

Expo further showcases the country that it has come to be. A young, confident nation with aspirations to be the best. The opening of Expo amidst the ongoing COVID pandemic itself was a strong indicator of the resilience of the country, about its systems and processes. The biggest takeaway is that the country is safe, welcoming and capable and a place to do business and enjoy the sun, sea and sand.

Future

Even as we reflect on the past half a century, our leadership is already working on a roadmap for the next half a century, as it focuses on inclusive growth and sustainable development. To my mind, ours will be a growth that is rimmed by the country's climate and conservation aspirations – and where our youth will be its chief drivers.

I have no doubt that we will have a smooth transition to clean energy – a transition that had already been set in motion with the establishment of Masdar City, the Barakah nuclear plant and solar parks across the Emirates.

I will paint a vivid picture. Vivid green. UAE will continue to grow; however, it will be largely green growth. It will continue to surprise everyone by its growth and development as it did in the last 50 years. The country has created the platform for the next fifty years of growth which will be more around scientific development, innovation, environment, and human development. If the past fifty years were more inward looking, the next fifty years will be more outward looking, with the UAE assuming more leadership role, especially in the field of human health and environment.

In my own field, the environment will continue to occupy a big space, driven by climate change and biodiversity. COP 28 to be hosted in Abu Dhabi in 2023, will be a landmark event. As in the words of Sheikh Mohamed bin Zayed, Crown Prince of Abu Dhabi and Deputy Supreme Commander of the Armed Forces, shortly before the UAE won the COP 28 bid – he said: "As a nation committed to international co-operation and positive action, the UAE is ready and willing to host this crucial global gathering aimed at accelerating efforts to address our planet's shared climate challenges."

Actions to mitigate climate change will be key, with the Net-Zero announcement, we will see a big shift towards energy efficient systems and transportation modes. We will move towards a circular economy (zero waste), see more electric vehicles on the road and transportation, both passenger and cargo by rail will be commonplace.

By 2071, we will have restored and recovered some of the most threatened ecosystems in Abu Dhabi such as coral reefs and mangroves. Our native plant nurseries and state of the art Gene bank will help in selecting the most resilient native plant species for restoring degraded terrestrial habitat as well as replacing non-native species in other green spaces. We will return to sustainable fishing ways, with over 90% of all fish caught sustainably. We have already turned the corner when it comes to sustainable fishing and there is no reason why we can't achieve this in the next decade itself. We will also see manifold increase in the development of the aquaculture sector, which will also help address the country's food security aspirations.

We will continue to protect all our species and their habitats through expansion of our Zayed Protected Areas Network. We will restore and rewild some of the most threatened species in Abu Dhabi and beyond and ensure their conservation status continues to improve. We have already integrated the best of technologies in our monitoring and regulation programmes, such as satellite tracking and drones, and will continue to make even greater push towards integration of AI and advanced data analytics to provide real time data to effectively protect our environment. We will build a strong and enduring public-private-partnership (PPP) and see much greater participation of private sectors and public in protecting our environment.

We will cut down on water abstraction and beef up our strategic water reserve and ensure that our air and water are clean more than 95% of the time. Finally, I believe that the UAE will be a leader in environmental field if we continue the path and align our strategies to local and global realities. I also have no doubt that Abu Dhabi will be among the most influential names when it comes to environmental leadership and shaping the global biodiversity and the climate agenda...

13. NURTURING NATURE

Sheikh Dr. Majid al Qasimi

"Give me agriculture and I will show you civilization"

Dr Majid trained as a veterinarian, receiving his Doctor of Veterinary Medicine from the University of Szent Istvan in Budapest. He has worked on projects, policy and regulation for agriculture, animal production, food safety, as well as conservation and sustainability. Of mixed ethnicity (Emirati/German) Majid has a broad cross-cultural perspective and this helps connect minds and ideas across the globe. Majid served as the Chief Veterinary Officer of the UAE and Advisor to the UAE Minister of Climate Change and Environment. He is a co-founder of a food security and sustainability consultancy SOMA MATER based in Dubai.

Earliest Memories

I was born in 1982, but my earliest memory is 1986 in Sharjah. My dad had just got a plot of land where we were building a house. The other side of the road was open desert, but if you walked to the right, there was a big water tower at the roundabout. You don't really see them anymore, but it was symbolic of life then in the UAE: it was a mixture of modern luxury, having fresh water, juxtaposed against the harsh desert environment in which we were building our home, and a reminder simultaneously of the scarcity of our resources. My dad still lives there today. Where we are sitting now, compared with my first home, demonstrates the journey the UAE has been on in my lifetime.

Journey

I didn't really know what I wanted to do, right up until my last few years at school. I just knew I liked Biology, and it struck me when I did some practical work with a family friend, at the Central Veterinary Research Laboratory, that a profession in Veterinary medicine would open up the world for me. Learning that there weren't any Emirati Veterinarians, meant I had a lot to contribute to my country. The ability to take what I was about to learn and bring it back to the UAE, was for me, my calling. After graduating and coming back, I have been working in the Environmental and Sustainability space my whole working life, spanning policy making, biodiversity, agriculture, and today, having been an advisor to two Ministers in this sector, I am now running my own consultancy. I believe I have given and continue to give to my country. I believe that the UAE has a big part to play in the Arab world and Middle East on re-addressing how we engage with Nature and Mother Earth.

HH Sheikh Zayed

HH Sheikh Zayed is someone who thought well beyond his own mortality and lifetime. A man with a simple understanding of the world, but able to scale it to his people. To say he was a North Star, would be selling him short. He really was a guiding light for the country. He was incredibly empathetic to bring so many people to the table and give them something bigger to work with and aim for.

There's one saying he always said which was "give me agriculture and I will show you civilization". It was his understanding that, being originally nomads, if we had resources and capabilities, we become a people, not a tribe.

Exponential Growth

Sharjah focused on a different sort of growth: education. To this day, we are the cornerstone of the country's heritage. My wife is from Dubai, and she always says Sharjah is where a lot of the learned people are; very academic. This is physically demonstrated in "University City".

For me the way I like to see it, as a federation, we are a team of seven Emirates. You have your centre of Government in Abu Dhabi, Dubai is commercial, but Sharjah is fostering education, design and culture. Everyone is playing to their strengths and that is really powerful. Ras al Khaimah doubled down on Eco-Tourism, as have the other Emirates chosen their own paths. It is the growth in every corner of the UAE.

Secret of Success

Visionary Leadership. We all say it, but let me explain what I mean by it. It is both the leadership of the country and the leadership for each Emirate. They come together and infuse the Emirati nationals with a sense of purpose. They call on each person's purpose to drive growth. Everyone has a national pride here which is very different to the pride I have experienced in other countries, which is centred on symbols like flags. We have a pride that is focused on our people, and a pride in our leadership. It's in the awakening of that spirit, that not only drives the engine of the country, but takes it into the world. Sheikh Zayed was trying to build a vision for the UAE that everyone could be proud of and be a part of. Akin to the American Dream, the UAE has a dream, and it's not only for the Emiratis, it's for Expats. That calling globally, that people not born here can feel a pride in the UAE, that is the secret to this country's success.

Challenges

The UAE has seven different players, in the form of each Emirate, and the challenge was finding out what each did best, and what were the unique characteristics. Own your own and play it well. I think coming out of the pandemic, you are seeing a confidence that each knows what it does best. I have no doubt that the world is going to see the UAE do more cool things in the future.

For me personally, a challenge has been how to transition out of government and into the private sector. There are private sector families that have built this country, and government entities that have shaped the growth, but it's the younger generation understanding the only goal isn't necessarily being a government servant, and that you can still grow your country and be valuable in the private sector. This is something I have personally learned, and it is a personal mission for me to figure out how I can also help that transition.

Opportunities

There are tech companies that can use the UAE as a testbed and launch to the region, using the logistics, while also enjoying a quality of life that promotes innovation and entrepreneurship and different thinking. Everything here is up for grabs in terms of disruption and development. The UAE wants to be the proud incubator for the world. When it comes to agriculture and tech, the UAE can leverage that incubator as we live in a very extreme environment. We stand at an opportunity to grow ideas and new technologies for food production that will be critical to the world's population living in arid and challenging environments.

Lessons

Long-term leadership. The short-termism of some leaders, ensuring they maintain power, skews their thinking. The motives when one can think long term means that a country can leapfrog others. In addition, and linked, is the ability to incorporate youth and bring youth into leadership. You can channel all that energy and naturally look more long-term. Infuse their vigour into solution finding. I'd ask other countries what their youth could do in terms of driving their growth.

Expo

Hospitality is not just our way of life, but it is the chance to connect. Expo is the manifestation of that hospitality. Come, be welcomed, get to know everyone. The themes and pillars of Expo are no accident: Sustainability, Mobility and Opportunity is how we can connect the world.

Future

I believe that the leadership will continue putting the peg further out, we will strive higher and further. And when you have that environment for the government and the people, continued exponential growth is possible. There is a reason I have heard us called Little Sparta: we are small but we punch above our weight. We are incredibly resourceful and tenacious, and that tenacity and capability is what we are exporting and that will be the model for tomorrow. The way the country has been run, developed and grown, will be something that other countries follow.

first graduate-level, research-based AI University. He serves on the board of Emirates Global Aluminum – the fifth largest aluminum company in the world.

In addition, Dr. Al Jaber served as Chairman of the Abu Dhabi Ports Company from 2009-2019. Over this decade, AD Ports has become a thriving business, turning a profit two years ahead of the approved business plan. During his tenure, Dr. Al Jaber oversaw the completion of Khalifa Port, Abu Dhabi's flagship, fastest growing deep-water port as well as Khalifa Industrial Zone Abu Dhabi (KIZAD), Abu Dhabi's first integrated trade, industrial and logistics free zone. Through strategic investments, AD Ports has grown to become a full-service transportation hub, leveraging Abu Dhabi's location at the nexus of three continents, and making significant contributions to the UAE's economy and diversification efforts.

Dr. Al Jaber served as Chairman of the UAE National Media Council from 2015 to 2020, where he led an organizational and governance restructure, while guiding the media sector's development as a responsive and responsible contributor to news and knowledge sharing in the digital and social media age.

Dr. Al Jaber has previously served on the United Nations Secretary General's High-Level Group on Sustainable Energy for All. He has received various awards including the United Nations flagship award "Champion of the Earth" in 2012, given to outstanding visionaries and leaders in the fields of policy, science and entrepreneurship. He was awarded the 2021 Energy Executive of the Year by Energy Intelligence for his role in mapping a path for the modernization of national oil companies within the energy transition and his contribution across the entire energy value chain.

In 2013 Dr. Al Jaber was appointed an honorary Commander of the Most Excellent Order of the British Empire (CBE) by Her Majesty Queen Elizabeth II. In 2019, Dr. Al Jaber received a lifetime achievement award from his Excellency the prime minister of India, Narendra Modi, for his contributions to energy security, building bridges to emerging Asian economies and for reshaping traditional energy business models. In 2021, Dr. Al Jaber was named Energy Executive of the Year by Energy Intelligence for his contribution to transforming the energy industry as the world navigates the energy transition.

Earliest Memories

From an early age, I always wanted to be an engineer and it was my dream to work at ADNOC. And growing up in the UAE of Sheikh Zayed, I was given the opportunity to fulfill that dream. Our founding father built a nation that shared its wealth with all its people and encouraged its young people to be all they could be.

My father was part of that generation. He pushed me to work hard and to never give anything less than everything I had to give. Importantly, he taught me to always show my love of country through my actions and by giving back. These values have guided me every day, every step of the way.

And if there is one thing I want to give back to my country today, it is to pass on to my children and the next generation of Emiratis the most important lessons I have learnt: That good work is hard and that hard work is good. And that you can forget you are tired if you never forget that you are making an impact.

It was my passion to work hard, deliver tangible results and make real impact that motivated me to join ADNOC as a young man and it's still what drives me today.

Journey

I began my career at ADNOC from the bottom, starting as a process engineer in oil fields and gas processing plants, working multiple shifts - reading pumps, compressors, pressure flow, air flow, water flow, filling out logbooks, managing control panels, you name it. After learning the ropes through hands on experience, I was gradually given more responsibility.

I was advancing in my career, when the call came from the leadership to explore how the UAE could diversify its energy mix and help establish a new economic model for our country. Back in 2006, some thought launching Abu Dhabi's Future Energy Company – Masdar - was a strange move for a major oil producing nation. In fact, our leadership viewed investment in clean, renewable energy as a natural and logical extension of Abu Dhabi and the UAE's role as a global energy leader and an opportunity to develop new partnerships, new knowledge, new skills and new jobs.

We began by learning as much as possible about the renewable energy sector. We discovered the sector needed a new ecosystem - an ecosystem that brought everything under one umbrella; from R&D, technology development, project development, project finance, capital and scale. This is essentially what we did at Masdar. We created a home for science and innovation, providing the space and the capital to turn good ideas into world-class projects. Fifteen years later, the UAE has three of the largest and lowest cost solar plants anywhere in the world, while our wind and solar portfolio has grown to 13 gigawatts in over 30 countries on five continents.

In 2016, I was asked to return to ADNOC - this time equipped with a greater understanding of how the various pieces of the energy mix fit together. The market dynamics then were challenging. Our leadership saw this as an opportunity that should not be wasted. An opportunity to transform our national oil company into a performance-driven organization that champions innovation, invests in people and maximizes the value of our resources. By doing so ADNOC, today, is delivering a more profitable upstream, more valuable downstream, more sustainable and economical gas supply and has a workforce composed of world class talent. At the same time we are delivering more value for all our stakeholders, as well as ADNOC and our shareholders.

And we will continue to do so in the future. We are expanding production capacity of the world's least carbon intensive oil to 5 million barrels per day, while also growing our renewable portfolio five-fold. We are growing our natural gas capacity by 30 per cent, enhancing our ability to supply more LNG. And we are exploring the potential of hydrogen, which shows great promise as a close to zero-carbon fuel that could be produced at scale as part of the existing hydrocarbon value chain. We are doing all this, with a strategy that is based on a sound business case and a belief that a realistic, well-planned energy strategy provides a resilient pathway for new industries, new jobs, and long-term sustainable economic growth.

In November 2021, the UAE Leadership asked me to become the UAE Special Envoy for Climate Change – the second time I have served in that role. Some may think it strange that the head of one of the world's most important oil and gas companies should lead the UAE's climate change policy but I actually think that having an understanding of the entire energy system is a plus, because the hydrocarbon industry simply has to be at the center of the conversation on climate change and part of the solution. I also see a role for the UAE, as the first country in the region to sign the Paris accords, to continue as a leader and convener of progressive climate action in the region.

HH Sheikh Zayed

Sheikh Zayed bin Sultan Al Nahyan dedicated his life to the long term, sustainable development of our people and our nation. He was not only a wise, generous and inspirational leader but also a father to his people, who had the capacity to imagine a better world and then execute against that vision. He invested the wealth of a nation in the health of a nation, building a nation that shared its wealth with all its people and encouraged its young people to be all they could be. He was the embodiment of the core principles of the nation, promoting peace, stability, prosperity, unity, tolerance and inclusion, at home and beyond our borders.

He transformed the UAE to become one of the most advanced, progressive, and forward-thinking countries in the world, balancing economic development with environmental responsibility, biodiversity alongside prosperity and laying the groundwork for the UAE's leadership in renewable and clean energy. He believed sharing made good nations great and guided the UAE to become one of the world's leading humanitarian donors. And more than this, he taught the people to aim for the stars, so that one day we would explore Mars, Venus and beyond.

Sheikh Zayed understood the UAE's development must also be economically sustainable, and placed an early focus on diversifying the UAE's economy. The multiple sectors the UAE excels in today from manufacturing, to healthcare, renewable and traditional energy, biotech, artificial intelligence and space exploration all have their roots in the vision of Sheikh Zayed.

Exponential Growth

As the UAE celebrates its Golden Jubilee, we have seen 50 years of unprecedented progress. Five decades ago, the UAE had a subsistence economy. Today, the UAE ranks among the most industrialized nations. The UAE's strategic location, strong financial reserves, large sovereign wealth fund, investor friendly business climate, consistent government spending, progressive policy of economic diversification, free zones and increased foreign direct investment all contribute to the nation's robust economy and rapid growth. In the next 50 years the UAE will continue to benefit from a sustainable and increasingly diversified economy, that is flexible in adopting new economic models, and able to capitalize on global economic partnerships to ensure long-term prosperity.

Secret of Success

Most countries that are oil dependent, focus on oil. But, I vividly remember His Highness Sheikh Mohammed Bin Zayed Al Nahyan at the World Government Summit saying 'I want to celebrate when we export the final barrel of oil 50 years from now'. It takes a visionary to say that; that we need to move away from oil and invest in the people. It takes understanding that we need to innovate. Our wise leaders are also what drives us. Everything they do is about how to improve our lives in every way, from government to services to having the best infrastructure and so on. So, we as citizens strive to do our best in return.

Challenges

To successfully navigate a complex transition to the energy system of tomorrow, we can't just unplug from the energy system of today. We must remain pragmatic, while being progressive. We need to make the energy system work more efficiently with less carbon and we should look for the solutions where the energy expertise exists. Above all, we should always remember our goal is to keep moving forward, while turning back the clock on emissions.

Opportunities

We understand the challenges, but we know that behind every challenge lies a greater opportunity. Let us focus on what's practical to produce real progress.

This region has specific advantages that can accelerate the transition to low or no carbon energy. Firstly, as long as the world continues to rely on oil and gas we can ensure reliable supplies of the least carbon intensive oil and gas available. We are leveraging this position to further drive down the carbon intensity through expansion of the first in the region carbon capture facility. We are also building on our unique capabilities in hydrogen to lay the foundation for a zero carbon hydrogen market. And, the UAE has been investing in the solar and broader renewable space for the last 15 years, and we are doubling down on this investment.

Net zero, for us, is about new industries, new skills and new jobs. For us, the business of tackling climate change is good business.

Lessons

Over the last 50 years the UAE has adopted a balanced, proactive and positive approach to its development, providing a number of lessons that will help guide the future of the country. Although our oil and gas resources have been the foundation for our development, our wise leadership long ago recognized that to thrive and prosper it was necessary to nurture a wide range of business sectors to give our people, our greatest asset, the opportunities to fulfill their potential. At the same time, the nation has adapted to thrive by modernizing in line with global trends without compromising on the traditional values ingrained in society. And, importantly, as we seize the opportunities of the fourth industrial age, the foundations have been laid for a culture of innovation through knowledge development, so that our people do not fear change but embrace it. By continuing to follow this progressive approach to the development of the country, we will ensure sustainable progress for all over the next 50 years.

Expo

EXPO 2020 was an unprecedented achievement for the region, bringing together the entire world in the course of a global pandemic. As a six-month celebration of creativity, innovation, humanity and world cultures, EXPO 2020, convened the global community in a spirit of hope and optimism and to help shape a better, post-pandemic future by inspiring new and exciting solutions to overcome some of the world's most pressing challenges. EXPO 2020 will not only inspire future generations of Emiratis but also provide models of excellence that people in other nations can adopt and adapt to improve their lives.

Future

As the UAE celebrates its 50th anniversary, our leadership has created a blueprint for sustainable prosperity for the next 50 years. And it is our guide to building a dynamic, world-leading economy. And at the core of that blueprint is partnership. No economy exists in a vacuum and we know progress is faster – much faster – when people work together.

When we began investing in the renewables space more than 15 years ago, our leadership had a theory of the future that has been proven right over time. Today, the UAE is home to the largest and lowest cost solar plants in the world. Globally, we see a bright future for the renewable energy sector as at least $3 trillion will be invested in renewable energy over the next 10 years. Through Masdar, we have invested in solar and wind energy projects in 40 countries around the world. Last year, under the direction of His Highness Sheikh Mohamed bin Zayed Al Nahyan, three of the largest energy companies in the UAE entered into a strategic partnership to consolidate Masdar's position and turn it into a global leader in the field of clean energy. And, as the first country in the MENA region to announce a Net Zero by 2050 Strategic Initiative, we are adopting a low carbon pathway to a high growth destination. We are keen to accelerate progress on this journey as hosts of COP 28, in 2023.

In alignment with our leadership's direction and the on-going preparations for the UAE Centennial 2071, we have launched Operation 300bn to make the industrial sector a key pillar of the national economy. The aim is to enhance its regional and global competitiveness, accelerate advanced technology adoption across the value chain and increase in-country value – all while creating thousands of new jobs for our citizens.

The next 50 years will bring many challenges. But we know that behind every challenge lies a greater opportunity. Our leadership has set out a mandate for further development for the next 50 years which is based on a low carbon, high growth economic model that does not put limits on what we can imagine for our future as we embark on an ambitious path to become a hub for digital, technical and scientific excellence.

15. NUCLEAR ENERGY

HE Mohamed Ibrahim Al Hammadi, Managing Director and CEO of the Emirates Nuclear Energy Corporation

"To understand how we work in this country; you have to have a dream, multiply it by 10, get your hands dirty, and deliver it to the highest quality in half the time it would normally take. It's in our DNA"

HE Mohamed Ibrahim Al Hammadi is Managing Director and CEO of the Emirates Nuclear Energy Corporation (ENEC). Established in 2009, it has grown from an energy startup with a handful of employees a decade ago into a world-class nuclear energy organization with a workforce of more than 3,500 people. With a responsibility to deliver the UAE Peaceful Nuclear Energy Program to the highest standards of safety, security, transparency and non-proliferation, the UAE has received international support and positive recognition for the manner in which the flagship Barakah Nuclear Energy Plant has been delivered.

Construction of the Barakah Nuclear Energy Plant commenced in 2012, peaking in 2015 when the site became the world's largest nuclear energy construction. It is an ambitious megaproject which has proven successful in many ways, setting the benchmark for other countries pursuing nuclear energy. With Unit 1 commencing commercial operations in April 2021, Unit 2 commencing commercial operations in March 2022, Unit 3 online and ramping up towards commercial operations in 2023 and construction concluding on Unit 4 so that all four units will be online by 2025, the Barakah plant is generating abundant clean electricity every day, leading the largest decarbonization effort in the UAE, and enabling the clean energy transition required to deliver the

UAE's Net Zero by 2050 initiative. Once fully operational, the Barakah plant will meet around a quarter of the nation's electricity demand, preventing the release of 22.4 million tons of CO_2 emissions every year.

Earliest Memories

Life was much more simple back then. Our time revolved around going to school, playing with friends, exploring – we were very active outside. Life ran at a quieter pace, without modern-day communications tools and social media. Back then, children would run from home to home - the doors were always open. Everyone took care of each other's children and families. Children played on the streets – a close-knit community.

Today, although it has changed in form, we still see this sense of community in the UAE – the culture of caring for others, for sharing. Although we have digitalized this, at the core, the principle of community is the same.

I remember a house next door to my home was a simple single story building when I was a child, then it was knocked down and replaced with a four--story building, and there's now an eight-story building there – I literally saw the exponential growth happening around me, reflective of the UAE's incredible pace of growth.

Journey

I have always had an interest in electricity, I remember fixing my father's radio, and making small radio transponders from a young age. This directed my educational focus towards electrical engineering, and later engineering project management, in which I received my Masters. In the early days of my career, my initial roles were in the utilities sector, where I took on the most remote, challenging projects that few others wanted. This enabled me to learn through practical experience and demonstrate my capabilities beyond my technical qualifications. Through this approach I was given more complex, larger scale projects to manage.

From working on the UAE grid, and then moving into managerial roles, I transitioned into the UAE's nuclear energy sector, which at the time, was a vision and a policy when I took the role on in 2009. I had been working on a project for the Federal Government to evaluate the UAE grid in terms of how we would maintain reliability and stability. To meet the growing levels of demand at the time, we were burning diesel, which was very expensive, and was also not going to enable us to meet the double-digit growth we were experiencing. I still remember the meeting we had to come together to identify the right long-term solutions for the nation. We looked at a number of options, including nuclear energy, systematically examining each source from a reliability, economic and environmental perspective. That was the moment: we went from problem to solution. UAE Leadership took the decision to develop the UAE policy on nuclear energy, which has guided us every step of the way and continues to do so today. As a result, we have developed a world-class peaceful nuclear energy program and the flagship Barakah Nuclear Energy Plant is one of the most strategically important infrastructure projects in the UAE today.

Through the Barakah Nuclear Energy Plant, we are rapidly decarbonizing the UAE's electricity grid, which is an enabler for achieving the UAE's Net Zero by 2050 initiative to tackle climate change. Barakah is a sustainable powerhouse for the nation, creating clean electricity, stimulating economic growth and diversification, growing the UAE's intellectual capabilities through the creation of high-value careers for UAE Nationals, as well as leading the creation of a brand new high-tech industry for the UAE, enabling UAE companies to join the international nuclear energy sector. We couldn't have done this without our people. Our teams have worked tirelessly to deliver on the vision of the UAE Leadership, HH Sheikh Mohamed bin Zayed Al Nahyan, Crown Prince of Abu Dhabi, to bring a new form of clean electricity to the Nation and in doing so, delivering another milestone and moment of pride for the UAE. A lot of people questioned whether it could be done in the UAE, but Leadership had the vision and the belief. And we have executed the project in line with the highest levels of accountability and transparency, meeting robust national regulations and international standards. We have had amazing engagement from international partners. My pride comes from the way our teams have worked together, UAE Nationals alongside 50 nationalities, like a beautiful mosaic of peoples and cultures, to deliver a world leading project that offers a new model for new build nuclear programs for other nations looking to make the transition to cleaner energy forms.

HH Sheikh Zayed

The late founding father of the UAE was a visionary for the Nation. He had the incredible ability to see the future and set a clear vision, while also being detail oriented to make sure the vision was achieved. He had the human touch, bringing people together, building consensus to make the impossible possible. Crucially he was "hands-on".

His promotion of women's roles in the workplace and spearheading women's education paved the way to our success today as we build a team of female nuclear professionals who are essential to the delivery of the UAE Peaceful Nuclear Energy Program, without the foundation Sheikh Zayed built in the 70's, this would simply not have been possible.

Some years ago now, we had a female electrical engineer that had resigned herself to back office, administrative work. I encouraged her to get out in the field and within months, she was putting the qualifications to use leading teams. Through her determination, she moved into the nuclear energy sector and trained as a reactor operator. She now trains other young men and women – this is the epitome of exponential growth in skills development, and the essence of the UAE, following in the footsteps of HH Sheikh Zayed's efforts to ensure women and men worked side by side in the workplace.

In terms of a personal meeting, I remember working on a utilities project, late in his life, in a very remote area of Abu Dhabi that had been instructed by Sheikh Zayed. The deadline was tight, and the project was critical. He set a very stretched timeframe, we had to work day and night and move mountains! Sheikh Zayed came to check on the progress being made to ensure the project was on track. He had a big smile and clapped, in recognition of those that had worked on the project. That was the motivation and reward we needed. His leadership in ensuring plans turned into deliverables on the ground set him apart, and I have used this model myself, both to ensure the work gets done, but also to personally appreciate those on the ground delivering.

To understand how we work in this country; you have to have a dream, multiply it by 10, get your hands dirty, and deliver it to the highest quality in half the time it would normally take. I see it in the DNA of the people in this country. Not just Emiratis, we have created an ecosystem that attracts likeminded people. This mentality helps them propel and excel.

Exponential Growth

For me, much of the UAE's growth comes from its tolerant, visionary approach, bringing the best international companies to come to the UAE and using this knowledge to create UAE-specific models.

We have over 200 nationalities residing peacefully together in the UAE, sharing knowledge and cultures together and is a global example of a tolerant, forward-thinking society. We are very collaborative, and through this approach we are able to accomplish so much more, in a very efficient manner.

Today, the UAE is home to almost 80% of the renewable energy projects in the region, and the first country in the Arab world with a multi-unit operating nuclear energy plant. Imagine if we can 10X that – we will become a true clean energy hub for the region.

Secret of Success

The UAE's success comes from creating a clear and ambitious vision, reviewed through a logical, scientific review process that looks at the benefits and costs from a people, environment, economic and cultural perspective.

The UAE looks at best practice and how that can be applied at a national level to work with the unique characteristics of our country. We have also been very transparent.

In my role as Managing Director and CEO, we have taken this same approach. We have set a clear vision for the delivery of the UAE Peaceful Nuclear Energy Program, and have brought in global experts from the international nuclear sector to share their knowledge and expertise to ensure the program, and the flagship Barakah Nuclear Energy Plant, is delivered to the highest national regulations and international standards.

Human capital is critical, and I think this is a real focus for UAE Leadership, and a secret of our success.

Challenges

Having the right knowledge to deliver on the vision is always challenging when starting out, whether personally, with a company or even a country.

The UAE has invested heavily in education for its citizens, setting up academic and vocational skills training centers across the country.

We took the same approach, initially sending our talented young

Emiratis overseas to complete their academic programs in nuclear engineering and related subjects, and in parallel creating academic programs here in the UAE. Most of our Energy Pioneers are now completing their education in the UAE, and today we have hundreds of young people that have benefitted from these programs, and continue to do so as we build our pipeline of UAE talent to operate and maintain the plant for the next 60 years, while also developing many of the other areas we are expanding into, in R&D and other clean energy technologies, acting as an incubator for other growth industries in the UAE, amongst others.

Opportunities

The UAE is leading the way in economic diversification and ENEC and the Barakah plant are enabling this through the provision of clean, reliable, 24/7 electricity.

Nuclear energy programs are a long-term strategic investment, with an approximate decade of development, followed by a minimum of 60 years of operations, likely to be 80 years with an extension.

The UAE is really at the beginning of the development of its local nuclear supply chain, with local companies and businesses in the process of enhancing their standards to meet the robust requirements of the nuclear industry. Not only does this open up a whole new market in the UAE, but creates opportunities to compete in the international nuclear industry, selling goods and services to other nations with nuclear programs. Ducab is a strong example of this, not only selling cabling to Barakah, but selling cabling to South Korea for their nuclear plants.

Green hydrogen will also become a growth market, and ENEC is well positioned to support this through the Barakah plant with the production of clean electricity and steam generation. This will support the UAE's transition to cleaner energy sources and further cement our position as a global clean energy leader.

Lessons

This goes back to setting a clear vision and delivering on it. Looking specifically at the UAE's energy planning, there are clear lessons for other countries. Over a decade ago, the UAE recognized the need to increase electricity production to meet demand, and diversify its energy policy while at the same time moving to cleaner, more sustainable sources. The UAE Leadership took a systematic, technology neutral approach to selecting which energy forms to use.

Today, the UAE is making significant leaps in decarbonizing its power sector and through the inclusion of nuclear energy in its clean energy certification, it is also enabling the decarbonization of related sectors by providing clean electricity to the oil and gas sector and heavy industry too. The UAE is driving the global clean energy transition and setting a clear example for other nations.

We want to be an example for the world on climate solutions.

Expo

This goes back to culture – Expo allows people from all over the world to come and experience the culture and latest developments from so many nations in one space. It represents the UAE in this respect, showing the diversity of our country and our forward-thinking, optimistic, inclusive and tolerant vision for the future.

The most beautiful thing that I have seen is the similarities between all the countries, for me personally, and also for my kids. The UAE pavilion was inspiring, following the story of a little girl experiencing the UAE's growth, that creates a vision for our younger generations to aspire to.

Future

When the 4th reactor begins operations in 2025, subject to final regulatory approvals, 85% of Abu Dhabi Emirate's electricity will be coming from a clean source. Each year, we will prevent 22.4 million tons of carbon emissions, more than netting out the emissions of all of the cars on the UAE's roads today. This is truly transformational and puts us at the forefront of rapid decarbonization of the power sector.

The next 50 years will see us build on the consolidation of the great efforts the UAE has already made, from space exploration, through to cleaner energy achievements.

The nuclear industry is currently moving into a new era as nations around the world recognize the important role nuclear energy will play in powering our future in a clean and sustainable way to reduce carbon emissions and tackle climate change. I do foresee that the UAE will be a forerunner in this space and a key player.

France, China, the US and the UK are already increasing their investments, and a number of companies are developing new nuclear technologies, such as Small Modular Reactors (SMRs) which will increase the use of nuclear energy by broadening the range of applications it can be used in. R&D is key to ensure the continuous improvement and advancement of the sector, and ENEC is committed to delivering its R&D strategy in the coming years.

The nuclear industry is poised to produce green hydrogen, with multiple pilot projects underway, and this will flourish in the coming years to meet the demand for green hydrogen in powering hard-to-decarbonize sectors.

The demand for electricity is growing faster than any other energy source. I foresee that much like oil and gas, clean electricity will become a strategic asset for the UAE, particularly as the possibilities for super grids using Ultra High Voltage direct current (UHVDC) lines will allow electricity to be transmitted across thousands of miles, allowing power generation and demand location to be decoupled. I see us being a hub and a conduit between Africa, Asia and Europe. The UAE could be the heart of the region with energy transformation.

Our ambitions for the use of peaceful nuclear energy go beyond electricity, and we will look to share our knowledge and expertise to benefit other related fields such as space exploration, agriculture and nuclear medicine.

Here in the UAE, by 2071, we will have had 50 years of safe and sustainable operations behind us as a strategic, sustainable powerhouse for the UAE. We will be powering growth from the four units of Barakah, and potentially from more units too should these be required, creating a clean energy economy, and a geopolitical asset for the Nation.

That is my dream and my personal mission, to make this happen.

16. SCALE-UP NATION

HE Abdulla bin Touq Al Marri, Minister of Economy

"The UAE was a Seaport, then an Airport, now a Brainport."

HE Abdulla Bin Touq Al Marri was appointed Minister of Economy in July 2020. Prior to his appointment, he was the Secretary General of the UAE Cabinet since 2017, during which he was instrumental in strengthening the interdependence between the federal and local governments. In this role, he also spearheaded many initiatives to get the pulse of the people and know their sentiments, as well as build the UAE's relationships with international organizations such as the World Economic Forum.

HE Abdulla is also the former Director General of the Executive Office of HH Sheikh Mohammed bin Rashid Al Maktoum. He was part of the high-profile team that was behind the launch of 'Area 2071,' the nucleus of the future envisioned in the UAE Centennial Plan 2071. In addition, he was the CEO of the Dubai Future Foundation, enabling him to play a vital role in the successful launch of Dubai 10X and other initiatives of national importance. The Dubai 10X initiative, in particular, aims to strengthen the Emirate's bid to become the city of the future.

Earliest Memories

My main memories are with the contrast between then and now. My earliest memories are of Sheikh Zayed Road and the beaches. You can see the UAE's growth all around.

Journey

I began working for HH Sheikh Mohammed's team back in 2007. I remember in 2010 I was tasked with proposing 50 KPIs for the UAE to reach in December 2021, the Golden Jubilee year. We wanted to help set the vision for the next 10 years and set specific goals in specific sectors. I was in charge of setting targets for infrastructure, the environment, energy and judicial. I started setting out ambitious dreams for the UAE to achieve over the next decade. I thought to myself "I'm going to put this out and see what happens in the next 10 years", I was not even sure I'd be around. Now a lot of them have ended up being my responsibility - I set a rod for my own back! I was lucky enough to be part of the "Dream Team", literally a team brainstorming and dreaming about what Dubai and the UAE could become.

HH Sheikh Zayed

HH Sheikh Zayed was a father figure. His words are still relevant today. You see them circulating in WhatsApp groups and on social media as inspiration for us all. His family and cultural values set the values of our nation, and he also set the dream for the UAE.

Exponential Growth

Look at a number of sectors: In shipping, as an example, our port at Jebel Ali was opened in 1979 and now DP World has more than 70 terminals in 40 countries across six continents. In aviation, look at the Emirates story. From a company that rented 2 planes, to a company that owns more than 250 planes 35 years later. I always say the UAE was a Seaport, then an airport, and now it's a Brainport. The exponential growth we are now undergoing is based on people. The recent changes that we have instigated with the Golden Visa, is all about talent. When you want exponential growth, you need to attract the best people. This will drive our growth. We are working according to an ambitious vision to double our national economy over the next 10 years to reach AED 3 trillion by 2031.

Secret of Success

Setting goals and targets. This helps you focus. However, I think the main reason are our people. We believe in humans. It's not oil, it's talent.

Challenges

One of the biggest challenges in the Ministry of Economy was the foreign ownership restrictions set out in the original Commercial Companies Law that required a UAE national to own at least 51% of the shares in the capital of a UAE company. The UAE had innovated over time, creating 40+ freezones that allowed 100% foreign ownership in some sectors and geographic areas, but last year we published amendments that largely removed the 51:49% restrictions for onshore entities, with each Emirate deciding if there were some sectors they wanted to exclude. As a Ministry we felt we needed to do this to drive the economy, and this was a big challenge to convince and convey to the stakeholders. We are also tackling other "taboo laws" such as the Commercial Transaction Law where we have decriminalized the bouncing of cheques. As of 1 Jan 2022, a bounced cheque becomes a civil case.

Opportunities

The UAE has a young spirit. There is a lot of agility. We are adaptable. We don't like to be too rigid. Laws and regulations can be changed to better the economy. The UAE's whole foundation is based on a focus on the economy. When President His Highness Sheikh Khalifa bin Zayed Al Nahyan issued the UAE's 10 principles for the next 50 years, the second principle was that "we will strive over the upcoming period to build the best and most dynamic economy in the world. The economic development of the country is the supreme national interest, and all state institutions, in all fields and across different federal and local levels, shall bear the responsibility of building the best global economic environment and maintaining the gains achieved over the past 50 years."

I believe we are a Scale-Up Nation. After the Abraham Accords, I joked with my Israeli counterpart that they were known as a Start-Up Nation and we are known as the Scale-Up Nation, so we are ideal for partnership! Israel and the UAE normalized relations in August 2020, and bilateral trade in goods alone reached nearly $500 million in the first half of 2021. That is big growth in less than a year.

Lessons

Focus on Youth. The youth is the future. I think that's vital. You need to create projects that excite the youth, like our Mars mission and Expo. Youth is at the heart of everything. You need to bet on the future and the future has to bet on the youth.

Expo

As HH Sheikh Mohammed bin Rashid al Maktoum has said, "we are not a country in a world — we are a world in a country." This is Expo. Lots of cultures and people all in one place. You can really learn about nations in all the pavilions. You can take Expo as an example of our growth. It was empty desert 5 years ago. That's the growth trajectory.

Future

To try and imagine the UAE in 50 years' time, in 2071, we built Area 2071. The idea of Area 2071 was based on the Creative Molecular Economy. The working definition for us was to look towards "An economy based on the integration of emerging technologies, with creative individuals, small groups and companies organized in interlocking networks, connecting and disconnecting constantly in processes of continuous innovation and transformation." In real terms, it meant that we saw the future as bringing 5 different stakeholders together: Government, Universities, Entrepreneurs, Investors and Companies, in order to solve the world's biggest challenges and to create a new economy that would be able to adapt to whatever the future holds. I don't know what that future will be, imagination is your only boundary, but we are creating an area, an ecosystem that will enable the economy to flourish in the future.

17. THE EMIRATI RECIPE

HE Mohammed Ali Al Shorafa Al Hammadi, Chairman of the Abu Dhabi Department of Economic Development

"The secret of the UAE's success, is in keeping pace with global development and progress, while still preserving the country's identity and its social and cultural heritage"

HE Mohamed Ali Al Shorafa Al Hammadi is a member of the Abu Dhabi Executive Council and the chairman of the Abu Dhabi Department of Economic Development (ADDED). HE Al Shorafa is currently the head of the Abu Dhabi Investment Office (ADIO) - an ADDED affiliate, Chairman of the Khalifa Fund for Enterprise Development (KFED), Chairman of Hub71 – a key initiative of the Abu Dhabi Government's development accelerators program, Deputy Chairman of the Board of the Securities & Commodities Authority (SCA), Chairman of the Board of Directors of the Abu Dhabi Securities Exchange (ADX), Chairman of Free Zones Council - Abu Dhabi, Chairman of the Etihad Aviation Group, and Vice-Chair of the Abu Dhabi Global Market.

Earliest Memories

The United Arab Emirates is my homeland. Although it was founded only 50 years ago, it has a rich history that brings its citizens and residents together, in a distinct cultural and social melting pot of our customs, values and principles. These elements have evolved and flourished to give us the UAE as you see it now: modern; distinctive; progressive.

The UAE is a country that never really leaves you, no matter how far away you go. I have fond memories of my childhood, how life felt simple, and society was cooperative, adhering to its customs and values, and always strived to progress and develop. In Al Freej, I have many amazing memories of my classmates, friends and relatives. All people were considered family, even if they were not, which instilled in me the values of love and benevolence that are cherished by Emirati society. Our schools, despite their simplicity, were scientific beacons, and our councils/Majilis were a source of warmth and safety for our society, in which everyone gathered to discuss their lives and affairs, and take advice from peers more experienced and knowledgeable than themselves. Our councils were a model and sign of a civilised society that continues to develop.

The UAE still drives to keep its social inheritance, in spite of significant progression and development in our economic and service sectors. We still honour traditions, which are embodied in our institutions and world-class scientific edifices.

The UAE has not changed in essence, but has developed in its external form, and has become a model for countries that still adhere to their identities and heritage.

Journey

I would describe my younger self as ambitious and driven, with dreams of creating a successful future for myself. Business management was the field I chose to study and excel at. Thanks to the basic education I received in my country, I was able to continue to study, eventually obtaining a certificate in the Harvard Business School Senior Executive Leadership Program, after also obtaining an MBA from the London Business School over 10 years ago.

I also graduated and obtained certification at the Sloan College of Management, from the Massachusetts Institute of Technology, a certification in Global Asset Management from Citibank, in addition to graduating from the Senior Executive Leadership Program at Harvard.

Throughout my scientific career, I have always had great ambitions to contribute to the work system within the Abu Dhabi government. I held the position of Managing Director and CEO of Danat Al Emarat Hospital, and I was a senior financial analyst at the Abu Dhabi Investment Authority for 7 years. In addition, I'm very familiar with the strengths and weaknesses in the economic development of Abu Dhabi, and the opportunities to become one of the most important global economic centres.

I am also honoured to be a member of the Executive Council of the Emirate of Abu Dhabi. In addition, I chair the Board of Directors of the Khalifa Fund for Enterprise Development, the Hub 71 Platform, the Abu Dhabi Securities Exchange, and the Abu Dhabi Global Market. I would state my most important position is as Chairman of the Abu Dhabi Department of Economic Development.

Throughout my career, I have been most proud of the great trust that our wise leadership placed in me, and the shouldering of many tasks and responsibilities, which I saw as a great honour for me to serve my country and my people in the Emirate of Abu Dhabi. I feel immensely proud whenever I contribute to the success of Abu Dhabi, especially in the economic field, which is an essential pillar for the nation's renaissance, and the continuation of our civilised march.

HH Sheikh Zayed

Sheikh Zayed, "May Allah rest his soul," is the father of every Emirati, a source of pride and inspiration. We continue to learn from him, and his lessons for life. Sheikh Zayed spent his life in the service of the UAE since it was founded by him and his brothers, the rulers of the Emirates.

Everyone is indebted to Sheikh Zayed for his generosity and vision, which realised that union and cooperation among the people of one nation is the basis for building a coherent and advanced nation. Everything we have is thanks to the wise vision of Sheikh Zayed, "may Allah rest his soul," as he created and outlined the path for progress and prosperity for the UAE, a path that our wise leadership still follows. From my point of view, the most important thing that Sheikh Zayed instilled in our society is cohesion, benevolence and tolerance, which made the UAE an oasis for humankind and goodness in the world.

At the economic level, Sheikh Zayed established a good foundation for the economy of Abu Dhabi and the UAE. He had an important vision that oil would be a source of wealth, one which we must use to build successful economic institutions. Most importantly, to build people to invest that wealth in creating new opportunities for the state in the post-oil era. Therefore, we see that Sheikh Zayed's efforts are still present in the projects of Abu Dhabi and the state, and also in what has been achieved regarding massive economic diversification.

Exponential Growth

I believe the growth of the UAE is a great role model for other countries. This country, founded only 50 years ago, has been able to lead many global indicators in several vital sectors, and become an influential player in the map of the global economy.

Certainly, the growth has been exceptional, and as mentioned, this growth is an extension of the vision of the late Sheikh Zayed "may Allah rest his soul" in establishing economic institutions and scientific edifices that were able to reshape the Emirati people, to keep pace with changes and challenges of the age, and even to enter directly, the global race towards worldwide progress and evolution.

We can see the exceptional growth in the Emirates on social, civilisational, cultural and economic levels, and I believe the multiple types of growth serve each other. Society is the basis of all this, and the UAE has been able to successfully invest in its human wealth until that wealth became the main driver of society, culture and civilisation. The features of Emirati growth are demonstrated in the welfare of society, and the improvement in the quality of life, in addition to the fact that the UAE attracts successful human wealth from all over the world, as it provides a fertile environment for development, progress and success.

We also find that Emirati growth has become an inspiring model for the state of the Gulf and Arab regions, through the approach of sustainability and cooperation with everyone, to exchange experiences and visions, and contribute to finding practical solutions to challenges of the human race. And even creating new opportunities for people in the future, which has manifested in several projects, the latest of which was the launch of the Hope probe towards Mars, and the start-up of the Barakah plant, which is the first peaceful nuclear power plant in the region.

Secret of Success

The secret of the UAE's success is in keeping pace with global development and progress, while still preserving the country's identity and its social and cultural heritage.

All of these elements created what I call the "Emirati recipe" which allows everyone to open up to one another, and cooperate while preserving the features of society, its customs and authentic values. The UAE's success also lies in creating its own experience, and thanks to its wise leadership, it has been designing this experience based on situation, capabilities and opportunities, as well as how and when to take new steps forward. Therefore, we see the growth process accelerating thanks to setting priorities, and every step and achievement served. From this experimentation, the success of the UAE was cumulative and depended on all of the elements, that then served the rest, within an integrated and complex work system. We see that all state bodies and institutions work in harmony and organisation, contributing to serving all the goals, so I believe that one of the most important contributing factors of the success of the UAE is teamwork.

The features of which were reflected in my thoughts, so cooperation and working within a team were the most important things I sought and implemented when trying to achieve professional success. My professional successes are the success of the team in which I was working at any given time, and I still believe this principle can bring success, not only to individuals and countries but also to the world if it wants to create a better future for humanity.

Challenges

One of the most important challenges the UAE faces is presenting itself as an ambitious country, that possesses the will and capabilities that qualify it to play a greater role alongside the rest of the world. The late Sheikh Zayed, "May Allah rest his soul," was able, with his diplomacy and wisdom, to present the UAE to the world through concrete efforts, and steps that imposed itself as a model of success. Hence, the UAE's launch of a new era has led us to advanced levels of progress, as the confidence of global investors in the UAE has increased, in addition to the confidence of individuals from professionals and innovators, who have confirmed that the UAE is a home for the future. The UAE is already reaping this success.

At a personal level, the challenges are the same. My childhood accompanied the establishment of the UAE, and I grew up witnessing its growth, which was reflected in my generation. I was, like my fellow classmates, among the first to receive new education, and afterwards, I was fortunate to then be able to obtain further education abroad. My mission was to present myself as a young man from a modern country, striving to acquire knowledge, learn the latest developments in the field of business management, and at the same time, be an ambassador for my country to the rest of the world. I am self-assured that I did all I could to learn of and present the UAE as a nation and a young country that will be, one day, at the forefront of developed countries.

Opportunities

There are many opportunities offered by Abu Dhabi and the UAE, to investors, entrepreneurs and owners of innovative ideas. There is tremendous economic diversification in various sectors, the most important being technology, agriculture, trade, logistics, finance, tourism, hospitality and real estate, in addition to culture, sports, energy, and anything related to sustainability.

Abu Dhabi and the UAE offer many economic incentives, the latest of which was the 100% foreign ownership law for companies, which allows various individuals to establish, or expand their investment activities freely and without any restrictions, and even benefit from economic initiatives that allow them to develop their businesses, and make the UAE a hub for their business.

Lessons

The most important lesson for other countries is the great economic diversity that enhances the competitiveness of the economy now, and in the future, especially in a number of vital sectors such as technology. However, this diversity needs to have a trained labour force and needs to attract other innovators and talent to be part of the process of diversity and economic progress.

I believe all of this must be achieved in an environment of stability, social security, justice and tolerance, and all these qualities are found to be deeply rooted in Emirati society.

Expo

Expo is a forum that brings the world together under the UAE flag, and it is an amazing opportunity for trade and cultural exchange. Governments, companies and individuals can build bridges of communication, friendship and cooperation to face global changes, front and foremost of which, is achieving sustainable development goals, and building sustainable economies to serve this goal.

I would say to anyone who visits the UAE, that besides visiting the tourist attractions and enjoying its high-end services, it is important to be keen to engage with Emirati society and come into contact with its noble customs and values. It is an honour to be part of this civilised society, that brings together more than 200 nationalities from different parts of the world, and to be an ambassador to convey our message to the world, that we are a peace-loving nation and welcome everyone for the sake of coexistence and the consolidation of good values for the good of man and humanity.

Future

The UAE is only a 50-year-old country, and 2021 is the year of preparation for the fiftieth year, in order to recognise what has been accomplished over the past five decades and to plan to build on it with a clear vision for the next fifty years. This, of course, serves the "UAE Centennial 2071".

The preparation for the fiftieth year reflects the determination of the UAE to move forward with its vision and the wisdom of its wise leadership, and to be the best in the world in all fields, as well as to confirm that the people of the UAE are determined to inspire the world with a unique experience, just as it has done in previous years.

We have learned from our wise leadership that good planning creates achievements and overcomes obstacles, which is a scientific and practical approach par excellence, and I believe that through this sound and informed planning, we will be able to carry out our tasks perfectly, especially in the economic sector, which is the main motive for achieving the UAE Centennial.

We already have ambitious plans to upgrade all economic sectors, and even to create new sectors that will contribute to the GDP of the Emirate of Abu Dhabi and the UAE, along with the rest of the Emirates of the country. Our goal will be to enhance the position of Abu Dhabi and the UAE on the map of the global economy, making it a centre for major global investments, and an advanced financial market that attracts capital from all over the world. All of this will be within the framework of a stimulating economic climate that gives everyone full opportunities for development and expansion.

18. UNITY THROUGH COMMUNITY

Badr Jafar, CEO of Crescent Enterprises and President of Crescent Petroleum

"Vision without implementation is hallucination"

Badr Jafar is CEO of Crescent Enterprises and President of Crescent Petroleum, headquartered in Sharjah. Crescent Petroleum, founded in 1971, is the oldest and largest privately owned upstream oil and gas company in the Middle East. Badr also serves as the Chairman of Gulftainer, the largest privately owned container port operator in the world. He attended Eton College and earned a Master's degree from the University of Cambridge, in addition to an MST from the University of Cambridge's Judge Business School.

In 2010, Badr founded the Pearl Initiative, a non-profit organisation committed to promoting a corporate culture of transparency and accountability across the Gulf Region, in collaboration with the United Nations Office for Partnerships. He is a member of the United Nations Secretary General's High-Level Panel on Humanitarian Financing, a member of the UNESCO International Commission on the Futures of Education, and a member of the Board of Advisors of the International Rescue Committee (IRC).

Badr, as well as championing numerous philanthropic causes and social entrepreneurship initiatives, is the Founding Patron of the Centre for Strategic Philanthropy based at the University of Cambridge, dedicated to enhancing the impact of strategic philanthropy both within and from the world's fastest-growing economies; and the Founding Patron of the NYU Abu Dhabi Strategic Philanthropy Initiative, the Gulf

Region's first centre to study and promote high-impact philanthropy.

Badr serves as Champion of the World Economic Forum's (WEF) EDISON Alliance which cultivates partnerships between leaders in government and industry to enhance the case for rapid digital development in the MENA region and beyond. He has been a member of the Young Presidents' Organization (YPO) since 2005 and served as Chair of the YPO Emirates Chapter. He was recognised as a Young Global Leader by WEF in 2011, is Co-Chair of the WEF Family Business Community and a member of the WEF Stewardship Board on New Economy and Society.

Earliest Memories

I was born in 1979 and raised in Sharjah. My childhood was very peaceful, with a house right on the beach in the Al Fisht district. We would stroll out and have barbeques on the sand– now there's a dual-carriageway between the house and the beach! I was schooled at the International School of Choueifat, right next to the Sharjah Cricket Stadium which I believe holds the global record for the most number of hosted One Day Internationals. We would enjoy the odd weekend trip to Dubai, a trip which my father remembers would take 10 minutes on a single lane road with zero traffic in the 70s, compared to a lot of traffic on 12 lanes today. A regular feature of these trips was to the Al Ghurair Centre, and being treated to Hardees which was right by the entrance. There was also an arcade centre on the top floor called Sinbad that was a must-visit! I also have many fond memories of family weekend excursions to Hatta.

There was beauty in simplicity to the UAE in the early days, and I'd like to think that we have managed to preserve that culture alongside our rapid growth, by retaining a community feel in the various neighborhoods that make up our expanding emirates.

Journey

My maternal grandfather was from Nazareth and was its Governor until the Palestinian expulsion in 1948, after which he created a base for himself in Beirut as a successful businessman. My paternal grandfather, Dhia Jafar, was from Baghdad and graduated with a PHD in Engineering from the University of Birmingham in the early 30s and returned to Iraq to work on overseeing the implementation of major infrastructure development as head of the Iraq Development Board which was responsible for reinvesting 70% of the country's oil revenues in national infrastructure and capacity building. He went on to serve as Minister of Finance and Deputy Prime Minister. He felt strongly that post the military coup in 1958 that the region's economic center of gravity was going to shift to the lower Gulf, and therefore advised his children, including my father, to establish themselves here. Which is why my father, who completed his secondary education in the UK, started visiting Abu Dhabi, Sharjah and Dubai in the mid-60s and eventually based himself in Sharjah in the late-60s.

My father first launched engineering and other businesses in Abu Dhabi, during which time he also met the Ruler of Sharjah and pursued an oil concession opportunity in the Emirate which was granted in 1969 offshore Sharjah. That was the genesis of what is today Crescent Petroleum, which has since grown over 50 years into the regions' largest privately-owned natural gas producer.

I had been exposed to business from as soon as I was able to speak. I was always interested, and sat in on many meetings and negotiations after school and on weekends. After I graduated from Cambridge, I was very keen to pursue an entrepreneurial path and spent time establishing a number of ventures, many of which failed but a few of which succeeded. My father, being an entrepreneur himself, encouraged me all the way, but I had to raise the money myself. My first successful business was in the fashion sector, which I launched with a GBP 50,000 loan from the Royal Bank of Scotland. I sold it 4 years later to a Japanese retail conglomerate. I also created a B2B e-commerce venture, but ultimately there was an expectation to return to the family business which I did in the early 2000s.

When negotiating my employment contract with my father, I remember having two requests: one was that I could continue to see out a few of the ventures I had established in a non-executive capacity, and two, that I could also pursue the diversification of the family business, for both defensive and opportunistic reasons. He agreed.

I worked in various departments at Crescent Petroleum before heading up business development for Crescent Petroleum and during that time we closed new deals and joint ventures for the company in Sharjah, Russia and the Kurdistan region of Iraq, as well as launching Dana Gas.

In 2012, and as part of the diversification efforts, we launched Crescent Enterprises, which today has four platforms: CE-Creates, CE-

Ventures, CE-Invests and CE-Operates. I had set a target of revenues diversification from the energy sector of 50% by 2020. Today, it has already surpassed that at 60-70%.

HH Sheikh Zayed

My grandfather had met HH Sheikh Zayed in Abu Dhabi and at my grandfather's home in the UK in the 1960s, as His Highness was at the time seeking general advice from Arab statesmen. After he met my father a few times, he offered him a job in government, and my father explained that he was eager to contribute to the country's growth in the private sector, which His Highness wholeheartedly encouraged.

In the late 60s, my grandfather recalled HH Sheikh Zayed telling him that he aspired for Abu Dhabi to be like Kuwait, which at the time was undergoing rapid growth in physical and social infrastructure. My grandfather also remembered Kuwaiti rulers at that time aspiring for Kuwait to be like Basra in Iraq. Two generations later, Iraqi youth look to the UAE for inspiration! This just shows you what great leadership can do in a relatively short space of time.

I had the opportunity and honour to visit HH Sheikh Zayed's Majlis growing up. HH was a true visionary, in every sense of the word. The UAE didn't have any real competitive advantage at the time. It's easy to acknowledge the UAE success story in hindsight, but as with all nation-building it was a complex adventure fraught with challenges, setbacks and excitement. A vision is always an important starting place, however, as the saying goes, "vision without implementation is hallucination" and a true leader like HH Sheikh Zayed doesn't just dream, but actually has the courage and tenacity to execute on that vision, and to do it with humility.

In many ways, HH Sheikh Zayed's legacy demonstrates that you don't need a fancy degree or even much experience to be a great leader. Great leadership is about courage, compassion, and consistency in execution, which for me is what HH Sheikh Zayed's legacy and that of all our founding rulers represent.

Exponential Growth

The scale and pace of growth across the UAE speaks for itself. However, it's also the quality of our growth that we need to celebrate and nurture, not just quantity. The UAE is now well on its way to becoming a truly diversified economy, and we see growth in new sectors including the all-important digital economy as well as the creative economy. On the latter, history has repeatedly shown that true innovation happens at the intersection of the humanities and sciences and hence the need to embrace the power of culture and the arts as being fundamental and not simply ornamental. The Emirate of Sharjah, under the vision and direction of HH Sheikh Dr. Sultan bin Muhammad Al Qasimi, has been laying the groundwork for a thriving cultural and educational hub over many decades, and is today home to a quarter of all UAE's museums and numerous world-class cultural and academic institutions. It is truly great to see this strategy for innovation pursued across the UAE today.

We are a truly global community, which is one of our core strengths, and so inclusive growth that propagates this diversity across generations is crucial. We also mustn't forget the UAE's ambitions to lead the way on sustainability, along with our Net Zero by 2050 target – so again, the success of our growth is measured alongside the success of our natural ecosystems which we have a responsibility and vested interest in protecting and nurturing. Which is why I believe that instead of blindly chasing the next billion-dollar business, we need to nurture startups that can harness the power of technology and innovation to address the needs of our society and the environment.

It's always nice to explore historical examples of what worked and why it worked, and I think the success of Baghdad in the 8th and 9th centuries which was termed the 'Golden Age' was largely due to the values the leadership then espoused including diversity, tolerance and creativity. I believe the UAE embraces these values authentically, which is why it has become the focal point for the region and increasingly, for the world's best minds, talent and creations.

Secret of Success

Other than great leadership, the UAE's model of success and growth is built on its unique governance model and Constitution, which provides an excellent example to the rest of the region of how to strike a powerful balance between the devolution of certain powers and a strong Union underpinned by a system of checks and balances upheld by our Federal Supreme Council. In many ways, this laid the building blocks upon which our beloved nation flourished. It is the only such example in the Arab world today, and perhaps why it is the most consistently successful.

Our core strength as a nation of course comes from our people, and the communities that collectively make up our nation. The uncompromising focus placed on providing opportunities for our youth to learn, be inspired, and reach for the stars – literally – has and will continue to pay major dividends in the years to come.

Challenges

It's a tough neighborhood! Also navigating the shifting sands of global geopolitics requires a tremendous amount of skill and is the ultimate balancing act. This is a challenge, but of course, also a huge opportunity that can continue to solidify our position as a truly global hub at the intersection between East and West that is open for business from everywhere, so long as our value systems and laws are respected of course.

Opportunities

Countless opportunities! A few that come to mind:

We've seen record sums of venture capital going towards new businesses across the region and especially in the UAE. Crescent Enterprises corporate venture capital arm CE-Ventures, for example, has itself invested $200 million in the past 3 years, over half of that in the region. Of course, we have a long way to go - venture capital funding as a percent of GDP in the MENA is 10 times less than in the US – but the momentum is there, and we now need to ensure we allocate more capital to growth stage businesses; improve the infrastructure to facilitate exits and returns on investments, and of course improve regulation across to make it easier for these businesses to raise money.

In addition to a thriving start-up community, we have a great opportunity to encourage our existing and well-established businesses to pursue innovation through business incubation. Our corporate incubator CE-Creates was built for this very purpose, and today we have over a dozen new ventures in the pipeline and a number already launched and profitable. This is not just to keep the entrepreneurial flame alive in our established business community, but the hope is it will also accelerate the creation of new businesses that 1) positively impact our social and environmental landscapes across our region; and 2) are able to export our success in the form of products and services such that the UAE becomes a truly diversified exporter.

Despite our historic credentials with inventions and discoveries, our region has greatly underperformed on this front. HH Sheikh

Mohammed bin Rashid Al Maktoum's Great Arab Minds initiative to search for exceptional talents among Arab scientists, thinkers, and innovators is exactly the sort of movement we need to encourage more inventors to step and create, and to generate globally valued intellectual property from the UAE and the region.

For far too long, philanthropy has been treated like the neglected child of our capital system. Here in the MENA Region, and in the broader Islamic World, we have a long history of charitable giving and today, anywhere between 400 billion to one trillion dollars is dispersed in Islamic philanthropy every year, between Zakat and Sadaqah. But do we know exactly what impact is it generating? With two-thirds of the population in the Middle East classified as vulnerable to poverty, what is certain is that we are not optimizing the use of this capital. The UAE is one of the most generous nations in the world, and we have a massive opportunity to create the structures and platforms needed to nurture a new generation of philanthropists and philanthropic ventures that can partner with government and business capital to address our most urgent challenges. This is why I was fortunate enough to collaborate with the likes of the University of Cambridge on the establishment of a new Centre for Strategic Philanthropy, exclusively on strategic philanthropy both within and from the world's emerging markets, and more recently with NYU-Abu Dhabi on a similar initiative dedicated to the Gulf Region.

Lessons

In the UAE's Principles of 50 to guide our next 50 Years, strengthening the Union is number one. In this spirit, a continuous focus on building and strengthening our communities is paramount. The second and I believe connected principle is a focus on building the most dynamic economy in the world, which really is core to the UAE's DNA. I say these are connected because the foundation of any strong economy is a strong society.

I would argue that one of the most acute challenges we face in the region, and in the world, is ensuring that our youth find and identify with a strong sense of purpose – everything else will flow from that. The root cause of many of our region's ills is that our communities are becoming increasingly fractured. As we continue to build world-class technology-powered cities and resilient economies, we must ensure we maintain and protect our strong community culture, which in turn will preserve a solid sense of purpose and belonging for members of society to thrive and generate positive impact. Also paramount is the creation of a culture of helping one another, such that together we become far greater than the sum of our parts.

Expo

The motto of Expo 2020 in Dubai is "Connecting Minds, Creating the Future", which is all about fostering creativity, innovation and collaboration between countries, cultures and institutions, and inspiring visitors to come together in order to develop shared solutions for a better future.

Whilst I am a big fan of exponential technology, I worry the world might soon over-rely on the metaverse. Physical connection and physical bridges are also vital. Expo 2020 has reminded us that people need to come together and co-create to overcome our challenges and properly embrace our opportunities. Expo 2020 is a "one-stop-shop" to convene the world, and I believe its legacy will speak for itself.

Future

The UAE is on track to be on par with the most advanced global change-maker nations of this world. In fact, I think we're almost there. When I say "change," I mean for the betterment of humanity and our habitat.

To me, an important measure of success for a nation, or a community, is the creation of a place where the brightest and most creative minds and hearts gather. This "Global Village" concept is not only one that we should celebrate as having worked, but one we should never become complacent about, and instead preserve and nurture relentlessly as a driving force.

Looking to the future, I'm confident we can continue to thrive, as a society and as business, if we stay true to these principles and value systems laid out for us by our leadership, past and present. This is key to achieving multi-generational, sustainable, and inclusive growth in the years and decades to come inshallah.

19. ADAPTABILITY

Marwan bin Jassim al Sarkal

"The bottom line is adaptability"

Marwan Al Sarkal is the Executive Chairman of the Sharjah Investment and Development Authority ("Shurooq"). His career with Shurooq began as CEO in 2009 and he held that position until mid-2018, when he became the Executive Chairman under a decree from the Ruler of Sharjah. Al Sarkal has led the authority by realizing the vision of the Ruler of Sharjah, Sheikh Dr. Sultan bin Muhammad Al Qasimi, establishing Shurooq as the driving force behind the transformation of Sharjah as a key investment, tourism, and business destination in the region.

Earliest Memories

My father used to be in the Ministry of Foreign Affairs and was an Ambassador, traveling the world. I was at Kindergarten in Japan. In those days it was harder to travel. We then went to Brazil. Now we have direct flights to Sao Paolo but not then. I think I saw the world in a different way.

We knew that historically, before the UAE, life in the Trucial States was about survival. The economy was centered around Pearl Diving, but was trashed when the Japanese discovered culturing pearls. The discovery of oil gave us new opportunities to develop.

I have always loved cars, and I remember some of the earliest ones being driven in Sharjah and the UAE when I was growing up, and I admired all the global models. For the 32nd anniversary of the UAE, I worked on the Super Race Truck world record which we attained with a speed of 281 km/h on the Emirates Road route towards Hatta. Considering there was not even a road there in the desert on the foundation of the Union, this shows the exponential growth of the UAE!

Journey

I graduated from the Dubai Men's College and then worked at the Sharjah Electricity and Water Authority before getting a job at the Ruler's Office of Dubai, being part of the Dubai Shopping Festival and helping to grow Global Village.

With HH Sheikha Bodour bint Sultan Al Qasimi, I was asked to set-up Shorooq in 2009. How can we develop projects in Sharjah that define Sharjah in a different way and put Sharjah on the world map? Sharjah is the industrial centre, cultural capital and education hotspot of the United Arab Emirates. It's a very vibrant city. Its diversified economy and carefully considered approach to investment and development have guided Sharjah through challenging economic times and laid the foundations for future growth. Shurooq is leading the continued transformation and economic diversification of the emirate. We strive to create a business friendly environment in Sharjah by identifying new investment opportunities across different sectors, developing breathtaking destinations and managing some of the emirate's most recognisable landmarks. Savvy investors and entrepreneurs will be impressed by the opportunities and recognise the tremendous potential that Sharjah offers. Being an independent government entity, we facilitate partnerships and connect investors, corporations, and entrepreneurs with the right opportunities.

We developed the culture in Sharjah with the "Heart of Sharjah" project, that included the Chedi al Beit and art galleries. We also went to the different villages in Sharjah like Khorfakkan and into the desert in Mleiah to tell the stories there. This tells the history of mankind. Everything from archeology to dune bashing. Our moon retreat has amazingly designed see-through tents in the desert. We also developed the Kelba eco-tourism strategy with the Kingfisher retreat, where you can say in a luxury tent overlooking the Indian Ocean.

The jewel of our projects is the House of Wisdom, a monument to celebrate Sharjah as the UNESCO World Book Capital for 2019. It opened on 9 December 2020, and is an iconic Library and Cultural Center, designed by international architecture firm Foster + Partners. We have redesigned the library experience. We have built Sharjah's first sustainable city in the desert where everything is recycled, uses solar and so on. We want to be a catalyst for investors and developers, and re-think what is possible. We took the old BP building and re-thought it for the Al Faya Lodge. The whole theme is how can we position Sharjah in a different way. Each Emirate is carving out a space.

HH Sheikh Zayed

HH Sheikh Zayed made us believe that everything is possible. He was not a ruler, he was a father. He made all citizens of the UAE feel like they are family. When he died, everyone was in mourning for a whole week. Everyone was sad and shocked. He developed a very strong bond between the leadership and the people. He just cared about the people. He looked at things in a different way to other international leaders. In some ways what Nelson Mandela did to South Africa, Sheikh Zayed did for the UAE and he should be noted globally for that achievement.

Exponential Growth

The progress is across the board: it is a constant desire to be number one. I would point to some of Shorooq's own projects to show what we have been able to achieve in 12 years. As a country, almost every week there is a new thing that helps accelerate growth. This year we have EXPO, we know that next year, and the year after, we will have something else, and so on. The UAE is also a catalyst for the region. If it can happen in the UAE, it can happen anywhere.

Secret of Success

The secret of the UAE's success is its people. Simple. The variety of people and an adaptive, disciplined government. The people who live here have a deep respect for each other and the leadership and vice versa. The law is the law, and no-one is above the law. Respect and peace mean that the people and the country can thrive.

Whatever I do, I do it because I love what I am doing for the change that I see that is happening. We are blessed with great leadership here in the United Arab Emirates. Sharjah has a visionary leader, Sheikh Sultan III, who gives us the opportunity to grow and the space to be creative, as well as giving us the support that we need. I have a fantastic leader in Sheikha Bodour, who was hands-on in a way that still gave us the chance to grow. That made me who I am today. But it all comes from within. You have to keep in mind that it is not about luck; it is about commitment, it is about hard work, it is about being passionate, and about having an idea of where you want to reach after a certain time. It is about loving what you do, caring about your life, enjoying it and believing that nobody can stop you except yourself. The passion that you have is what will drive you. Success never comes easily. Everything takes time. You have to practice, you have to believe in yourself, you have to believe in others, and I think that is the only way to succeed.

Challenges

Covid was a huge challenge, but this was a good example of how the adaptable government made changes, but also was disciplined, and the people respected and supported. When vaccination started, the leaders lead from the front, and it was rolled out very successfully. No-one was left behind. Our government repatriated non-UAE nationals to the UAE who were residents here. It is in tough times that you see the true spirit of a government, and ours demonstrated the respect and support for our people.

Sharjah has always redeveloped its economic strategy every time there has been a challenge. We have moved from being an oil-based economy to focusing on non-oil sectors such as education and tourism, among others. The bottom line is adaptability. We have seen many changes over the past decade. Today, the oil sector comprises only 30% of our economy. Sharjah is now a more diversified economy. It does not solely focus on any one sector. It has played a major role in the UAE developing into a light industrial hub, an educational hub, a heritage hub, and a cultural hub. Sharjah has hosted several international events and activities.

Opportunities

The UAE has a very dynamic economy. We encourage companies to not just see the UAE as a market they can sell to, but to move here, scale and partner. Renewable energy, education, tourism, manufacturing, R&D – there is a lot of opportunities for unicorns to be created here.

Lessons

A while back, people used to say "why should I go to the UAE"? now they say "why shouldn't I go to the UAE". The UAE made itself somewhere that people want to travel to, to do business, to live. It is a desirable destination. Education is critical, starting with schools and then universities. Other countries could learn from this.

We saw what happened to Singapore, we learned from them. Legal system, ease of doing business, a government that listens. We created a Youth Council to listen to our youth. Our government is hugely dynamic, we look at our laws every 6 months to check they are still fit for purpose.

With peace in the UAE, we can also thrive and grow. We try and help our neighbours when they have issues. This is a lot of responsibility to spread the word of peace. With the recent Abraham Accords, it shows what can be done when nations commit to peace, and the opportunities that come out of that.

Expo

I went to Expo in Shanghai and Milan – I loved visiting as it is a great way to see the host country. I never thought we would host an Expo here! Bigger than ever in a location that used to be desert is now a city itself. A great opportunity to bring people who have never come here. I implore them to use it as a way to visit the whole UAE.

Future

I think the UAE will continue to evolve exponentially!

The UAE will be a beacon for sustainability and is at the forefront of a post-oil economy. The future is here already, you can glimpse it and see it in the vision of our leadership.

20. TRADING GOODS AND IDEAS

HE Dr Thani Ahmed Al Zeyoudi, Minister of State for Foreign Trade and Minister in charge of Talent Attraction and Retention

"The trade in goods and ideas, talent attraction and development, business empowerment, a global transport hub, an incubator of new energy solutions… these are the pillars of our success."

HE Dr. Thani is the Minister of State for Foreign Trade and Minister in charge of Talent Attraction and Retention. As Minister, he is responsible for leading the development and expansion of the country's non-oil foreign trade, enhancing national polices and measures to enable increased inflows of foreign direct investment to the UAE, and implementing initiatives to attract and retain strategic global talent in the UAE. Dr. Al Zeyoudi is also the former Minister of Climate Change and Environment for the UAE, where he was instrumental in elevating the UAE's global presence and contributions in climate mitigation and adaptation.

Earliest Memories

Like most people, my first memories are of home… our house, the streets around it, the route to and from school. Looking back at those times, I think the element that stands out is the community, the sense of belonging. We knew our neighbors, knew the families around us, and it felt safe, nurturing and reassuring – and I'm happy to say it still does. I don't think there was any sense, as there never is when you're young, that where I was living was special, different or undergoing some transformation – it was just home, and every new development in the country was simply something new to explore and enjoy. I hope my own children have the same feelings about growing up in the UAE as I do.

Journey

I come from a petroleum engineering background, that was the field I studied and in which I was first employed – working as a petroleum engineer. From there I moved to Masdar and that was where I led the team to secure Abu Dhabi as the new home for the International Renewable Energy Agency. That's something that gives me a good deal of satisfaction as it helps create a new narrative around the UAE – that this is a place for the development of new energy sources, not simply the extraction of old ones. It's clear that this led directly to the successful award of COP28 that was announced a few days ago.

In 2016, I was then honored to be named the UAE's first-ever Minister of Climate Change and the Environment. I think that role was key to understanding the global nature of the challenge and how multilateral approaches and integrated solutions must be pursued to deliver the best results – incorporating industry, education, policy, etc. The message was clear: no nation can work alone or succeed in isolation.

As the Minister of State for Foreign Trade, I am responsible for leading the development and expansion of the country's non-oil foreign trade, facilitating FDI inflows, and implementing initiatives to attract and retain strategic global talent in the UAE. I believe these are all strongly linked to sustainable development – so it's a continuation of the mission. Long-term prosperity built on environmentally responsible foundations. I wouldn't claim to say that I have played a role in the UAE's growth, but I am honored to be serving the nation and committed to working to help achieve its goals.

HH Sheikh Zayed

HH Sheikh Zayed is a tremendously important figure in the history of the UAE and someone whose life and career set the best possible example for all Emiratis to follow. I never had the chance to meet him, but we grew up hearing stories of his wisdom, his compassion and his generosity, which extended well beyond the borders of the UAE. He was also the pivotal, driving force in the establishment of the nation whose 50th anniversary we're celebrating this year. He had the vision and foresight to recognize that our seven emirates needed to unite to accelerate development and prosperity.

From a personal perspective, Sheikh Zayed has always been an inspiration. He was a champion of the environment and someone who believed we could create broad-based, sustainable development – both of which are very important to me in my current and previous roles. He also wanted the UAE to look outward and to build connections with the rest of the world, and that's a legacy I have been entrusted to build on.

Exponential Growth

It's difficult to signal one thing as emblematic of the UAE's growth; there are so many economic indicators, so many physical symbols. I think, though, speaking in 2021, we have to say Expo. Our nation is only 50 years old, yet we are able to host the world in a showcase of humanity's endless innovation and creativity. Looking at the themes of the event – sustainability, mobility and opportunity – it's clear that they have been critical to our nation success, and that we have now become a global leader in conversations around them. The trade in goods and ideas, talent attraction and development, business empowerment, a global transport hub, an incubator of new energy solutions… these are the pillars of our success.

Secret of Success

I'd say there are three things that we need to look at:

First, is the vision of the leadership, from the events leading up to the union in 1971 to the present day. They understood that only by coming together as a single nation could our emirates prosper. They realized that the discovery of oil was a means to accelerate our goals, not the goal itself. From day one, their mission was to elevate the standard of living for the people of the region and build a modern, dynamic nation that could take its place on the global stage. The recent Projects of the 50 confirm that the same vision remains very much in place.

Secondly, our geographical location between three major continents and our desire to use that as a platform to connect the world – and connect with the world. Trade is central to our history, the foundation stone on which the modern nation is built. From the spice trade to pearls, we have been a country that has always prospered by looking outwards rather than inwards. As global trade accelerated, we leveraged our position between three continents to become a regional and international hub. We have developed a state-of-the-art logistics infrastructure and a network of trade deals to facilitate frictionless trade to suit the modern world. We have become a place where not just products are exchanged but ideas, innovations, solutions as well.

Third, is the energy sector. This provided the fuel to advance our ambitions to become a modern, dynamic nation capable of providing opportunities for all its citizens. Although we are transitioning to a post-oil economy, oil continues to provide economic growth through power generation, petrochemical industries and manufacturing. It has been a key catalyst to development, and created the platform on which new industries, new capabilities and new opportunities could be built.

In terms of personal success, I wouldn't be in the position I am without all the above. I continue to benefit from the nation and society that our leadership has created. Above all, nothing can be achieved without hard work and teamwork – and that's ultimately the story of the UAE.

Challenges

The biggest challenge the UAE has faced is to meet the ambitions of our founding fathers. They could see the potential of our nation, even when our population was just 180,000, when our nation was largely desert with a difficult climate. But they could see what was possible, and every step of our development brings us closer to realizing their vision. Not many people in 1971 could foresee the economic and cultural success story we see today. But they did. And we continue to work to fulfill their vision.

Opportunities

That's a question that could take a long time to answer! In general, I think our response to Covid and our ability to emerge from the pandemic perhaps faster than any other nation provides the biggest opportunity. We're open for business and every indicator points towards growth and expansion.

In terms of sectors, we have robust financial, aviation, logistics, real estate and hospitality sectors, as I think everyone knows. I'm very excited about opportunities in new sectors such as Renewable energy, particularly hydrogen and solar; Agri-tech and food security, which is essential for our sustainable growth; Biotechnology and life sciences, which are leading to better health outcomes; Mobility solutions, particularly automated transport, drones, and the hyperloop, and Smart Manufacturing. I think all these will play a major part in the success of the UAE going forward.

Lessons

Every country has its own unique circumstances and challenges, so I would be reluctant to suggest our model can be replicated anywhere. If I would suggest one, however, is that a nation's ambitions shouldn't be restricted by what's possible today or even tomorrow. Set the highest bar for what you want to achieve, and you are far more likely to deliver positive outcomes. Again, the fact that the UAE became a thriving, modern, innovation nation in 50 years was possible only because someone had the ambition to see it.

Expo

Expo is a huge opportunity for the UAE to introduce government officials, business leaders, investors and innovators from all around the world to the UAE and showcase our vibrant, open economy. We're welcoming representatives from the public- and private-sector from 190+ nations over six months, so the opportunity to build lasting, mutually beneficial relationships is significant. Also, the themes of Expo create potential for joint-ventures and collaborations in the vital sectors of energy, water, transportation and healthcare – all of which are central to the UAE's future. I hope the takeaway for visitors is that the UAE is an open, welcoming, dynamic nation that is an ideal place not just for business but for living, studying and growing.

Future

The roadmap has been laid out for our nation, so it's up to every minister, every business leader, every teacher, and every citizen to fulfill it. The vision is very much the same as it was in 1971: to create a prosperous, open and tolerant society that enables and champions success in every sector. It's not about skyscrapers or world records, as nice as they are, but the society we have created for our children and the forthcoming generations. I look at the work we have done in the last 50 years, and I look at the foundations we have laid, and know we can continue to create a model nation.

21. FLOW

HE Sultan bin Sulayem, Chairman & CEO DP World, Chairman Nakheel

"The energy and vibrancy of the place was incredible, with all the elements coming together like a giant jig-saw puzzle to turn our little desert kingdom into one of the most modern and prosperous states the world had ever seen"

HE Sultan Bin Sulayem is Group Chairman and Chief Executive Officer of DP World and has spearheaded the rapid expansion of Dubai's infrastructure, including ports and free zones, contributing significantly to the stellar growth trajectory of the United Arab Emirates. He is a leader in developing the infrastructure supporting Dubai's successful tourism industry, among various other sectors. He has led marine terminal operator DP World's expansion internationally, including the purchase of the P&O group for $6.8 billion in March 2006, which propelled it to one of the largest global port operators and trade enablers in the world; oversaw the development of the Jebel Ali Free Zone (Jafza) into a business park; established and led Nakheel, a real estate and tourism property development; established and led Istithmar World, a major investment house focusing on private equity; pioneered the Dubai Multi Commodities Centre (DMCC), a market for gold and precious metals, diamonds and coloured stones, energy and other commodities.

Earliest Memories

When I was a baby, Dubai had no running water, no electricity, no international airport and not even one hotel. As late as 1961, when I was six, the influential French newspaper Le Monde carried an editorial condemning the developed world for ignoring 'the poverty, disease and backwardness' which afflicted the Trucial States, including Dubai.

I have a very clear memory of visiting the Ruler's palace with my father when I was about seven where I discovered the miracle of running water. Dubai finally got electricity in 1959 when I was four but the supply of fresh water, although it was an even more urgent issue, took longer and disease was rife.

There had never been any lack of fresh water around Dubai – the Bedu in the desert, including the Sheikh who remained close to his desert roots, always knew where to find it. There were wells of what my father called 'sweet water' under the city, one near the Al Fahidi Fort and several at Deira, across the Creek, but the major source was a huge aquifer of fresh water on the old Bedu oasis at Al Oweir, fifteen miles south of the town. It was fed from the winter rains falling on the surrounding mountains, and carried into the city in jerry cans on the backs of donkeys, which is how we got our water – as everybody did, rich or poor, master or servant, there was no difference.

I had never seen running water until one day we were invited for lunch with the Sheikh and I was sent out to the yard to wash my hands before we sat down. I found a tap set in the wall from which water flowed when I turned it, but I couldn't figure out where it was coming from and ran around to the other side to check. 'There was nothing there,' I told my father excitedly as we sat down to eat. 'Where does it come from?'

'From a well of fresh water deep in the ground,' my father explained patiently. 'It is pumped up through a pipe to a tank on the roof, which is always full of fresh water. Then it flows down through a pipe hidden in the wall to the tap you used. That's what we mean by running water.'

Even at my tender age, this seemed a development of enormous importance.

'It's amazing – but so simple," I said, wondering why no one else had thought of it.

Sheikh Rashid, who treated me like a favourite nephew, listened to this with a tolerant smile. 'I want all houses in Dubai to have running water in the next three years,' he said.

Within a few years almost everyone in Dubai did, another major milestone along the road to prosperity. Bit by bit, the infrastructure of a modern city was coming together under the rule of a visionary Ruler.

Journey

I studied abroad with my wife, obtaining a BSc in Economics from Temple University in the USA. Shortly after my return I paid a courtesy visit on Sheikh Mohammed. My reason for seeing him was to pay my respects and to tell him I had finally graduated from Temple and was ready to get down to work. I had my own little property company, Asteco, but the state had paid for me to go to university and I had an obligation to pay it back. He was courteous as ever, inquiring after my family and step-mother, before we came to my future. We discussed a few roles in government service and he said he would make some inquiries and be in touch.

A few days later I got a call from his office to say he wanted to see me. 'We are sending you to the Dubai Petroleum Company,' he said formally. 'And tomorrow is your first day.' That suited me fine. The oil price was over $30 a barrel at the time, new fields were coming on stream, and the Dubai Petroleum Company was growing in leaps and bounds. It seemed a good place to be, even for a lowly management trainee with no experience of business. I was actually looking forward to it when I got a call the next morning from one of Sheikh Mohammed's officials, telling me to stand down. 'Don't go to the petroleum company,' he said. 'They're out of jobs. We'll be in touch.'

A letter arrived a week later requiring me to report to the director-general of customs, once run by my father. He greeted me with a cheery: 'I have good news and bad news.' Sheikh Mohammed, he said, was appointing three assistant director-generals to take charge of the customs at Dubai's ports, Port Rashid, Al Hamriya, and the new port of Jebel Ali. 'The good news is you've got a job,' he went on. 'The bad news is it's in Jebel Ali.'

That wasn't just bad news – it was terrible news. Everyone in Dubai knew that Jebel Ali, Sheikh Rashid's most ambitious infrastructure project yet, was a disaster – including the head of customs who had responsibility for it. 'I feel sorry for you but it's all we've got and you'll have to make the best of it,' he told me discouragingly. 'That place will never work. They should shut it down, level it to the ground, fill it with sand.

Today there are over 8,000 companies, including 100 of the top Fortune Global 500, operating in the Jebel Ali free trade zone, and we have virtually run out of space. Almost 150,000 people work there, driving traffic through the port which has grown into the biggest in the Middle East region and one of the largest in the world, impossible to conceive when I first went there in 1982. The area around the port and free zone, once dismissed as being 'too far' from the centre of Dubai, now accounts for 40 per cent of Dubai's GDP and a third of its foreign direct investment (FDI). JAFZA alone generates trade worth almost $100 billion a year, a quarter of the total UAE GDP of $400 billion (2019).

It has exceeded even Sheikh Rashid's wildest dreams when he first conceived it in 1976, and Sheikh Mohammed freely admits he never thought it would be such a success when he appointed me chairman in 1982 at the age of twenty-eight. I am pleased to have played my part.

HH Sheikh Zayed

Sheikh Zayed and Sheikh Rashid had the vision for what the UAE has become. The UAE is inclusive, fair and welcomes everyone. We are modern but we don't lose our traditions.

Exponential Growth

As a general point, the UAE has had to innovate with everything. We have built everything that you see around you from this harsh desert.

In terms of exponential growth for me, the years between 2001 and 2007 were the busiest and most productive of my life. I established DP World, bought CSX and then P&O, creating from scratch the world's third biggest ports operator which we floated on the stock market for more than $20 billion, the most important listing ever done by a Middle East company until Aramco in 2020.

As chairman of the government-owned holding company Dubai World and also of its main subsidiaries, Nakheel and Istithmar, I oversaw a high-profile investment programme in which we acquired some of the finest properties in Manhattan, a share stake in MGM, and a major portfolio of prime properties and prestige assets.

Looking back now, I can't imagine where I found the energy – and time – but in those years I was responsible for some of Dubai's most ambitious projects, building almost 800 miles of new beaches, 130,000 apartments, 6,000 villas, two giant shopping malls (each more than 1.5m sq ft), two golf courses, and half a dozen new hotels, including the 1,500-room Atlantis. Dubai Waterfront was the largest development of its kind ever attempted, and the project to build fifty new islands in the sea in the shape of a map of the World capped everything else. No one had ever done that before.

These were wild, exciting times when everything was happening, Dubai was growing in double digits, and we were borrowing and investing billions of dollars in imaginative and ground-breaking construction projects which were right out on the cutting edge of technology and entrepreneurial achievement. The world looked on in amazement as new man-made islands emerged from the sea, buildings designed by the best – and only the best – architects reached for the sky, shopping centres, a giant theme-park, a huge indoor ski resort, new roads, bridges, fly-overs, an international airport bigger than Heathrow and so much more materialised where a few decades before there had been sand and sea. Visitors gazed in awe at the forest of cranes stretching into the distance and the huge quantities of building materials which arrived at - and left - Jebel Ali every day. Companies from every corner of the world arrived to set up factories or warehouses in our free zone which grew in size and importance every year. In those years Dubai became an international destination for bankers, financiers, traders, merchants, manufacturers, agents and – most important of all – tourists, whose numbers increased ten-fold in a single decade. Money flowed in, property prices soared and the local merchants and traders made fortunes.

The energy and vibrancy of the place was incredible, with all the elements coming together like a giant jig-saw puzzle to turn our little desert kingdom into one of the most modern and prosperous states the world had ever seen, the envy of the Gulf. Nothing, not even Hong Kong or Singapore at their height, had seen anything like it. It was a joy to be at the centre of it.

Secret of Success

I would say our resilience, and our ability to adapt to changes.

One of Sheikh Mohammed's great strengths is that, like his father, he can look well into the future, see what needs to happen and then find a way of doing it.

Sheikh Mohammed always says that the success of Dubai, which many countries envy and try to copy, is based on the principle, originally established by his grandfather Sheikh Saeed, that the economy should be 'the most transparent and liberal in the Arab world, and the one most closely linked with free-market factors'. If Dubai had embraced the left-wing doctrine of Colonel Gaddafi for instance, it would be a ruin in the desert today, like Libya – or indeed Venezuela, Cuba or North Korea. 'My father learned from my grandfather, Sheikh Saeed, that Dubai's economic lifeblood, the qualities that make it special and unique,' says Sheikh Mohammed, 'are its openness to the world and its relations with other people across the globe. This is especially significant when it comes to business.'

Challenges

After the Global Financial Crisis, Dubai World would be criticised for the speed at which we expanded and the apparently indiscriminate nature of the companies we acquired. We would also face criticism for over-paying for assets at the height of the boom, and for borrowing too much money. My response to that is to point to what Dubai is today: a city in the global top ten most desirable cities to live in, the most important financial centre in the Middle East, the world's leading hub for international flights and, as the Economist described us: 'the pearl-fishing village which became one of the world's great entrepots'. The strong foundations that Dubai put down at the end of the twentieth century and early 2000s were more than enough to withstand a financial shock which brought other countries to their knees, some of which took years to recover. Dubai, by contrast, always had a clear investment strategy, agreed with and supported by Sheikh Mohammed, which was carried out to the letter. It is true we borrowed many billions of dollars; but Dubai has trillions in trade and what seemed to the outside world to be a serious financial crisis now looks no more than a hiccup which even the financial community has already forgotten.

Opportunities

DP World is global. We are evolving and solving logistical problems globally, improving the journey from factory floor to customer door. The supply chain is still inefficient though. That provides amazing opportunities for people who can solve for that. The world is also so fast changing, that anyone that makes advances in technology will find opportunity in the UAE.

Lessons

The UAE is a federation of 7 emirates that could have been independent. The unification, the harmony between tribes, nationalities and faiths provide lessons for other countries. Politics tends to get in the way: we should all work together for one goal to improve the lives of everyone.

To this day the UAE is, in the words of Sheikh Mohammed, 'the only viable Arab country conceived by genuine union, rather than arbitrary lines drawn on a map; and the only country that was built by Arab leaders through agreement rather than force'.

I knew nothing of the Abrahams Accord, the agreement between Israel and the UAE (Bahrain and the Sudan joined soon after), until August 2020 when it was signed in the White House. My immediate reaction was joy and admiration for the wisdom of our leadership and the courage of Sheikh Mohammed bin Zayed and Sheikh Khalifa who decided that enough was enough and we should be co-existing with the world. It is by far and away the most significant breakthrough in the Middle East peace process in my lifetime.

Expo

I have been to other Expos, but this one has been truly special. Every country has come together and invested so much. The themes of Expo have also really resonated.

When I unveiled the DP World pavilion at Expo 2020 in Dubai, the biggest event ever staged in the Arab world, I remarked that our pavilion, of which I was very proud, concentrated on the concept of trade, 'the energy that moves mountains, builds new cities, creates a new world, drives change and transforms economies.'

That, I said, is what DP World is all about: we make global trade flow, faster and more efficiently, 'to change what's possible for everyone'. That's more than an abstract aspiration. It's a fact, as we proved during the Covid pandemic when a shortage of shipping containers and a sharp rise in shipping costs led to severe congestion and long delays at the ports. Our heavy investment in the logistics chain over the past six years proved its worth and we kept trade moving, growing our business and our market share right through the crisis.

The opening of Expo, the most spectacular display any of us had ever seen, was a great day for Dubai and a great day for DP World. From the first time I heard about it, I was a big supporter of Expo, another visionary project from Sheikh Mohammed's extraordinary mind, and through our global network we played an integral role in making it happen. It added yet another dimension to Jebel Ali, occupying a 438-hectare site on the edge of the free zone; after a six-month run, the exhibition closed and the exhibitors moved out, leaving behind some of the most spectacular architectural designs on the planet which have now become the entirely new District 2020. The Saudi pavilion alone is said to have cost $1 billion and some of the others, including the Dubai and UAE pavilions, were not far behind. They now house a mixture of commercial and residential spaces, with hospitals, schools, a university campus, film studios and so much else.

The spectacular opening of Expo was a time for me to reflect on just how far DP World had come from a local port operator in Jebel Ali and Port Rashid to become an integral part of the supply chain, moving 10 per cent of global world trade, or more than $2 trillion of goods and services. It was only twenty-two years since its creation and fifteen since we took over P&O, yet in that time we have developed ports and terminals that set the bar for innovation and efficiency. We have established economic zones, including the first one in the UK, based on the success of Jebel Ali, and we have added shortsea and inland services around our ports. DP World operates in sixty-one countries across six continents.

The port of Jebel Ali is at the centre of it all. From virtually nothing in 1983, when I joined as a humble customs officer, the Jebel Ali complex now accounts for nearly 30 per cent of the sheikhdom's GNP and 20 per cent of all of the UAE's. The Free Zone has doubled in size in the past decade and now has 8,000 companies, employing 135,000 people with another 500,000 indirectly employed in businesses related to it.

Future

We're still bubbling with ideas of where we go from here. I took the opportunity at Expo to reveal some of the futuristic developments we are working on. Over the next decade, we plan to introduce new systems and new modes of transport which will be every bit as significant as the invention of the container which has revolutionised world trade. Outside our pavilion was a Hyperloop pod in which one day cargo – and people - will travel at the speed of sound to destinations all around the world. I have already witnessed the protype myself in the desert north of Las Vegas, where in 2020 the electric-powered vehicle had its first experimental run through a 500-metre vacuum tunnels using magnetic levitation tunnel. We hope to have our first commercial operation running, probably in India or Saudi Arabia, by 2027. Our studies have already shown that Hyperloop will cut the travel time from Riyadh to Jeddah to only 46 minutes, compared with 9-10 hours by car. One day there will be a network of them across the globe, under the sea and over the ground, and it will be the safest and most environmentally friendly form of transport ever designed.

We are planning new ports, and improvements to others, all the time making them faster, safer and less costly. In October 2021 we announced a new partnership with the British government agency CDC to invest $1.7bn in ports, inland container depots, economic zones and other logistics across Africa to increase trade. We already have significant port facilities in Dakar in Senegal, Sokhna in Egypt and Berbera in Somaliland and by 2035, the new ports will create 140,000 jobs and indirectly support employment for about five million people.

We have invented Box Bay, a unique system of stacking containers on shelves rather than on top of each other which allows us to get nearly 50 per cent more containers in the same space on the terminals.

And so it goes on, year after year, with new ideas, new technologies, new ports in new parts of the world. In 2016, when I again took on the job of chief executive of DP World, I expected to stay only a few years. Now, five years later, I feel I am just beginning…

22. DIAMONDS IN THE DESERT

Amit Dhamani, CEO of Dhamani Jewels Group

"The UAE's extraordinary growth is evidenced to me by the growth in the whole ecosystem: people, places, culture, trade and tourism and being the global leader in transformational ideas"

As one enters the Burj al Arab, or Dubai Mall, one of the first boutiques one sees is "Dhamani". Amit Dhamani is a second-generation jeweler who leads the brand with his two brothers and their three wives. They are the archetypal family business, and indeed take it to another level by all living together. In the last 30 years, Amit Dhamani has become a driving force in transforming the Dhamani Brand to a well-recognized Jewelry brand in the region. Amit Dhamani is a Director on the Global Board of Harvard Business School Alumni and is on the Board of Directors at the Dubai Diamond Exchange (DDE) & The Dubai Gold and Jewelry Group and is on the Board of Governors of GIA (Gemological Institute of America). Indeed, Harvard conducted a business case on the Dhamani family business.

Earliest Memories

I vividly remember my first visit to the UAE in 1992 when I accompanied my father on a sales trip from Bangkok where I was based at the time. Since day one, I found it very welcoming and embracing for new businesses and young entrepreneurs. During that trip, I was able to meet key businesspeople and families in a very informal and welcoming way. The loose gemstones and diamond business was in its nascency and as a gem dealer with offices in Bangkok and Jaipur, we were a unique addition to the market here.

The business spirit with a personal touch was a key factor that we found across all the people we met in UAE. We still cherish the great bonds and relationships formed in those early days.

Journey

My professional journey has evolved alongside with the growth and development of the UAE. Beginning my career as a loose gem and diamond merchant, we navigated the manufacturing of fine jewelry and became an important wholesaler in the region. As time evolved, we further aligned ourselves with the vision of the UAE leadership, which is to be an important center for trade and tourism for people from around the world. We emulated this by stepping closer to the consumer through establishing Dhamani retail boutiques in 2000.

Dhamani Group became an avid supporter of the Dubai and UAE vision to become a key center for the jewelry industry and did so by participating in various key platforms to support this vision. In early 2000, we started with being a part of the various brainstorming sessions during the pre-launch of the DMCC and were one of the first companies to register with DMCC. To enhance the trade of diamonds, I was appointed as a founding board member of Dubai Diamond Exchange in 2006 to date, contributing to the decision-making process and the growth of the diamond industry in UAE.

On the other spectrum of the jewelry industry, retail, I am appointed on the board of directors of the Dubai Gold & Jewelry group, a non-profit organization, which works hand in hand with all industry segments and is instrumental in making the Dubai – City of Gold and Jewelry destination of the world. I am very humbled and proud of Harvard Business School writing a case study about Dhamani Jewels, which is used for teaching purposes at the Harvard University.

HH Sheikh Zayed

HH Sheikh Zayed is the father of this great nation. His legacy and teachings are a source of personal inspiration. His vision transformed not only the UAE but also the lives of millions of people who now get to live and experience the country.

Exponential Growth

The UAE's extraordinary growth is evidenced to me by the growth in the whole ecosystem: people, places, culture, trade and tourism and being the global leader in transformational ideas. The quote by HH Sheikh Mohammed Bin Rashid AL Maktoum "We should always be practical, realistic, and optimistic" has always resonated with me because it keeps us aspiring while being grounded.

Secret of Success

The secret of the success of UAE is the can-do attitude of "nothing is impossible". Having full conviction on the vision of the leadership and align the strategies to implement and reach the vision has been a key to UAE's success. Moreover, the openness of having all nationalities and their culture work hand in hand to grow the economy – is the recipe for success.

We as Dhamani family, are unified to achieve the vision of being a global fine jewelry brand through the global strategic positioning of the group with a vertically integrated model – from mine to consumer.

Challenges

On a personal and business level, the biggest challenge is to keep focused on achieving the vision and periodically align the on-ground execution with a dynamic global environment.

The UAE as a country has overcome many challenges such as the 2008 global financial slowdown and the recent COVID-19 pandemic. This has been possible with a forward-looking positive attitude and integrated cohesive teamwork in various levels of government and the public sector. Adaptability to the changing dynamics is the key attribute, which helps the UAE overcome the challenges.

Opportunities

The UAE has a vast horizon of business opportunities in all segments, I see the growth in trade and tourism due to amazing infrastructure facilities and global connectivity. In the gem and jewelry industry there are vast opportunities for the UAE to play a hub role for regional and global expansion due to the industry's favorable policies.

Lessons

The most important lesson that other countries can emulate from the UAE is openness and a positive attitude of growth at all levels of society. The ease of communication of best policies and suggestions for improvement for the betterment of growth are always welcome in the UAE.

Expo

Expo 2020 Dubai is one of the best-executed Expos in history. Within a few square kilometers, a visitor can experience the ecosystem of nearly 200 countries. Expo brings diversity of culture, the social and business aspects of each country and is a revelation to all the visitors. The theme on being green and sustainability is a big takeaway for all the visitors to EXPO. My visit to Expo was a mesmerizing experience, looking up into Al Wasl Dome and seeing the creativity, I truly saw the quote of HH Sheikh Mohammad Bin Rashid Al Maktoum come to life - "Nothing is Impossible."

Future

From the past success we believe that UAE in next 50 years will be one of the most advanced countries in the world in the aspects of trade, tourism, fintech, space technology, and all new and upcoming industries, which the UAE will be the first to embrace.

In the Gems and Jewelry industry, we feel the UAE will be the global leader in trade and distribution and as HH Sheikh Mohammed says, "The race for excellence has no finish line"!

23. STANDING ON THE EDGE OF TOMORROW

Alain G. Bejjani, CEO Majid Al Futtaim Holding

"The secret of the UAE's success is its mindset. It is a welcoming society, genuinely tolerant, open and trusting, inquisitive and progressive. What makes it exceptional is the sense of community and belonging citizens and residents have for the Nation."

The manifestation of its founder's simple wish – great moments for everyone, everyday – has seen Majid Al Futtaim grow from a single mall in one of the oldest parts of Dubai to become a powerhouse across the region, recognised and lauded for its veracity, innovation and drive.

At the helm of the organisation is Alain Bejjani. Appointed as CEO in 2015, Alain has led its evolution from local stalwart to globally-recognised regional powerhouse, transforming the conglomerate's diverse operating companies to drive value creation for the long-term. Appointed as co-chair of the World Economic Forum 2020 Stewardship Board for the Middle East and North Africa, and a key private sector figure in shaping the regional agenda, Alain is recognised as one of the most successful CEOs in the Middle East. But he puts the company's success firmly down to the inspiration, leadership, boldness and passion of his mentor, and company founder.

At the end of 2021, Mr. Majid Al Futtaim passed away. Described by HH Sheikh Mohammed bin Rashid Al Maktoum as one of the Emirates 'most important merchants and senior men', his death was a source of immeasurable sadness for the company.

"For generations, Mr Majid Al Futtaim was a North Star - for us and millions of others. His wisdom, humility, kindness, generosity, energy and relentless drive to make things better inspired, enriched and improved us all. Mr. Majid was an exceptional visionary. In his drive to build towards a sustainable tomorrow, his certainty and clarity of purpose often saw him rallying against conventional wisdom. Because in founding our company, Mr. Majid's ambition was never to build a business, but rather an organisation that sets an example of what a single man can do to better his community and society at large. He wanted to create an enterprise that would serve as a beacon for the private sector and actively demonstrate how meaningful and enduring contribution to our economies creates a better today, tomorrow and future for the generations to come. Mr. Majid used to tell me "When I walk in our malls, I see joy, I see life". His mentorship was a gift. His leadership was a blessing. Today more than ever, we are committed to bringing his vision to life, to uphold his legacy and his dream to create great moments for everyone, every day".

Earliest Memories

My earliest memory of the UAE was seeing Emirates Towers when I first moved to the UAE in 2003. The Towers had just opened at that time, and I clearly remember they stood out in such stark contrast to anything else I had seen in the region. Today Dubai, Abu Dhabi are brimming with perhaps even more impressive buildings that bring cutting-edge advancements to life, but for me Emirates Towers will always represent the modernity, ambition, progression and bold aspiration that has become the hallmark of the United Arab Emirates.

Journey

As one of the largest privately held organisations in the region, Majid Al Futtaim is proud to take an active role in contributing to the development of the countries in which we operate. I joined the organisation in 2006 and it was immediately clear that Mr. Majid had huge ambitions for his company. I was honoured to be appointed CEO in 2015, and together with my leadership team we set about ensuring we were well-positioned to attain those ambitions. We have made incredible progress to date, and I am extremely proud of how we have continued to work in partnership with government bodies, local communities and global thought leaders to live our purpose and deliver on our vision.

It's been an extremely challenging, exciting and rewarding role… after all, on any given day you are challenged to understand now and be ready to adapt to tomorrow.

The most difficult thing is not just to dream and make that a reality, but to then dream bigger…to continuously push the boundaries of what you are told is possible. One of the first areas of focus I wanted to define is a 25-year strategic direction that would ensure we remain relevant and fit-for-purpose for the long-term. Today I ask, how do we ensure we can be successful for the next 100 years – how can we reshape to ensure we become a truly sustainable business, driving value creation for the long-term locally, regionally and globally.

As His Highness Sheikh Mohammed says, the journey to be number one never ends. This is what we think at Majid Al Futtaim. We want to create great moments for everyone, every day. Once you have created one great moment, you have to move on to the next, and never stand still. It is a journey of continuous improvement. What made us relevant 10 years ago won't necessarily be the thing that keeps us relevant now or in the future. What was great yesterday becomes expected tomorrow.

The world around us is evolving fast. We stand on the event horizon of the Fourth Industrial Revolution, technology and digital advancements are set to redefine how we interact and engage. The UAE stands at the forefront of progress in that respect, and we are delighted to be able to contribute to its success. It's an incredibly exciting time.

HH Sheikh Zayed

This is almost impossible to answer. Sheikh Zayed was an incredible visionary, he did not just lead one generation, but rather he continues, and will continue to inspire millions of people for generations to come. He was a man with an unwavering clarity of purpose and the ripple effect of his leadership continues to drive the UAE's collective drive, passion and aspirations. He was a truly great man by any and every measure.

Exponential Growth

This subject is as large as its topic! Just looking out of my office window at Dubai Creek and reflecting what it meant for the pearl divers and merchants in the 1900s, and then considering Jebel Ali, the world's ninth biggest deep-water port is a few minutes' drive away…the foresight of the UAE's leadership is truly incredible. It becomes even more so when you consider that foresight is weaved into our everyday experiences. For a country to grow in just half a century from a desert trading stop to a hyperconnected global talent hub known for cutting-edge innovation and a progressive society ...the UAE has not only evolved in itself, it has done so in a way that has become a role model for the region and indeed the world. Now that's exponential and extraordinary growth!

Secret of Success

The secret of the UAE is its mindset. It is a welcoming society, genuinely tolerant, open and trusting, inquisitive and progressive. What makes it exceptional is the sense of community and belonging citizens and residents have for the Nation.

Our community is one of the most cosmopolitan in the world but has a genuine admiration and respect for the country and its aspirations. Perhaps most importantly, we have a phenomenal sense of connection to the UAE, which drives a great sense of loyalty to both the Nation and its leaders. You feel you belong and that you have a role to play in the wider community. No matter where you came from, the UAE very quickly becomes home.

Challenges

I strongly believe our challenges are as big as our ambitions. However how we experience those challenges is wholly dependent on the team you have around you. At Majid Al Futtaim we pride ourselves on the scope of our ambitions, but we know to achieve them we need the best talent and the brightest minds to work on them – which is why we consider our human capital as important as our financial capital.

That said, it is one thing to meet a challenge of your own making, and entirely another to be able to rise and overcome one that presents itself...take COVID, for example. The UAE's response set the global bar not just for its initial response to the health crisis, which was remarkable in itself, but also the understanding of the potential broader impact and the swift, decisive and sustained steps the country took to mitigate socio and economic ramifications.

What really stood out for me is how every part of society; individuals, businesses and government came together, united by a common purpose to do what was right to protect our communities.

The UAE's collective response to the health crisis proves that with the right mindset seemingly insurmountable challenges can become great opportunities.

Opportunities

On the business side, the sky is the limit. The last century was defined by 'the American Dream', now it is really the UAE dream. I don't believe there are boundaries as to what the UAE can achieve when its sets its mind to it. There is simply no such word as impossible. The UAE's incredible entrepreneurial spirit permeates every aspect of life here and is bolstered by an infrastructure that supports and rewards those with the grit and perseverance to bring their ideas to life. Any new global sector or industry can come here and thrive.

Lessons

I don't believe there are lessons learned, per se, but rather a bar to reach. It has been truly humbling to see how the UAE has grown through the foresight of its leaders and experience its hugely ambitious plans come to fruition. No matter where you turn, be that security, community, technology, environment, the UAE is role modeling what good can look like in one or more areas. If I had to pick one aspect that had the largest impact, it would have to be the sense of togetherness across the public and private sectors. It may have started with Sheikh Maktoum's merchant majlis, but today it is organic, almost innate and it has made the UAE a blueprint for the world. There is a continuously evolving and progressive framework that supports entrepreneurship and the Government is there to help the economy thrive providing stability, agility and an unbridled drive to do what's best for its citizens.

Expo

Having Expo 2020 here in Dubai is a huge source of pride, and a great opportunity to shine a global light on the incredible innovation, energy and forward-thinking culture that defines the UAE. Each and every experience is part of a simple, sensorial and seamless omnichannel journey and it epitomises the UAE in so many ways, from the blend of technology to the outstanding hospitality. Expo 2020 is a crystallisation of what our future looks like. It is the beginning of tomorrow.

Future

The UAE has proven time and time again that it will achieve anything it sets out to do, so I am sure that the Centennial Plan will be in full swing! I believe that it will be the mindset of this remarkable place that will drive the milestones and ambitions that see the country grow exponentially and sustainably between then and now. That is to say challenging ourselves and each other to understand how we can collectively thrive, and how can we create an environment where our people can lead fulfilled and happy lives. This question starts at the very centre of Government and permeates every aspect of life here. Majid Al Futtaim's entire vision hinges on this simple question, how we can create great moments for everyone, every day? As human beings we are on a continuous quest for more fulfilment, for more meaning. We want to build connections and be part of a story that is bigger than ourselves - the UAE is a superb embodiment of that drive, that purpose-filled existence and I am incredibly grateful to be able to contribute to its mission.

24. PARTNERSHIPS OF TRUST

Patrick Chalhoub, Group President, Chalhoub Group

"The Founders of the UAE had a vision to create a country where the whole of civilization can meet and live. It is in the roots of the country."

It was in 1955 that the late Michel Chalhoub founded the Chalhoub Group in Damascus, with his wife Widad, by opening the first Christofle boutique at the age of 23. The Chalhoub Group now operates over 700 retail stores in 14 countries, employing more than 12,000 people. Nicknamed the "Wandering President", he was convinced of the growth potential of the Gulf and worked hard to establish the Group's business, operating in different categories and countries. Michel Chalhoub had to face major crises during his career while running the business in a turbulent region. He moved from Syria to Lebanon to Kuwait and then ultimately Dubai and operated during unprecedented periods of war and instability. He was always able to react to changing environments with speed and agility to rebuild the Group and make it even stronger.

Michel Chalhoub drove the Group's growth until the early 2000s when he became Chairman, handing over the Group's management to his two sons, the late Anthony Chalhoub and Patrick Chalhoub. In recognition of his endeavor to promote the French art-de-vivre culture and language, Michel Chalhoub was appointed Officier de la Legion d'Honneur, the highest French distinction, as well as other honours.

Patrick Chalhoub continues to fly the flag for the Chalhoub Group and has driven its growth over the last 20 years. He and his wife

Ingie are part of the fabric of the UAE.

Earliest Memories

My personal journey is linked with my family journey. My father, having started the business in 1955 in Damascus, very quickly found Syria too small. Luxury was in its infancy, but he believed that it would grow in the region. Lebanon was the most developed at the time, so we moved there in 1965. From there we travelled throughout the Gulf.

My first memories of the UAE were from traveling with my father. I would not have been 10 years old at the time, when I first arrived with my father in the late 1960s. There was no real market in the UAE, just a few families who could afford the goods. Our meetings were one-on-one and he loved it. I remember the friendships he made and loyalty he forged with clients, whose families are still our clients today.

I remember staying in the Al Ain Palace who had a famous Greek General Manager. The city was buzzing and had a real vibrancy. Once I had to sleep in the lobby as there was no room, and my father shared a room. However, we could feel something happening. This was not the luxury of today, but there was an excitement, a vibrancy.

Journey

I remember HH Sheikh Rashid, at the time, Ruler of Dubai, on one of my father's early visits, HH patted on my father shoulder and said, "Come back here often my son, it will be the new Hong Kong!". I joined the family business in 1979, and I continued to come to the Emirates to visit. Around 1985, I really felt that the UAE should be the hub for our business. It was a home for merchants. In 1989 I convinced my family to move the business to Dubai. We must have been among the first 50 businesses to move into Jebel Ali. As a business, our role was to import and distribute, and this was only possible because Jebel Ali existed.

When we arrived, HH Sheikh Ahmed bin Saeed welcomed us personally. Friends of my parents helped us establish here. The trust and friendships that my parents had made meant that we felt extremely welcome in the UAE.

We opened our first Louis Vuitton boutique in 1994 and I am

proud that by the time I came co-CEO with my brother in 2000, we had played our part in establishing the UAE as a luxury retail destination.

HH Sheikh Zayed

My father, on one of our earlier visits, had spent two months trying to see HH Sheikh Zayed to no avail. One day the Greek GM who I mentioned approached my father and said two other French guests were in urgent need for a French-Arabic translator as they had a meeting with HH Sheikh Zayed about an aircraft order. My father joined the meeting and facilitated the deal which culminated in 5 aircraft being bought. The interesting thing was that he was offered a commission for helping but turned it down, as he said that all he wanted to do was to explain to HH Sheikh Zayed what he did. That honesty and transparency was repaid when HH Sheikh Zayed put in an order, and my family have continued to supply the palace for the subsequent 60 years! My father's interaction with HH Sheikh Zayed was a lesson to us that patience and trust will be rewarded, and to not be greedy.

Exponential Growth

It is the People. The Founders had a vision to create a country where the whole of civilization can meet and live. It is in the roots of the country. This is not just talking about at an event like Expo. They have created a place to welcome to meet and mingle. There is a trading mentality, infrastructure, ports and airports. They are always looking ahead. Security is also key. Not just geopolitical security but personal security.

Secret of Success

Leadership here is building and leaving a legacy. Having this clarity in the mind of the leaders, and the companies asking how they are going to be relevant in the future is a great combination. Countries need to adapt and move quickly. We are not just competing amongst ourselves in the UAE, we are competing against the world. If the UAE wins, we also win.

Challenges

The Global Financial Crisis took us all by surprise. It was a great lesson that also helped us adapt in the recent pandemic.

Opportunities

Generally, I see great opportunity as everyone adapts to the digital world. We empower our teams to have the start-up mindset. Not just about having physical hubs and places but embed in the culture. We also need to put ourselves into the mindset that competition is not just local but Global.

Lessons

The UAE can be admired, amongst other things, for how future-oriented it is and in its success in planning and implementing long-term visions. There is also learning about creating security: health, education and ability to be entrepreneurial. The vibrancy that you find here. The tolerance and inclusiveness in a population that is around 90% expatriates.

Expo

Even just opening Expo in this climate is amazing. Success of Expo isn't a question of visitor numbers, but their appreciation of the country and attraction to come back and eventually invest. True success is a long-term success. Expo can be a tool to put the UAE on the world map, showing Dubai as destination for people to come and visit, attracting tourists but also increasing the awareness happening in the region. With the UAE being a luxury retail destination, the Chalhoub Group is playing our part to create an engaging experience so people will come back even after Expo.

Future

My hope is that we can maintain the UAE as a place where people are happy to live and maintain the warmth that I experienced when I visited in the late 60s.

It is important for us to continue to invite the best infrastructure and technologies to be implemented here, and I believe we are uniquely based to continue to be a hub for that and bring together the best people from East and West.

25. ENRICHING LIVES

Dr. Amina Abdulwahid Al Rostamani

"In a world of AI and digitization, creative jobs will be critical: the human element"

Dr Amina al Rostomani regularly features in the region's "power lists", most recently in the Forbes "Middle East Power Businesswomen 2021". It is well deserved: Dr Amina is currently Executive Director and COO of her family business, the AW Rostamani Group, She also oversees the Group Properties division, being the Chief Executive Officer of AWR Properties. Her father, Abdul Wahid Al Rostamani started a small Dubai bookstore in 1954 and laid the foundations for what now is the AW Rostamani Group, which has grown exponentially over the years to become one of the region's most progressive and innovative businesses. Today, the group has 14 companies with more than 4,000 employees and turnover has reached $2 billion.

In addition, Dr. Amina sits on number of International and UAE Boards, such HSBC Bank Middle East Limited, and two of Non-Profit Organizations; Al Jalila Foundation and at Sandooq Al Watan.

However, it was joining the TECOM Group fresh out of university where Dr Amina really made her mark. TECOM pioneered the "business cluster" model. TECOM is a subsidiary of Dubai Holding, the Holding Company of the ruling Maktoum family of Dubai. Beginning with Dubai Internet City in 1999, the idea was to create sector-focused business communities and work environments that provide innovative ecosystems. These would allow digital, technological, media and design companies to flourish. In a few short years, Dr Amina was promoted to CEO of the TECOM Group, and was instrumental to the development of Dubai Design District, Dubai Wholesale City, the Dubai Institute of Design and Innovation, and other projects. TECOM freezones are now home to 6,500 companies ranging from start-ups to multinational corporations with a total workforce of 95,000.

HH Sheikh Mohammed bin Rashid Al Maktoum summed up the success of TECOM and Dubai Internet City in particular when he tweeted on 26 May 2019: "In 1999, many people questioned our idea to establish Dubai Internet City in the desert. Two years ago, Amazon acquired the multi-billion dirham Souq.com and today, Uber acquired Careem for Dh11 billion. These giant companies flourished from the "desert" of Dubai."

Earliest Memories

My first memories are of going to school. You wouldn't believe the change. My mother didn't go to a traditional school, she learned the Quran with a Mutawa (religious teacher). This is the main difference between the generations and explains the main change that the UAE has undergone. They wanted me to have something that they didn't have.

Journey

I was lucky enough to get a scholarship in the USA, and ultimately got my Ph.D. in Electrical Engineering at Georgetown University. I was passionate about research, and on returning to the UAE had applied for various jobs at universities. One of my friends told me about what was going on at Media City and they had some interesting projects related to engineering, so I got a job, working as a project engineer, carrying cables, doing design.

I never thought I would become CEO. I was not interested in power — what drives me is challenges, and developing people. The first thought in my mind when I woke up as CEO was that I was serving my country, which is a great feeling. You go through your life and you go through major changes. To move out of research and become a simple project engineer was a big change. But the transition from just looking at the media sector to looking after everything was not a big surprise for me. It was something I felt ready for.

HH Sheikh Zayed

Whenever I see HH Sheikh Zayed's image, I think of a father

figure. Uniting the UAE was no easy task. He, Sheikh Rashid and the other rulers of the Emirates needed to have a long-term vision. They needed to invest in infrastructure: schools and people. Literacy and education were key, but also female empowerment. We are seeing the fruits of the results now.

Exponential Growth

The entrepreneurship I witnessed with the companies that were founded in the various TECOM freezones I oversaw. Seeing them each grow and interact with each other in each cluster fueled some of the amazing growth the UAE has seen.

Secret of Success

The UAE is like an engine that is constantly renewing itself, driving the whole country. It is about self-drive and self-improvement. Also the leadership stresses that failure is ok, as long as it is a path to improvement, and creates the environment for success.

On a personal level, my advice to succeed is you need to love what you do. A CEO has to be patient, and have experience of leadership and management. You need that ability to motivate people to do their job. I believe it's better to use the carrot rather than the stick. But this comes with experience, and the different situations I had to deal with… I was never really daunted by having to take on such a big role. The first question in my mind when I got the job was can I do it?

Challenges

Life is full of challenges. At the end of the day, when you face difficult times, you have to re-engineer your approach to the way you do business. The UAE is dynamic and so you have to be dynamic with what's going on in the market. There have been previous events like the Gulf war, we always had flexibility. Even during the Global Financial Crisis in 2009, when I was running TECOM, if I was told we would had have 654 new companies registering two years later, I would be very happy, I mean, really happy with that figure.

It was a period of huge uncertainty. I got a lot of phone calls saying this place will become a ghost town. We had some companies leaving, but we were very careful to understand what the customers were going through, especially those who had been here for ten years — we made sure we listened to them to see how we could support them, and help them sustain their business.

We started running networking events and sessions for them to learn from different people. We had sustainability sessions with consultants and legal firms, and various schemes to support our people.

The growth we had was tremendous and as human beings to have been here, and to see that growth, was amazing. But you really learn so much also from challenges, you learn how to reverse your thinking and look for efficiencies.

Opportunities

For the next generation, I see great importance for creativity. In a world of AI and digitization, creative jobs will be critical. The human element.

Lessons

What we learn from the founding fathers of the UAE is that you should always prioritise relationships, values, integrity and transparency. It is about long-term sustainability of a country before anything else.

Expo

I would personally encourage them to see the other side of the city, the desert life, the simplicity. It's very important to see the heritage and cultural story of the UAE.

Whenever I would meet new investors coming to set up in the UAE, I would always ensure that we were looking to a win:win for all. I believe that if you focus on that, you will see exponential growth.

Future

More success inshallah! I think the UAE is continuing on a very exciting journey. Growth in the economy and the development of people will always be fundamental to our future.

26. TRAVELERS WELCOME

HE Mohamed Khalifa al Mubarak

"Culture is the foundation of any society"

Louvre Abu Dhabi is itself a work of art. Designed by renowned French architect Jean Nouvel, it is simultaneously historic and futuristic. From afar, it looks like a collection of whitewashed buildings, that would have not looked out of place at the birth of the UAE in 1971. Looking closer, what catches the eye is a huge domed roof, that looks like a flying saucer has landed. Made from nearly 8,000 metal stars set in a geometric pattern, it allows shards of sunlight to enter, giving the interior a dappled effect like one is walking through the shade of a palm grove.

Appearing to float on water, like a desert mirage, Louvre Abu Dhabi stands as the physical embodiment of the emirates' past, present and future, and a symbolic cornerstone of the nation. The opening is just one of the remarkable milestones achieved by HE Mohamed Al Mubarak, member of the Executive Council of Abu Dhabi, and Chairman of the Department of Culture and Tourism - Abu Dhabi (DCT Abu Dhabi) to which he was appointed in 2015. In his role, he oversees the cultural development of the emirate and its promotion as a global destination, through the integration of tourism regulations and the active engagement of local, regional and international audiences.

Al Mubarak has a range of roles and titles. He leads the teams behind many of Saadiyat Cultural District's array of institutions; he is a father and mentor; he is Chairman of Aldar Properties, as well as DCT Abu Dhabi. This is what he does, yet it does not fully speak of who he is, which is revealed within vibrant anecdotes of a life lived within a fast-changing UAE, spending time among the nation's elders and founders, including Sheikh Zayed himself.

Earliest Memories

Some of my earliest memories are spending time with my grandparents, listening to their stories at our farm in Al Ain, or visiting the Cultural Foundation with my mother. My aunt worked there and I can recall exploring all of the inspiring programs, wandering through the vast library and seeing all of the vibrant performing arts. I would spend hours just roaming the Cultural Foundation, just letting my imagination wander.

I have stirring memories of our leaders from my youth. I can recall when Marina Mall had just opened, and it was one of the first shopping malls we had in Abu Dhabi. Sheikh Zayed would love to visit people there. Everybody was so happy to see him and have the opportunity to greet him personally. One hot day, he saw kids running around and he said: "Give everybody cold drinks and ice cream inside the mall". Everybody – every single person inside the mall. That level of care, consideration and inclusivity still inspires the way I think and approach solutions, because acts of kindness and words of wisdom have inspired me more than anything else.

The objective to enhance quality of life is a message that His Highness Sheikh Mohamed bin Zayed imprinted on my mind from a young age. He taught me that a city filled with attractive architecture is nice to have, but it's all about quality of life. That's what we are here to build – it's not about the structures themselves. This has been a guiding principle for me for the past 20 years and it will always stay with me. So when I say our intention is to enrich quality of life, that's directly where it comes from.

From a young age, Japanese anime and western comics were influences that fed into my creativity. Now, today, Arabic content and Arabic comics are all created here. Everyone can visit nearby attractions that we would only dream about, including Metropolis and Gotham City at Warner Bros World Abu Dhabi. You can only imagine how these experiences will inspire young minds to pursue art, or archaeology, or marine biology. It's something special.

To this day, I take inspiration from the joy-filled experiences and cultural insights from my childhood. They remain more relevant than ever as I help deliver the vision to grow Abu Dhabi as a destination, as a home, and as a vibrant cultural center. Together we are shaping a better place to live, work, learn and play. The dreams I had in my youth have helped shaped my duty to dream as a leader, for the benefit of Abu Dhabi.

Journey

Growing up, we traveled abroad to visit museums, and now those experiences exist here in Abu Dhabi. Young minds are like sponges, freely absorbing history, culture and creative concepts, and this generation now has instant access to iconic institutions that were out of reach just a decade ago. This also applies to more entertainment-focused experiences, like our theme parks, which inspire us all to be innovative, imaginative and playful.

Future-thinking leadership places creativity at the heart of all we do, which is reflected in our investments in cultural and creative industries. One of my first ever responsibilities at DCT – Abu Dhabi was the restoration of the Cultural Foundation – which is a beautiful link from one of my earliest memories. It was the very place that inspired me to become an artist, with a love for music, art and performance. That all came as a result of the Cultural Foundation, and these institutions are critical for influencing and enabling our youth, and I am living proof of that.

We believe that culture is the foundation of any society. This is why the nation's heritage underpins so much of our strategy – connecting with our past to pave the way for the future. We continue to invest in our cultural ecosystem as it will lead to a long-lasting, resonate legacy for the entire UAE.

HH Sheikh Zayed

HH Sheikh Zayed is truly an icon of leadership, continuing to inspire the world through his writings and documented wisdom. With humility and kindness, he understood that the true value of a nation is its people. As a leader, he was passionately driven to provide a better quality of life for all. He worked tirelessly to make sure the UAE will continue to grow and prosper, while also ensuring the preservation of nature. He loved and cherished this land, with a deep understanding of our ecology.

If I could go back in time I would tell myself to keep my eyes and ears open. I would watch and listen to everything Sheikh Zayed was doing. These things will teach you how to be a better person, a better father, a better husband and a better mentor. Sheikh Zayed taught us to love our environment, he told us education is key, he told us that no matter what happens, equality is always there. He told us to never forget where you come from, and that you should help somebody when you have the opportunity.

He taught us all of this through his actions, as well as his words. While the Federation was being formed, he never stopped giving and visiting those who were in need. You hear so many pieces of learned wisdom that got passed on from Sheikh Zayed to Sheikh Khalifa to Sheikh Mohamed, ensuring that we have a living legacy of mentorship. We have individuals who inspire us every single day, which is an opportunity that many don't have, and something I do not take for granted.

Exponential Growth

In its 50 years of development, the UAE has made incredible advances on all fronts to become a nation that embraces innovation and modernity while maintaining a deep connection to our heritage.

For me, the most iconic symbol of this extraordinary development has to be Louvre Abu Dhabi. This renowned institution carries an essence of the UAE, with stunning, cutting-edge architecture inspired by palm leaves and the oases of the desert. Inside, the unique range of collections span the entire globe, across millennia, telling the universal story of shared humanity.

Founded on an incredible diplomatic partnership, the museum is among the nation's proudest achievements, and will soon form a central part of an expansive cultural district including the Zayed National Museum, Guggenheim Abu Dhabi and Abrahamic Family House. This is a tangible example of the UAE's progress towards being one of the world's most prominent, vibrant and diverse cultural centers within the next 50 years.

Opportunities

I see a very exciting future for the UAE, with sustainable business and career opportunities across all sectors – from Culture and Creative Industries (CCI), heritage and archaeology, fine arts and performance, filmmaking and video game development, to tourism and real estate.

Creativity and the arts are vital pillars of social development, as well as important economic contributors – with global revenues of more than US$ 2.25 trillion a year and 30 million people employed in the sector. We are embracing this potential, with CCI fully integrated into our vision for progress.

Abu Dhabi has developed a thriving CCI sector, with 20,000 industry jobs already created. Over a 10-year period, beginning 2016, the emirate is investing more than AED 30 billion into growing this sector further, accelerating growth across large-scale developments such as Yas Creative Hub and Saadiyat Cultural District, soft infrastructure such as flexible visas and business licenses, and talent development to create opportunities and training for new generations of professionals.

This robust and ambitious strategy is creating an environment where the entire culture and creative sector can grow, thrive and contribute to a diversified economy – with the CCI expected to enter the top·10 economic sectors of the UAE before too long.

Abu Dhabi is known for its broad range of hospitality, retail and residential developments, offering the public a multitude of options to enhance the way they live, work and play. Our ambitious tourism strategy will see the number of hotel jobs alone grow from 28,000 in 2020 to around 68,000 by 2025, contributing more than AED 30 billion to GDP.

On the real estate front, I also serve as Chairman of Aldar, driven by a vision to develop quality, comfortable, desirable destinations where people live, work at and visit. Aldar is managing the AED one billion development of twofour54's media and creative campus. Yas Creative Hub on Yas Island will add another creative dimension and drive significant weekday footfall to the island.

The AED 500 million redevelopment plan for Yas Mall is also

set to repurpose 40% of its GLA toward high-impact experiential retail, as well as F&B. In addition, new co-working office spaces will provide additional room for creative talent to collaborate and work on Yas Island.

With tens of thousands of long-term career opportunities being created and a continuously evolving cultural landscape attracting and inspiring all kinds of creatives and entrepreneurs, I see incredibly exciting opportunities in these sectors for the years and decades to come.

Lessons

The fast-paced development of our nation provides a model with many lessons other countries or communities can draw from. Firstly, by welcoming residents from around the world, we have built a highly diverse society where social cohesion, peaceful coexistence and mutual understanding are cherished. There is a considerable sense here of being one strong community, no matter your background.

Secondly, the UAE's leaders have always understood the critical importance of investing in the foundations of a thriving society: infrastructure, education and innovation. Whether it's the Emirates Mars Mission, the Barakah Nuclear Plant, or the vast Ghadan 21 economic accelerator programme, sufficient investment is vital to ensure people, businesses and industries have the ability to grow, thrive and become self-sustaining in the long term.

Thirdly, the UAE has always been highly ambitious, resilient and visionary, as we look to be at the forefront of 21st century advances. At the same time, we have retained a deep connection to the ancient heritage of our region and the cultural roots of our past. These help to bring balance to our unique society.

Expo

To have hosted the first World Expo in the Middle East was an incredible achievement. Countries from around the world came together in a space of collaboration, ideation and exchange to explore ways that the global community can improve lives and protect the planet for decades to come. It was a truly impressive platform for change, and a chance for millions of international visitors to experience the UAE.

The main takeaway for a first-time visitor has to be the warm hospitality and incredible diversity of experiences that our country has to offer. Tourists and residents have endless choices, whether they're looking for inspiring art and museums or ancient heritage sites; contemporary urban architecture or expansive, restorative untouched deserts; award-winning performing arts or exciting global sporting events; miles of pristine beaches or thrilling roller coasters; peaceful nature reserves or buzzing nightlife. There is truly something for everyone to discover, at their own pace.

Future

The UAE's Golden Jubilee marks a half-century of rapid and ambitious development across all aspects of the nation; I can only imagine how much more we can achieve over the next 50 years. As we look forward to our next decades of progress, we are rapidly diversifying our economy to embrace knowledge, entrepreneurship and innovation.

The UAE's ongoing investment in growing the industries of the future – as diverse as next-generation digital advances, tech-enabled food production, clean energy, and creative media production – is already making a socioeconomic impact, and this will only continue to grow in the future.

As we think ahead to 2071 and prepare for progress in all that we do, the UAE already established as a leading tourism destination, global hub for business and trade, and as a center for culture. The vast array of cultural institutions will continue to attract brilliant, creative minds from around the world – from top-tier universities and global museums to smaller galleries and grassroots initiatives, providing platforms for innovative young artists.

What will never change is the UAE's commitment to its core values of harmony, diversity, cross-cultural understanding and passionate dedication to progress, all underpinning this exciting vision for the future.

27. HELLO TOMORROW

Sir Maurice Flanagan

"You can chew the dynamism in the air"

Many people's first experience of the UAE is with Emirates Airline. Emirates has become a globally recognized brand, built largely on innovative sports sponsorships that mean the brand is known all over the world. However, travel back to the beginning of 1985, and the airline did not even exist. At that time, Maurice Flanagan was running the Dubai National Air Travel Agency when HH Sheikh Mohammed bin Rashid al Maktoum, Ruler of Dubai, asked him to launch the airline. Remarkably, nine months later, on 25 October 1985, Emirates' inaugural flight, EK600, flew from Dubai to Karachi with Maurice Flanagan and his wife Audrey on board. He went on to be Executive Vice-Chairman and was knighted by Her Majesty the Queen in 2010. Sadly, Sir Maurice passed away in 2015, but I had the privilege of knowing him for 10 years. One night in the Capital Club, after he retired, he delivered a speech, that with his family's kind permission, I have adapted below into the same format as the other interviews. What he said is as relevant now as it was then.

On his passing, HH Sheikh Ahmed bin Saeed al Maktoum, Chairman of the Emirates Group said: "The Emirates Group and Dubai, have lost a great friend. Maurice was a man of great character and a legend in the aviation industry. He was generous with his time, forthright in his views, and a person who gave 110 per cent to everything he did."

Earliest Memories

When I first arrived in the UAE in 1978, if you wanted a pint of fresh milk you had to be at Spinney's before it opened. If you stood on the top of the new World Trade Centre and looked down the Abu Dhabi Road the only building on the horizon was the old Chicago Beach Hotel, on the site of today's Burj al Arab. But you could chew the dynamism in the air. In our first month or two the Creek Sheraton, the Trade Centre Hilton, the Grand Metropolitan and the Meridian near the airport all opened. There was an ice rink at Al Nasr and soon another, and a revolving roof at the first Hyatt.

DNATA's town office at that time was high up above Al Nasr Square reached by a staircase so shabby that a travel agency at ground level, owned by my friend Abdulla Ansari, charged Dnata customers Dhs20, gave them a cup of coffee, and they waited in comfort for a messenger to go up for their DNATA ticket. My wife seeing the premises said " My God what have you come to" She reckons I said "I've come for the way it's going to be." Surely, I didn't say anything that pompous. Dnata was in any case a step ahead. It was already building the Airline Centre. Unfortunately, the Airline Centre was equipped with a job lot of airline check-in counters, which had probably fallen off the back of a lorry. Sales counters they were not. Fortunately, the Airline Centre caught fire – I had an alibi – I then furnished it fit for purpose, which included a proper IT system.

Dnata thus became like an airline without its own aircraft. That's why it was later possible to launch Emirates within the time limit.

Journey

Early in January 1985, my wife Audrey and I were in London having Christmas leave to celebrate our 30th wedding anniversary with our family. I had a call from Brigadier Michael Barclay, Sheikh Mohammed's advisor, telling me to get back quickly as His Highness was talking about an airline. Gulf Air were asking Sheikh Mohammed to declare Dubai its national carrier to give it access to more traffic rights to Pakistan. His Highness refused because it conflicted with his policy of Open Skies in Dubai. This allowed all airlines unlimited access to Dubai and has been crucial to its growth.

Sheikh Mohammed asked me to plan as if we were to start an

airline. It had to be secret. We held project meetings all over the Airline Centre with a few dummy meetings to divert suspicion. One day in May I was going to a meeting at what was then the Intercon on the Creek, when I was called to reception to take a call from Sheikh Mohammed. "What did you say was the best time to start the airline" he said. "October 25th, Your Highness, the start of the airlines' winter schedules". "We go ahead" His Highness said. "Come and see me this evening". When he asked how much I needed to start the airline. I said "Ten million dollars, Your Highness." Of course it wasn't enough but I had to give a figure I thought was acceptable. "Right" Sheikh Mohammed said. "And don't come back for any more". He made it clear there would be no protection from competition, Open Skies stays. He said the airline had to be good, look good, and make money. There would be no subsidies. The Gulf Air Board were called to a meeting at Zabeel Palace, expecting to hear good news. I heard later that when they were leaving His Highness said "By the way gentlemen, I'm starting my own airline."

The critical path for the launch ran through the selection of corporate identity. It goes into stationery, tickets, uniforms, airport signage, travel agents' windows, the livery of the aircraft. My ideal was that Emirates Inflight Service should be that of early BOAC, when an airline trip was an occasion in itself. We obviously could not choose our own aircraft and put them in service in the time available. So we decided to lease two aircraft from PIA. We held our breaths as launch day approached. The two aircraft had been painted in Emirates livery as secretly as possible. The sheikhs of the Gulf had been invited, the red carpets were laid. And then appeared from the east two Emirates aircraft with an escort of UAE fighters. We'd done it.

Secret of Success

Why has the Emirates Group been such a success? Several reasons. Our Chairman, its geographical position, making a perfect hub, an enlightened ownership in the government, whose policy towards tourism has made it possible for us and other airlines and hotels to feed off each other and enhance the Emirate's prosperity.

For the UAE it was the culture: Firmly Islamic but tolerant, the perfect combination of magnificent desert and 21st Century fun, safe, welcoming, modern but with Eastern mystery and culture and with a hospitable indigenous population.

Challenges

The main challenge for us was getting known. At that time the rest of the world didn't know about Dubai ("Isn't that in Saudi Arabia"?) let alone Emirates. We had a good ad agency Grey's but advertising never produces the same exposure for the money as the right sponsorship, especially on TV. Our greatest success in sponsorship has been with the Emirates Stadium and shirt at Arsenal. Another is the umpires' shirts in top level cricket. They always have their backs and Fly Emirates to the camera. There is golf, the Americas Cup with Prince William and Catherine in our New Zealand boat. The Emirates Cup is attached to the richest horse race in the world. The Emirates Literary Festival brings the world's intellectuals and writers who might otherwise think Dubai too lightweight but go away reeling with admiration of a city where Islam, Arabic culture and an international community, can live happily together.

Exponential Growth

Some airlines can't understand our growth, they think there must be some sort of trick in there. [As mentioned above] my Chairman, HH Sheikh Ahmed and I were given $10m to start the airline in 1985. And HH Sheikh Mohammed said don't come back for anymore and don't expect any subsidy or any capital injection and it's been like that right from the start. So the rules of the game were quite rigorous.... In the first 10 years, the airline grew on average of 30% per year in capacity: that's 10-fold growth in 10 years.

28. DOING YOUR DUTY

Colm McLoughlan, CEO of Dubai Duty Free

"The UAE continues to open, not shut, its doors, making it one of the most competitive and open markets in the world economy"

Colm McLoughlin began his retailing career in London in the 1960s, working for high-street chain Woolworths, before moving back to his native Ireland to work for Shannon Duty Free. As General Manager of Shannon Duty Free, Colm was one of a team of ten from Aer Rianta (the Irish Airport Authority) who moved to Dubai in 1983 at the request of the Dubai Government, to set up Dubai Duty Free. Following the successful opening of Dubai Duty Free in December 1983, Colm was asked to remain and head up the operation, which in its opening year had a turnover of US$20 million. In July 2011, Colm was named Executive Vice Chairman and CEO of Dubai Duty Free. Under Colm's direction, Dubai Duty Free has become one of the leading airport retailers in the world with annual sales turnover of over US$2 billion in 2019 and is a recipient of over 700 awards presented by international, regional and local entities, which bear testimony to its retail success.

Earliest Memories

I arrived in Dubai on the evening of July 15, 1983. It was the eve of my 40th birthday and I recalled the wave of intense heat that hit me as I was walking down the steps of the aircraft. I had never experienced anything like it in my life.

I remember being met by Norman Turnbull from Dubai Airport and we went to the International Hotel near the airport, now Le Meridien. The airline had lost my luggage so I went the next lunchtime to the Al

Ghurair Centre to buy a new shirt and so on, but did not realise that they closed between 1pm and 4pm in those days, so was standing outside waiting for the shops to re-open in the summer heat!

Luckily my meetings with the then Director-General of Dubai Civil Aviation Authority, Mohi-din Binhendi, went very well and we were given the go ahead to set up the duty free operation in the basement of the existing terminal, where there had been a former kitchen. We had barely six months to do everything, from working with contractors on the construction, to hiring staff, to buying stock, everything.

In addition to the hard work in the setting up of the business, we had to learn a good deal about doing business in Dubai. The very first thing that we did was to get hold of a copy of the Dubai business directory from the Chamber of Commerce and looked up local distributors of products that we wanted to stock. We eventually chose our suppliers and we still have many of the same to this day and have a great relationship with them.

I certainly got a sense right from the start that things had to move quickly in Dubai, and I liked that. I very quickly got the sense as well, that everything had to be of a very high standard. At that time, there were around three million passengers using the airport and only about 250,000 people living in Dubai, compared to over 89 million passengers in 2019 and a UAE population of over ten million.

Before the arrival of the current golf courses in Dubai, we played golf on sand and you had to hit off a little patch of AstroTurf you carried around with you. Rather than 'please repair the greens', the signs read 'please brush the browns.' Golf has grown up so much in the time we've been here and now there are more than twenty golf courses in the UAE.

Indeed, a lot has changed. When I arrived in Dubai all those years ago, I certainly did not envisage that I would still be here, over 38 years later, but I'm glad I am!

Journey

I was one of a team of ten from Aer Rianta (the Irish Airport Authority) who came to Dubai in 1983 at the request of the Dubai Government, to set up Dubai Duty Free. The contract was for six months but following the successful opening of Dubai Duty Free on 20th December 1983, I was asked to remain and head up the operation. The idea appealed to me. I talked to myself a lot about it. And eventually whilst I was supposed to return to Ireland in March 1984, as per my six-month contract, I decided to retire from my job in Ireland and come and work as general manager of Dubai Duty Free.

Since then, Dubai Duty Free has grown from strength to strength and with it my love of this city and the organisation I work for. Our business grew from sales of US$20 million in 1984 to over US$2 billion in 2019. We have been recognised as the single largest duty free in any airport in the world many times. Our staff grew from 100 to a high of 6,000. Our business has won over 700 awards. During our time, we also set up the Dubai Duty Free Foundation, which is very active and is focused on charities that help women and children in particular. We have had great support from the Government of Dubai and especially my boss, HH Sheikh Ahmed bin Saeed Al Maktoum, President of Dubai Civil Aviation Authority and Chairman of Dubai Duty Free.

In addition to our retail business, Dubai Duty Free also operates a Leisure Division, which includes The Irish Village in Garhoud, Studio One Hotel and Expo 2020 Dubai, The Century Village, the Dubai Duty Free Tennis Stadium, home to the Dubai Duty Free Tennis Championships, and The Jumeirah Creekside Hotel.

HH Sheikh Zayed

I have to say 'inspirational' when you consider the tremendous changes that have happened since the formation of the UAE in 1971 to today's modern and vibrant nation.

I did not meet HH Sheikh Zayed in person, but I know that he was a great man of the people and he was regularly seen driving around Abu Dhabi by local residents.

During the course of my career, I have met with many other senior members of the UAE Ruling families, in particular HH Sheikh Mohammed bin Rashid Al Maktoum, Vice-President and Prime Minister of the UAE and Ruler of Dubai. I remember being called to meet HH in the early days of Dubai Duty Free and he expressed his support of the operation and encouraged me to ensure that it was the biggest and best in the world!

We are also very fortunate to have HH Sheikh Ahmed as our Chairman and of course he is overall head of Dubai Airports as well as Emirates Airline and many other entities. I report to HH directly and greatly admire him as a hard-working man as well as being extremely approachable and down to earth.

Exponential Growth

As a Dubai resident of 38 years, I have seen the UAE grow dramatically during that time to become a strong and vibrant nation that cares for its citizens. and I'm very proud of the role played by Dubai Duty Free in doing our part to put Dubai on the map through our own business success as well as through our many international sports sponsorships.

Secret of Success

The success of the UAE is attributed to the wise policies drawn by the founding fathers of the nation and in particular the late HH Sheikh Zayed Bin Sultan Al Nahyan and the late HH Sheikh Rashid bin Saeed Al Maktoum. They have put the UAE on the world map as an ambitious nation that nurtures its history and culture, while building for the future.

For my own success and that of Dubai Duty Free, our operation is owned by the Government of Dubai and there is a very positive attitude among the government members that everything in Dubai should succeed and support is given to ensure that success. That positive attitude permeates through organisations, including our own and we have tried to build a family-oriented team. We value our staff and ensure they are fully trained for the job and I think they are the main reasons for our success.

Challenges

Without a doubt, the Covid-19 global health crisis affected all aspects of life and business and represents the biggest challenge the likes of which we have never seen before.

It has changed the world as we know it, and I am very proud of the way that the UAE government managed the pandemic from the very beginning. Also, the way that they rolled out the Vaccine programme is admirable and I think we are all very lucky to have been living in the UAE over the past 18 months.

It was an extremely challenging year for the global travel retail industry and those challenges, which included the closure of Dubai International Airport for three months and the continued closure of Al Maktoum International Airport, are reflected in Dubai Duty Free's sales of US$697 million in 2020, which is 65% down on the previous year. Yet, despite the challenges, we managed to gradually and safely re-open our retail operation at Dubai International Airport which is now operating 100 per cent full capacity with the opening of Concourse A last week. Also, we returned to profitability earlier this year, which is a good indicator for us.

Today, the UAE has overcome the worst side of the Covid-19 crisis and ranks among the top countries globally in addressing the pandemic. The UAE is also the most vaccinated country, with over 21.8 million vaccine doses administered. Almost 100 per cent of the UAE population has received at least one dose of the vaccine, while 90.31 per cent are fully vaccinated with two doses.

Opportunities

The UAE has become one of the most sought-after places for living and doing business in. With tax-friendly policies, top quality social and economic infrastructure, and a strategic location, it comes as no surprise that so many companies and entrepreneurs have chosen to set up their business here.

But what excites me the most is the range and quality of retail in the UAE, which raises the bar in terms of customer service, quality retail outlets, diverse products and availability. In addition, the UAE and Dubai in particular, remain hubs for retail e-commerce growth in the MENA region. Many companies had a significant investment in online sales activity during the pandemic and managed to grow or keep their businesses going.

Lessons

From the very start I liked the welcoming and courteous nature of the people in Dubai, both the UAE nationals and expatriates. The 'can do' attitude was very much in evidence even in back in the 1980's and everyone was willing to help or to point you in the right direction.

In the face of overwhelming numbers of expatriates and other effects of globalisation, the UAE continues to open, not shut, its doors, making it one of the most competitive and open markets in the world economy.

Expo

The Dubai Expo 2020 is absolutely fantastic, and I have visited it several times, the last time was to watch a performance of Riverdance (the Irish dance troupe) which was world class. So, in addition to the entertainment value, Expo 2020 has created thousands of jobs in Dubai which is good for the overall economy. Previous Expos have left a real legacy with the products that were launched, the inventions that came to the world and this Expo is no exception. Following the six months of Expo, the site will be transitioned into District 2020, re-purposing 80% of the Expo's built environment to develop a sustainable and human-centric smart city, that will continue to attract business and people to work, live, visit and enjoy.

For someone visiting the UAE for the first time, I would say take inspiration from the UAE and what has happened in just 50 years.

Future

The UAE is committed to the environment, to sustainability, to space exploration and to many more things that will drive the future. I think the UAE will become the best country in the world, with an even better quality of life for its citizens and residents. They will develop more parks, a better spread of three to five-star hotels, an extension of a very successful metro, new suburban cities and a bigger population

When I retire, I plan to live here for the best part of the year. I consider Dubai very much my home and I am very excited about the development plans that are in place and those of the future.

29. STAY DIFFERENT

Gerald Lawless

"Vision is one thing; ambition, courage and the energy to be able to implement the vision are something else"

Gerald Lawless joined Jumeirah in 1997 as its Founding CEO. He started with a team of less than 30 employees and grew it to more than 14,500 by the time he stepped down in early 2016. During this time Jumeirah's international portfolio expanded to 23 hotels in 12 destinations by February 2016 with more than 100 food and beverage outlets. Gerald built Jumeirah's service philosophy on its brand promise of "Stay Different". It recognises that everyone is different which is why each of the Jumeirah properties is different and has a solid connection with its local community and culture.

Earliest Memories

I began my career with Trust House Forte, as it was known then, later to become Forte Hotels. In those early career days we were transferred quite frequently moving from Southampton to Swindon and then to Glasgow between 1974 and 1978. At that stage I had decided that I wanted to have an international career, so I kept calling my head office until one day they finally called me in Glasgow and said, "Are you still interested in going overseas?" I said, "Yes, I must go overseas", and they said, "Okay, we've got a possibility for you in Dubai. Would you go there?" I said, "yes of course". I then paused and said, "where exactly is it? I know it's in the Middle East…" They laughed and said, "you're right. Look it up!" No google in those days!

So, by July 78, everything was finalised. My wife, Neasa and I flew out here on 26th August 1978 – a hot time of the year to arrive! We had never experienced weather like that before. My role was as assistant food and beverage manager, working on the opening of what was then to be known as the Dubai International Hotel, which was under construction and is now Le Meridien at the airport. That was our first experience of Dubai and we were accommodated in the Astoria Hotel in Bur Dubai. We really enjoyed being in Dubai. We will always treasure those early memories… walking through the souks, crossing the creek in an Abra. Neasa and I still take our house guests through this special area. We always say that if you visit Dubai and you haven't visited Bur Dubai, the Creekside and the Spice Souks then you have not really seen Dubai!

Journey

After four years in Dubai, my company offered me a position as General Manager of their hotel in Durban, South Africa. We spent two and a half years there, and then went to London for 14 months at Heathrow Airport, however both Neasa and I really wanted to get back to the Middle East.

Forte offered us Bahrain, so we came to Bahrain in 1985. It felt so good to be back in the Gulf – we were home! Then in 1988 we transferred to Dublin and in 1990 to London where they said okay, you can eventually return to Dubai where you can run our existing hotels and be responsible to develop the region for Forte. However, in the meantime, you will also be responsible for Forte Hotels in the Caribbean, and be based in Slough, West London! When you have sufficiently expanded the region in the Middle East and North Africa you can set up the regional office in Dubai.

So, at the end of 1991 we finally returned to Dubai with our three children. Home at last and never to move again! Forte then took over Meridien hotels in 1994, but in 1996 the whole company was unfortunately taken over in a hostile bid. However, fortunately for me, I was then contacted by the Ruler's Office to see if I was interested in opening the Jumeirah Beach Hotel and to establish the corporate team for what was to become the Jumeirah Group. The Jumeirah Beach Hotel opened in late November 1997, and then the Burj Al Arab in December 1999. In April 2000 we opened the Emirates Towers and then in 2001, we started the construction of the Madinat Jumeirah complex. Busy times!

There was great excitement around the Burj al Arab because everybody knew this was going to be groundbreaking. This was going to be different than anything that had ever been done before. In fact, at one stage we had a promotional campaign that said for this hotel we've had to invent a whole new star grading system, so we designed a seven star image in the shape of the Burj – that seemed to catch the world's attention!

Right from the beginning of the whole concept, when you speak to people like Tom Wright from WS Atkins, it was obvious that HH Sheikh Mohammed had a very clear vision for the Burj al Arab and it was going to be a "World-Beater". It was going to be something that had never been done before, and probably would not be repeated in the way that it was an island, coming out of the sea. It represented the tradition of the sailing dhows that still race offshore in the UAE. HH Sheikh Mohammed was very involved in every detail and knew that it would become the symbol of Dubai.

With Jumeirah, one of our straplines was "Stay Different". In fact, people at the time questioned the phrase and said it should be "Stay Differently", and although that might have been grammatically correct, we wanted to emphasise that you are an individual, you're different to everybody else. We want you to stay that way: Stay Different. We wanted to use the word "Stay" so people would understand it's a hotel. You stay in this place a bit like Emirates used to have "Fly Emirates" to link with what they do.

Over my career, I have also come to understand that luxury is very much about individuality and generosity as well. You always know when you're in a hotel that's nickel and diming all the little bits and pieces, you feel it as a guest. We also used to say that we would "surprise and delight" our guests.

HH Sheikh Zayed

I think of the example that HH Sheikh Zayed and the leadership have given in the caring approach they have for their people. Many leaders around the world say that they care for their people, but here they truly do. In return, they're loved by the population. This has been a great example to all of us expatriates coming to live here, to make our lives here. We could see that there is this respect from the population to the leaders and it goes both ways. I can see with the decisions of the leadership, how everything is always done for the good of the country, and the population of the country is allowed to prosper under their leadership. People can come to this country and be allowed to become successful in their own right and deservedly so.

Exponential Growth

Well, I always remember a couple of years after we arrived here, my father-in-law and my mother-in-law came out for a holiday and he was an engineer. I managed to take him along to see the building of Jebel Ali Port. At the same time, they were building the dry dock for the biggest oil tanker that was ever built. People were asking why these were being built, but at the same time, you could see then the ambition of the leadership here was way beyond the imagination of most people: not only people within the country, but people outside the country. That is something that really struck me at the time that this place is going places. It was incredible that somebody had the ambition, the vision and the courage to go forward with projects like that.

Secret of Success

Everyone is treated with great respect, but you have got to prove that you know what you're doing. You also have to have the energy and you have to have the work ethic, and we at Jumeirah got this example from HH Sheikh Mohammed bin Rashid al Maktoum

Challenges

For us, 2008/2009 was a very difficult time because we had the situation where business had just collapsed worldwide, and business in Dubai was no exception. Yes, we had to have some redundancies, but we tried to do it in a way that reflected our principles at Jumeirah. One of the great cornerstones of Jumeirah was that we recognized that the most important people were actually the people who interacted with the customers more than anybody else. They were often the most junior people in the organization. They're the doorman, the waiters, the serving staff, the receptionist, the toilet cleaner: these are the people who talk to our customers. We tried as much as possible to reduce the layoffs in those areas and we focused on more middle to senior management roles. However, I believe, we were still very caring in our approach. We brought all the people together whose jobs would actually be affected, and we spoke to each one of them individually. We asked them if they were going to try to stay on in Dubai, because there were still jobs here. There were hotels under construction that were going to open anyway and have to employ people, so we actually contacted all of our colleagues in competitor hotels. From my recollection, everybody who wanted to get a job and didn't want to go back to their home country found another job. In challenges like these we forged the foundations of Jumeirah and understanding the importance of our colleagues in Jumeirah is key to the success of the development of the brand.

Opportunities

First of all, I believe so strongly in the "United" part of the United Arab Emirates. I've seen HH Sheikh Mohammed be so instrumental in this with his brothers, and the other Sheikhs of the other Emirates, really getting across this understanding to Nationals and to expatriates, that this is one united country. In the late 70s, if you asked somebody where they're from, they would have said Dubai, Sharjah, Fujairah etc. You ask them today where they're from and they say the UAE. This is really significant, and I think it has made such a difference to the respect other nations have for the United Arab Emirates.

I think the opportunity for the United Arab Emirates is what they have done now in relation to welcoming people from around the world to come and live here. The new Golden Visa process is re-invigorating the country and you can see the results of it in the last several months, with companies, individuals and entrepreneurs coming into the UAE to set up because it's a great place in which to live. If you attract talent into your country, that talent is going to be fostered, developed and encouraged, with the resulting opportunities.

Lessons

Well, I think first of all it is to have leaders who really care for the people like they do in the United Arab Emirates. It is great to be under a leadership that really does care and wants to see people prosper. We want people to be good to each other and to care for each other. Which I think is something that other countries can learn.

"Vision" is one thing. Ambition, courage and the energy to be able to implement the vision are something else. Also, the UAE is not afraid of competition. In fact, it is encouraged. HH Sheikh Mohammed once said to me of competitors, that it means that they respect what we have already done if they're doing the same thing as we've done, so it means that we're on the right track ourselves.

Expo

As a member of the advisory board of Expo, I can tell you it's been a great journey. It's something that, for me, has been a just reward for the United Arab Emirates, and for Dubai, to have been chosen as the Expo city. I think we're only just beginning to appreciate the potential of having hosted Expo here in Dubai, because you see already all these countries from around the world, their ministers are coming here, everybody is coming to have a look and see what their pavilion looks like and see how they've been represented. Of course, they're getting exposed to the dynamics and to the to the example of what has been achieved within the United Arab Emirates.

I think that Expo will very much be a new starting point, a new point of positive departure for where we're going with the UAE, the whole area of District 2020, the pavilions that will be kept and be used either by the countries or by other organizations. I think that the UAE is very much on the map already internationally, but this has taken it to a new level of respectability from the international community. People are really saying "wow, when they do things in the UAE, they do it so well".

Future

I think the UAE will continue to be an example of tolerance and coexistence, and that is a foundation for whatever humanity can achieve. If the conditions are right, if you have peace, if you have security, and most of all, if you have inspired and benevolent leadership, this country will continue to prosper. I think the UAE will be known as one of the beacons of peace, security, innovation and industry for the world.

30. DESERT TO DIGITAL

HE Omar Sultan Al Olama, Minister of State for Artificial Intelligence, Digital Economy and Remote Work Applications

"Technology is Global. It doesn't respect borders. We need less friction and less restriction."

His Excellency Omar Sultan Al Olama joined the Federal Government in 2017 as Minister of State for Artificial Intelligence and was appointed as Minister of State for Artificial Intelligence, Digital Economy and Remote Work Applications in July 2020. HE Al Olama has been responsible for enhancing the government performance by investing the latest technologies and tools of artificial intelligence and applying them in various sectors. As such he was the world's first Minister of AI. In addition to his role as a Minister, HE Al Olama is also currently the Managing Director of the World Government Summit Organization, and the Deputy Managing Director of Dubai Future Foundation. HE Al Olama contributed to the preparation of the UAE Centennial 2071 strategy and the UAE 4th Industrial Revolution Strategy. He is also the Chairman of the Dubai Chamber of Digital Economy which aims to make Dubai one of the top 10 digital economies in the world.

Earliest Memories

My earliest memory was walking around my grandfather's house. I was very fond of the well that he had. I had lots of questions about it – they just said don't fall in! It was a symbol of the importance of water to our life here. It was a simpler time. There was a continuous sense of community. All the people around us were family. In modern life we don't retain a lot of that, but we don't forget our roots.

Journey

I was educated in the American University in Dubai. The UAE created dreamers and allows anyone and everyone to achieve their dreams. Honestly, I think my personal story captures this. At 5 years old my mother was taking a video of me and asked me what I wanted to be when I grew up. I said I wanted to be a Minister. However, did I think it would happen? No - I didn't plan it. As I grew up, I realized that we as a country needed to do a lot. Everyone was trying to be the best in the Middle East. We were an upstart nation. As a kid I felt like an underdog; an outlier. Slowly but surely in the 90s, we made great progress, compared with other countries in the region, but we didn't feel the exponential rate of growth, the snowball effect until the 2000s. With the new millennium, things completely changed. They changed on multiple fronts. The scale of the projects, the ambition, the buzz in the city. The Burj al Arab was symbolic, followed by the Burj Khalifa. The four lane highway became an eight lane highway, then a 16 lane highway – that's exponential growth in front of your eyes! Sometimes it felt like we were in the plot of a movie, it felt so surreal. I always thought that if the country could do this, then I could. I was inspired by everything that happened while I was growing up.

On graduating, I applied to work with the government, and I just thought if I learn a lot I can give back. I grew up knowing that I got dealt lucky cards. My mother always said, "out of every place on earth, you were destined to be born here and under a leader that wants the best for their country". That's why I always had the inclination to give back. I wanted to be a part of the government and was lucky to be accepted to work in the Prime Minister's Office. I was chosen to work on the 4th Industrial Revolution Projects, tech and policy. In 2017 I was then lucky enough to be chosen as the first Minister for Artificial Intelligence.

HH Sheikh Zayed

My life's dream was to meet Sheikh Zayed. If I had a time machine I'd love to go back and meet him. As a kid growing up, my hobby was collecting pictures of Sheikh Zayed – seriously! I loved finding pictures of him that were not well known. Why? Everything we heard about him at school and about his family, was that he and Sheikh Rashid just wanted the best for us. Sheikh Zayed is my role model. I'd love to think he would be proud of what a young Emirati boy has been able to achieve.

Exponential Growth

Imagine in the 80s and 90s, a startup nation that was making claims that they were going to be the best country in the world. It sounded so audacious.

The UAE's exponential growth just teaches me that we are only limited by the limits of our ambition. I think the most powerful thing in this world is a driven person with a dream. Nothing can stop that person. Sheikh Zayed and Sheikh Rashid planted a seed in the mind of every single Emirati and Expat that we could create a society driven by a common dream. Most dreamers have an ego. I believe the UAE is a place where ego has been put on the side, where everyone tries to help each other, and we are all working towards one goal.

Every time there is a ceiling, the leadership makes us break through the ceiling. I remember when Sheikh Mohammed walked into the office in 2013 and said that we were going to Mars in 2021. I remember thinking "hang on, we already have all these other targets for 2021, do we want to carry on building the nation and going to Mars, do we want to do both?" If you asked me at the time, I'm afraid I would have been dubious we could do it. But we did. He assembled driven people with a dream. If we continue to do this, anything is possible.

Secret of Success

There is no real secret. The only reason why people think it's a secret is that they think it's a path that's hard to follow. As Sheikh Mohammed bin Rashid says: "the tougher the path, the more I like to walk it". With that mindset, if the UAE attracts people like that, if everyone believes the country is for them, it is a recipe for success. If everyone thinks tomorrow will be better than today, they will carry on working towards the future. There is a fundamental requirement for every society which is to have equal opportunity, equal rights, fairness for everyone – this is what we strive for. It is not a secret, but a tough path to follow.

Challenges

For me personally, the stigma around 9/11 was tough. We launched a lot of projects in 2001, when the world was looking at the Middle East with a wary eye. 2008 and the crisis were tough. We are not an isolated part of the world. Anything that is global in nature, also affects us. If we plan well and adapt, we can overcome any challenge. A great example of a challenge to opportunity was Covid. We locked down quicker and faster, then opened up quicker, and put in a range of safeguards. As long as we try and be agile and adaptable, we should be able to tackle challenges. The UAE has a history of turning challenges into opportunity.

Opportunities

The first huge opportunity is the fact that the UAE has 200 nationalities. Why do I think that's a huge opportunity? AI is built on data and speed of that. We have cutting edge infrastructure to get data immediately. Think about what this means for spotting global trends and analysis. If you want to create a global product, you can trial and test it here and export it to the world. We have the best from every country. The UAE invests in infrastructure that ensures we're ready for positive disruption and innovation. When countries stop investing in infrastructure you have dwindling opportunities. We are right at the centre of the world, attracting the best: we are a bridge between east and west.

Lessons

Technology is Global. It does not respect borders. We need less friction and less restriction. Tech pushes us as individuals. We need to be in a continuous learning mindset. Governments need to stay on top of technology and be curious. That is something that every government needs to learn from. If your country just has bureaucrats that want to put in restrictions and too many regulations, I think it's not going to be good.

Expo

I have visited Expo and I have been blown away by the vibrancy and opportunity. When the whole world has been shut down, if you want to visit the world, go to Expo. The impact of Expo will last a long time. It is an extra engine of growth for the UAE, supplementing all the other growth to date.

I remember showing people around Dubai Design District, it was desert and portacabins, and I was saying that this would be a fashion hub, with designers and architects from all around the world: they looked like I was hallucinating. Going there now it is exactly what the UAE is about. Expo has done the same. We have realized the hardware of

Expo. We have the software of people. It will now combine and be a nucleus for the next phase of growth.

Future

If you look at the UAE, we will continue investing in the quality of life, allowing people to thrive. The quality of life will be second to none. We want to invest in talent – constantly attract the best.

31. DEEP THOUGHT

Peng Xiao, Group CEO G42

"My job is to digitize a physical problem and then tackle it with computing power. I believe that this is the key to solving all the challenges that we face."

Peng Xiao is a global technology and business leader with a track record of building breakthrough products, delivering customer successes, and achieving commercial results.

As Group CEO of G42, Peng is responsible for crafting the Group's business and product strategies, and overseeing the operating companies across numerous industry verticals, including smart city, healthcare, energy, finance and education. G42 develops world-class solutions in Artificial Intelligence, Big Data Analytics, Mobile Technology, and Cloud Computing, and its offerings are delivered to a wide range of commercial and government clients.

Previously, as Senior Executive Vice President, Chief Technology Officer, and Chief Information Officer of MicroStrategy, Peng spent a decade in the enterprise software industry. Responsible for the management of over 1,000 engineers, Peng led the R&D of the company's entire product portfolio, including Business Intelligence, Secure Identity, and Mobile Commerce.

Over the years, Peng established a partnership ecosystem to promote joint technology and business development with his counterparts at Facebook, eBay, Citigroup, PayPal, Alibaba and other Fortune 500 companies, rapidly creating and deploying cutting-edge analytics, security, and commerce solutions.

Peng is a member of the Board of Trustees of the Mohamed bin Zayed University of Artificial Intelligence, the first graduate-level, research-based AI university in the world, launched on October 2018 in Abu Dhabi.

Peng is on a mission to advance Artificial Intelligence from its current narrow scope to a much more generalized state, in order to exponentially enhance our cognitive abilities and turn profound global challenges into opportunities for humanity.

Earliest Memories

My wife and I arrived at the end of 2014, during the Christmas season. We were making a family decision on whether to make the UAE our home from Washington DC. For me, it was a professional decision, however for my wife, it was a personal decision to see if we could live here. What she saw was that the UAE was celebrating Christmas: there were more Christmas trees than in DC! It was impossible to have imagined and, as a Christian, she immediately felt at home. The trip was meant to last for one week – we stayed in the end for a month!

Journey

I was born and raised in China, however I left China to study in the USA at the age of 16, so most of my academic and professional life was in the USA. I worked for MicroStrategy from 1999-2014, which is a leader in big data and analytics. Our clients all had access to data, but they were struggling to monetise their services. We helped them better understand their customers.

I give credit to HE Yousef al Otaiba, the UAE Ambassador to the USA for introducing me to the UAE. He had explained when we met, that the UAE was switching from an extractive economy, from oil, to become a knowledge economy, with data being the new oil! I realized up until that point that the clients I worked for were all one dimensional. They were companies that looked at one part of life, for example social media or shopping. The companies were very industry specific. The opportunity to work with a country rather than a company meant that it would be multi-dimensional. As a nation, we can centralise information. There is a richness: a multi-source, large data repository. With this opportunity, traditional methods couldn't keep up. The tech stack we were used to was one dimensional. We wanted to scale and grow to a whole new level.

We called the company Group 42, then evolved to G42, as the number 42 is, in The Hitchhiker's Guide to the Galaxy, the "Answer to the Ultimate Question of Life, the Universe, and Everything," calculated by an enormous supercomputer named Deep Thought over a period of 7.5 million years… We thought this was a good analogy for what we wanted to do.

When I first came, G42 was about traditional analytics: to use data to create actionable insights. With large data sets, we have to cut through the noise. No longer deterministic, more probabilistic. AI helps to give us patterns and trends. We now use data analytics for national decision-making. We believe that we can solve the most profound problems facing us.

HH Sheikh Zayed

It's a great personal regret that I never met HH Sheikh Zayed. He symbolized tolerance. To do this in his time, when there were social and religious biases is even more incredible, and the DNA is in the spirit of the country. However, I think another attribute is courage. In life, one doesn't always make the right decisions, and when we don't know for sure what decision to make, the default position is to do nothing. That's not what HH Sheikh Zayed did, or our current leadership. They have evidenced a courage in decision making. Waiting is never the winning strategy. Courage is even more precious when you have more to lose. There is a fine line between courage and recklessness. Those that have nothing to lose can be courageous. The courage when you are making decisions for a whole country is important and profound.

Exponential Growth

There are so many wonderful examples, but I will choose one example that I was proud to be a part of. In just 18 months, we were able to build two of the world's top supercomputers here in the UAE. We put them to use in Oil & Gas and setting up a cloud infrastructure, but they came very useful with the COVID pandemic and healthcare. I would put this up there with going to Mars. Now we're going beyond supercomputers and into quantum computing. My job is to digitize a physical problem and then tackle it with computing power. I believe that this is the key to solving all the challenges that we face, and this computing power will help us do that.

Secret of Success

One of the main secrets of success is the foresight. The leadership has taken a long-term, architectural view on how to build a society. This is for the next generation and beyond. In the UAE, success is measured by more than pure financial return: it is about impact and improving lives.

Challenges

We live in a world of intensifying global polarization and I think 2022 will be a big year of transition. We need to be ultra-careful to see how this plays out. Globally, there could be cooperation or conflict: there lies our greatest challenge. Many would think that we're being asked to choose sides, but I don't subscribe to this. I think this is a gross simplification, amplified by local pressure groups. We work with the USA and China. If the superpowers are occupied with each other, we're left with a bit of a vacuum here in the region. I believe that this gives the UAE a real chance to take a lead and strive for harmony.

Opportunities

As mentioned, in the same way that the UAE brought together 7 Emirates 50 years ago, I think the region can unite: not in just a political way, but with people and society. I think we have a golden opportunity to come together and work with each other. The Middle East is really well positioned for the future if we start talking and collaborating. Nothing can stop us. We can have an equal seat at the table with the global superpowers.

Lessons

I think the story of the UAE's unification is a lesson that can be spread. The ability to create harmony out of conflict. The UAE has a unique form of government and market dynamics that is very successful and should be studied: whether one calls it 'UAE Inc' or the 'UAE Family'.

Expo

Expo is a great showcase of the values of the UAE. It is even more special to have this platform after the pandemic. I think it will be pivotal with a true legacy in what it stands for.

Future

I'm a digital native. I see in the future a world where we erase physical boundaries. I think the UAE will be a digital thought leader at a national level. We can build a new global digital framework. That's truly exciting: we can break through the boundaries and lead the world. We want to establish new digital standards. I believe the World is going through a big transition and we have to find our footing in this transition, but absolutely we can be an open lab to the world to show them that maybe by doing this we can create greater harmony among nations.

32. DELIVERING THE GOODS

Fadi Ghandour, Executive Chairman of Wamda Group

"'Build it and they will come' is the original story that has been proven year-in and year-out"

Fadi Ghandour is an entrepreneur, investor, and philanthropist. He is the Executive Chairman of Wamda Group, a platform that invests, nurtures and builds entrepreneurship eco-systems across the Middle East and North Africa. Fadi is also the Founder of Aramex, one of the leading global logistics companies. Fadi spent the first 30 years of his work life as CEO of Aramex, building the company, making it the leading emerging market logistics company, employing over 15,000 people working in over 250 offices in 90 countries. He took the company public twice, first on Nasdaq making it the first company from the Arab world to do so, then on Dubai Financial market. He continues to be active on the Aramex board.

Fadi is a serial entrepreneur. In his career, he was involved with founding, investing and launching tens of companies and non-profits, ranging from digital tech, hospitality, fitness & wellness to security. Passionate about impact and social entrepreneurship, Fadi founded and chairs Ruwwad for Development, a private-sector led community empowerment platform that helps marginalized communities, across several countries in the MENA region, overcome marginalization through activism, civic engagement, education and financial inclusion. He has also co-founded and continues to support Al-Riyadi, one of the leading not-for-profit sports clubs in Jordan. Fadi also served and continues to serve on several global and regional boards of companies, education institutions and non-profits.

Earliest Memories

My first memory of the UAE was landing at Dubai airport in late 1982, to explore and understand the Dubai market for "courier deliveries". I was just about to launch Aramex then and wanted to establish an office in Dubai. The airport was a fraction of what it is today; Jebel Ali was just an idea then - Port Rashid was the main port. Dubai business activity at the time started and ended between Deira and Bur Dubai. Maydan Nasser was the hustling and bustling center of Deira, where I eventually launched the first Aramex office. Driving to Abu Dhabi was a two-lane road, dangerous to drive because of camels crossing the road. The nicest hotel in town at the time was called the "Galadari Galleria" in Deira on the Creek, which eventually became the Hyatt Regency. The country has come a very long way from my first landing.

Journey

My 30-year career at Aramex is closely aligned with the exponential growth of Dubai, specifically as it has become the logistics, transportation and travel hub of emerging markets. From Jebal Ali to the launch of Emirates Airline and building a super-hub airport, Aramex grew and evolved with each logistics infrastructure development in Dubai. As you know Aramex grew out of Jordan, my home country. As a last mile delivery and logistics company we couldn't have scaled the business and gone global without a presence in Dubai and establishing our operations hub out of Dubai airport. As Dubai became a global hub, Aramex mirrored that growth. And when the Dubai financial market boomed in the early 2000s, Aramex decided to list on DFM after being a Nasdaq listed company. We felt listing on DFM was like coming back home, where our brand was strong, our story was appreciated and thus we were able to get our fair value, today Aramex continues to be listed on DFM becoming a multibillion-dollar company.

HH Sheikh Zayed

The late HH Sheikh Zayed was a man of vision and a man in love with nature, and extreme generosity. A consensus builder the father of an Arab Federation that has thrived for decades attracting talent from all over the world.

Exponential Growth

The UAE is a global model for a state that delivers high quality standard of living, the country's leadership understands diversity, tolerance, and innovation. It knows very well what it takes to create a state that competes for global talent to fuel its growth and maintain the quality of life for people living in it.

I was a founding investor in Maktoob, that was acquired by Yahoo in 2009, and an investor in Careem, that was acquired by Uber in 2019. The Maktoob sale was an amazing catalyst for the region's entrepreneurial ecosystem, but the Careem - Uber transaction has had a 10X impact. A new era has arrived and this is going to be the era of the Careem graduates taking the region to the next level of innovation and company creation – creating new jobs, and new wealth. This liquidity event has generated wealth to so many Careem employees like the region has never seen before. Not only have the founders got a huge infusion of funds, but the generous stock option plan of the company meant that there are tens if not hundreds of people who will either get millions or hundreds of thousands in paychecks. This matters, because that is what entrepreneurship is all about – creating value and generating new wealth away from the traditional wealth generation in the region from inheritance or family businesses. This is completely new and unprecedented in its scope for the UAE and the region.

Secret of Success

Visionary leadership that talks the talk and walks the walk.

Challenges

Competing with giants required building a passionate team that believed a small company from Jordan with a center of operation in Dubai can go global … So attracting talent, finding funding, and finally overcoming regulatory hurdles to establish our operations were my biggest challenges.

Opportunities

One of the consequences of the pandemic for the world's digital ecosystem, was that what we had previously predicted would take 10 years, in fact took a couple of months. Everything digital is effectively growing exponentially: e-commerce, fintech, crypto, health tech, edtech…. Everything digital and "new economy" is therefore very exciting in the UAE. We live in a consumer-based region. So e-commerce, payments and last mile logistics are really taking off. I like tourism and everything that comes with it in terms of the hospitality business.

Lessons

I think the UAE has shown that you can build world class infrastructure and create a multi-cultural, tolerant environment that attracts global talent. “Build it and they will come” is the original story that has been proven year-in and year-out. In the beginning it was a story of hard infrastructure, today and specially after the pandemic, it is a soft infrastructure that continues to attract talented people, professionals and investors from every corner of the world.

Expo

I think Expo is a continuation of the UAE story. It is about top-notch infrastructure, beautiful design, focusing on sustainability, and the future of cities. The story continues.

Future

You don’t need me to predict the next 50 years. Just follow what the country has been saying that it wants to do in 50 years’ time, and you will know it will happen, because that has been our experience in the past 30 years.

33. EVERY DAY LIFE MADE SIMPLE

Mudassir Sheikha, CEO and Co-Founder of Careem

"Exponential growth comes from coupling big dreams with a disciplined focus on improving every day, and the UAE is constantly dreaming big and not afraid of putting in the work to reach really ambitious goals."

Mudassir Sheikha is the CEO and co-founder of Careem. He grew up in Karachi, before graduating from the University of Southern California with a degree in economics and computer science and then completing a Masters Degree in computer science at Stanford.

Mudassir's career in tech started with Silicon Valley startup "Brience". Mudassir then moved back to Pakistan and co-founded "DeviceAnywhere", a company that was acquired by "Keynote" in 2008 before joining McKinsey in Dubai. In 2012, he left to form a new company with ex-McKinsey colleague, Magnus Olsson. The idea was not just to build a big business, but start one that would have a big impact, be meaningful, and with a mission to simplify and improve lives and create an awesome organisation that inspires. From that came Careem. Today, Careem is the leading technology platform across the greater Middle East and was recently acquired by Uber in the largest industry transaction seen in the region. Careem operates in more than 100 cities across 14 countries with more than 1,300 colleagues and well over one million captains on its platform. Careem personifies an "exponential company" and the founders chose their home to be the UAE.

Earliest Memories

I came to Dubai in April 2008. At that time there was a lot of development happening, and my earliest memory of Dubai is as one big construction site. There were buildings going up, roads being paved, the Burj Khalifa was coming up - it was a little messy. But amidst all the construction, there was an overwhelming sense that the future looked promising and that the country was driving towards a version of the UAE that would impress us all. The lessons there are that if you're as ambitious as the UAE's leadership is, you have to be okay with disrupting things in service of a bigger vision. You also need to make sure the people following you are aligned with you. They may not always see the bigger picture as clearly as you do, but they need to trust that you're headed in the right direction so they too can identify with your vision. Even during the chaos of increased construction and traffic diversions in Dubai, things were planned and communicated well; we knew where the leaders were taking us, and it wasn't long before we saw the benefits of their vision.

Journey

What I'm most proud of is what we've been able to do for over two million Captains across the region including tens of thousands in the UAE. The fact that they can make a living and support their families and create even better opportunities for their children is part of the opportunities that the UAE has also offered to millions of people for years. We've always aimed to simplify and improve people's lives. In a region where unemployment is so high, and in a country where people come from all corners of the world to make a life for themselves, I'm proud that Careem is playing its part.

The second thing I'm proud of is the Careem Mafia - Alumni that have gone on to build their own startups. Around 2013, we talked internally at Careem about being a talent factory for the region. We wanted Careem to be akin to what General Electric was in the U.S. at one time - or in relation to the Tech industry, Google - where we produce excellent quality talent that go on to do bigger and better things, and extend the legacy we're building. That is really aligned with the way that the UAE creates a conducive environment for people who have big dreams and the will to see those dreams through. Inspiring people is hard. But in small ways, we've managed to do that with our Alumni, and the UAE does it at an even greater scale across multiple industries.

HH Sheikh Zayed

Sheikh Zayed was a unifier at heart - he saw the value in a country and a region that was connected and that found strength in its close ties. Collaboration is one the key elements of building for the long term - I would not be where I am now without the contributions of so many loved ones and colleagues. Careem needed partnerships with different government entities, private sector players, investors and our amazing Customers, to help us get this far. Sheikh Zayed saw the magic in working together, and the way the UAE's leaders operate now is a testament to his legacy.

Exponential Growth

The UAE is an unusually ambitious nation. The idea of shooting for the moon, or even Mars, is embedded in almost every aspect of life here and that has been a big inspiration for me personally. Careem's journey started here, and what continues to make our exponential growth possible here is the commitment to constantly pushing the boundaries on what we think is possible.

The UAE is also one of our biggest markets, in part due to the exceptionally talented colleagues who call the UAE home. This country has been both an attractor of global talent and innovative companies, and an incubator for them. It's a country of 'firsts'; filled with smart, ambitious people who aren't afraid to be pioneers in their fields of expertise. That takes courage, faith, and the firm belief that life is far more meaningful when we're contributing to moving the world forward and making it a little better every day.

The UAE is also a country where quality isn't compromised - there's a habit of doing things at a large scale, and doing them excellently. Exponential growth comes from coupling big dreams with a disciplined focus on improving every day, and the UAE is constantly dreaming big and not afraid of putting in the work to reach really ambitious goals. The sort of ambition that I've found here can be infectious, it can encourage you to aim a little higher and give you the confidence that truly amazing things are possible.

Secret of Success

Careem is on a mission to simplify and improve lives, and simplifying lives of people is functionally important here. There are basic, everyday challenges that stop people from focusing on creating life changing ideas. When you have to focus on the minute, everyday problems like unstable power supply, poor education standards, and unsafe transport, you struggle to think beyond tomorrow. In the UAE, we take a lot of things for granted - a stable economy, reliable infrastructure, everyday convenience and the quality of life - all these things are incomparable in any other part of the world. That reliability makes room for people to innovate and challenge the status quo. That, in turn, leads to success.

One of the other things is the diversity here. It's not just a source of top talent, it also naturally creates connections to other countries through people's heritage. It was always easier for Careem to expand to the 13 countries we're in now, for example, because of the talent that we hired here who were from all over the region. A lot of our colleagues here care deeply about their home countries, and when they take their ideas home, they want to execute them with the same level of excellence. That makes for a ripple effect that is important to mention when speaking about the UAE.

Opportunities

The tech industry in the UAE is super exciting at the moment; the number of companies that are using their platforms, services and products to change the way our region operates is remarkable. Not only are tech unicorns more common, but subsets of the industry like fintech and payments services are shifting the way we transact and bank. This opens up a whole segment of Customers who are continuously looking for simpler and more convenient ways to live their lives. We definitely see Careem Pay growing exponentially and branching into more financial products, and we can see the same of our competitors. It's an exciting time to be in this field because the bar gets higher and higher, and the products get more and more essential to our everyday lives.

Expo

The Expo is a culmination of the different things the UAE stands for in my mind – progressive thinking, courageous business decisions, refreshing products and services, innovative approaches to infrastructure, governance and more. And sustainability here isn't just a hot topic - it's the backbone for the longevity of the country's success, and a responsibility that the UAE has taken on fully. This goes back to the UAE's commitment to excellence and high standards, always.

The Expo theme is “Connecting minds, Creating the future” - an apt theme for a country like this. Visitors have the chance to see what we residents see every day; a glimpse of what the world will look like years from now. The UAE has an extraordinary ability to bring a part of the future into the present, while reminding us how important the past was to its journey. Through the Expo, we’re seeing this on a grand scale, with countries from all over the world coming together to reimagine the future. The Expo leaves you with a sense of hope, of wonder and of progress, and that’s what will stay with visitors once they leave the UAE.

Future

The UAE will become the best country to live in globally. From what I have seen in over a decade of being here, we’re definitely going to see a country that’s driven by a commitment to high living standards, investing in growing sustainably and inviting the world to take part in that growth. This value proposition will continue to draw in top global talent which will fuel a virtuous cycle where the things being invented and developed in the UAE inspire the region and people around the world, who will in turn want to make the UAE their home. I believe the UAE will keep surprising us with out-of-the-box, disruptive thinking across different industries. It will continue to be a country that hosts pioneers, visionaries and those consumed with the idea of making a mark on the world.

In 50 years, the question won’t be whether the country has achieved what it set out to do, it will be how much the country has exceeded those targets, and how much more can be done to further develop the economy and make a mark on the world.

34. TOGETHER MATTERS

Mohammed Omran, Former Chairman & CEO of etisalat

"We like to see others come to the UAE to win"

One of the first companies that most people encounter when arriving in the UAE is Etisalat. In fact, as soon as your phone is switched on you get a message from Etisalat saying "Welcome to the UAE" or "Welcome back". The Emirates Telecommunication Corporation (Emirtel) was founded in September 1976, and over the last 45 years, it has grown exponentially. Now rebranded to Etisalat, it serves approximately 150 million subscribers in 16 countries across the Middle East, Asia and Africa. Etisalat has been ranked the fastest mobile network globally and was named "The Most Valuable Portfolio Brand" in MENA by Brand Finance. As a group, it is now worth more than USD 70 billion.

To give a further sense of the growth, the first phone directory for Dubai was produced in 1961. It had just 30 pages listing a few hundred numbers. Most pages were adverts, many of them hand-drawn. Only 60 years later, the UAE has achieved the first place amongst the Arab countries and the fourth position globally in launching and deploying 5G networks, and uses AI and Machine Learning to optimize performance across the whole network and customer experience. Over 90% of the population have smartphones. Etisalat's success also has meant success for the citizens and businesses of the UAE, and as their motto says, "Together Matters".

Mohammed Omran has been instrumental in etisalat's success story. Joining Etisalat in its first year of existence, he retired 35 years later in 2012 as its Chairman & CEO. He is also Chairman of RAK Bank and has held various other positions, such as Chairman & Chancellor of the Higher Colleges of Technology, member of Board of Trustee of Khalifa University and member of the Board of Directors of the Emirates Foundation. He has written a wonderful memoir, entitled *Milestones in career and life*.

Earliest Memories

I was born in Al Jazirah al Hamra in the Emirate of Ras Al Khaimah in 1953. The life of the inhabitants of this region was strongly linked to the sea. Most of them were pearl divers and fishermen. Fortunately, the first modern school of RAK was built in my village. Modern schools started in the 1950s in the region. Kuwait helped the region by building schools, providing teachers and all other necessities in many parts of the now UAE till the early 1970s. Books and exams used to come from Kuwait as well. That was an impressive hallmark in the history of Gulf cooperation that we should share and remember with successive generations.

I completed my high school education at RAK Secondary School in the sciences branch. As there were no universities in the UAE at this time, the Government sent students on scholarships to universities abroad. I opted to go to Egypt where I joined Cairo University's College of Engineering. I graduated 5 years later with a degree in electrical engineering, majoring in telecommunications and electronics.

Journey

I was fortunate enough to witness and be part of one of the greatest revolutions of our time: telecommunications. I joined Emirtel (now Etisalat) in November 1977. The company was one year old by then and the whole UAE had less than 30,000 telephone lines. I became Chairman and CEO in 2005. Our vision was to work harder and put Etisalat in the top list of world telecom operators while enhancing the UAE operation to become the best operator in terms of quality of service and customers satisfaction. It was a great privilege to be one of the first telecommunication engineers in my country. That was a source of pride indeed, as it enabled me to serve my country wholeheartedly and contribute to its development by sparing no effort to turn each and every project into a success. I retired in 2012, an exciting 35-year career journey punctuated by challenges and tough times, hard work and achievements.

HH Sheikh Zayed

The wisdom and the long-term vision of the Late Shaikh Zayed and Late Shaikh Rashid were behind a strong unified Emirates. This was strongly supported by other Emirates rulers and the people of the whole Emirates.

Exponential Growth

Etisalat for me is the perfect example, as, in effect, the total value of the shares of Etisalat increased 548 times in the 33 years that I was there, which is a very high rate, perhaps one of the highest in the world.

Not only that, but in 1979, 20% of Etisalat shares had been offered to Emiratis. It was an unparalleled step, as the Government offered shares to its own citizens at a subsidized rate and enabled them to own shares in a vital sector. Thanks to that unprecedented method of sharing wealth amongst its citizens, some of the Emiratis who took advantage of that opportunity become senior shareholders in the ensuing years. It can safely be said that the UAE was a world leader in allowing the private sector to own shares in the telecommunications sector, at a time when most telecommunications companies in the world were wholly owned by governments.

Secret of Success

The mentality used in Emirtel-Etisalat was the main reason for success coupled with dedication and hard work by both UAE nationals and expats who were working in the company. We encouraged and awarded new ideas and out of the box thinking. This happened all over the journey since beginning.

Challenges

The region used to be prosperous due to income from pearl diving activities. During the 1930s and 1940s Japan introduced cultured pearls at a fraction of natural pearl prices. This resulted in abandoning pearl diving and other related activities in the region and the whole region was deprived of its main source of income. All suffered because of that. Thanks to Allah we have been compensated by oil and with leaders who loved their countries and their people. This helped in changing challenges to opportunities and all benefited from it.

Opportunities

From my experience and interaction with many countries, I strongly believe that the UAE is the ideal place for achieving entrepreneurs' dreams and ambitions. It is of course obvious for big businesses that there are many benefits rarely found in other areas.

Lessons

No success can be achieved without education. Means and ways are changing but the objectives never change. We need our young boys and girls to be among the best educated youth of the world and they are capable and dependable to do so.

Expo

The whole country is encouraging new ideas. We like to see others come to the UAE to win. The UAE is a country with great vision supported by a strong bond of loyalty and dedication between leadership and society. Successful people come from all over the world to participate in this vision and achieve their goals. Expo provides the visitors with real time interaction where they will learn and will love the UAE and the way it thrives.

Future

With the vision the UAE has, which is shared by leadership and the whole society, I am sure the UAE will be among the top 10 countries in the world in terms of innovation and prosperity.

35. THE ART OF SCIENCE

HE Hussain al Mahmoudi

"What motivates us all is love of our country and love of the work we are doing."

HE Hussain Al Mahmoudi serves a dual role as the CEO of the American University of Sharjah Enterprises and CEO The Sharjah Research, Technology, and Innovation Park Free Zone. Both these entities were established through royal decree by the Ruler of Sharjah, who tasked Hussain to create collaborative long-term relationships between industry, academia and the public sector, fostering an ecosystem of enterprise and innovation.

Previously, Hussain served as the Director General of the Sharjah Chamber of Commerce and Industry, a Member of the UAE Chamber Federation, and GCC Chambers for 8 years. He was responsible for the overall management and operations of the Chamber including the provision of services to its members. In this role, he launched several strategic economic initiatives for Sharjah such as the SME Act, Sharjah Export Centre, Sharjah Commercial Arbitration Centre, and the Sharjah Business Forum.

Hussain has held leadership roles at leading regional and international companies such as the Royal Dutch Shell Group, Emirates National Oil Company (ENOC), and several Dubai Holding entities. He currently serves as an honorary board member of both the Tatweer Forum and of Maastricht University in the Netherlands, and as chairman of the Emirates Business Council for Sustainable Development. He also serves as a board member of the Sharjah Entrepreneurship Center

(Sheraa).

The Sharjah Research, Technology, and Innovation Park aims to develop and manage an innovation ecosystem that promotes Research and Development and supports enterprise activities and the triple helix collaboration of industry, government and academia.

Earliest Memories

My earliest memory was playing football around the houses in my neighbourhood. This was in the early 1970s. There was sand everywhere as there weren't enough roads. We used to walk to Dubai back then. We'd often pick up food from traditional small grocery shops and then picnic under the trees. I could see the construction beginning, and the future was being built in front of our eyes.

Journey

I was lucky to have the country sponsor me to go and study in the US. I was actually sent to a Christian school – this was an example of the openness of the country.

I began my career with the Emirates National Oil Company (ENOC), but I soon joined Dubai Internet City which was essentially a start-up, attracting the best tech companies in the world to come and set up in the UAE.

I then joined Royal Dutch Shell Group, persuading them to relocate more of their business units to Dubai. I went to Holland for 2 years, and while I was there, I created a non-for-profit called the Sharjah Development Forum. This was a think tank that fostered public-private-partnership and soon got on the radar of HH the Ruler of Sharjah. He actually requested to become the Chairman and it was a turning point in my career. He subsequently asked me to become DG of the Sharjah Chamber of Commerce and Industry in 2008. This was ironic as only 10 years before, I had applied to them for a job and they said there is no job for you! Over the next 8 years we launched a lot of initiatives for SMEs in Sharjah.

In 2016, HH the Ruler called me and asked me to start the Sharjah Research, Technology, and Innovation Park. Since 2016, and despite COVID, we have created one of the most innovative hubs in the region. We have a transport and logistics innovation centre, an additive manufacturing lab, a mixed reality lab and Agtech to name a few. The

Sharjah Research, Technology, and Innovation Park has generated $100m investment in R&D and we are just getting started. We have created a model for commercialisation and have been training young nationals on cutting edge technologies.

This is the culmination of my whole career and draws on all the elements of my education and experience over the years.

HH Sheikh Zayed

I see HH Sheikh Zayed as my father. I felt his presence and warmth without ever meeting him. In every move he was a father to me and the country.

Exponential Growth

The UAE has in no time developed from a country that had nothing, to today being one of the best in the world. When you look at every sector that has been huge growth. The economy, human capital, international relations, energy, defence…. Our military is now one of the best in the world from being only 50 years old. Very professional. Art, culture, healthcare, education: day by day our schools get more sophisticated. The growth is universal.

Secret of Success

Love. Love of my country. We were brought up to do good. What motivates an 82-year-old ruler who has everything? The leadership still continues to give.

Challenges

People thought the Union would die in one year. Now we're talking about Mars!

Opportunities

The opportunities are massive. The UAE is genuinely focused on innovation, science and tech. These areas have not been leveraged so far. We have use of investment and infrastructure for whoever wants to come. The UAE is an amazing place to thrive and live. The Sharjah Research, Technology, and Innovation Park has been designed to accelerate those opportunities. For example, we are committed to engaging with relevant stakeholders, including the UAE government, the private sector and academia with the aim of developing the longevity industry and creating new opportunities for our communities, while putting the health and wellbeing of our senior citizens and residents on top of our development agenda.

Lessons

Develop your country and do not be selfish. Nothing happens out of the blue: you need to make sacrifices and work hard. Unity is important, and therefore tolerance too.

Expo

Expo is all about connecting. It opens your mind and heart. An opportunity to learn about every country: not just commercial. You can learn about the heritage and soul of each country. Of course, this can all lead to economic prosperity, and I believe it will reboot the economy post-COVID.

Future

The UAE will become a knowledge-driven country and will become a hub for tech. Not only in the next 50 years, but you will see this more and more in the next 5 years.

In this Golden Jubilee year, we begin a renewed tireless and ambitious journey towards greater achievements in all fields, driven by the 'Principles of 50' document.

36. CULTIVATING CLUSTERS

Badr al Olama, Chairman of Strata, Chairman of Emirates Post, CEO of HUB 71, Executive Director of Mubadala Aerospace

"For the first 50 years of the UAE, it was all about "catch-up", where we benchmarked ourselves against countries which had been around for hundreds of years. We put in the infrastructure, the roads, networks, schools, and created businesses like ADIA, ADNOC, Mubadala, Strata – we developed all the necessary clusters. Now, for the next 50, we have no excuse why the UAE can't be better than any other nation. We have everything we need to excel. The next 50 will be about outperforming. That is the opportunity."

Badr holds a Bachelor's Degree in Shari'a and Law from the UAE University, and a Master of Law Degree from Harvard Law School, Harvard University. On returning to the UAE, Badr began working for Mubadala where he became Chief Executive Officer of Strata, and was instrumental in positioning the company as a global tier-one supplier to both Airbus and Boeing, forging strong and value-adding partnerships with leading Original Equipment Manufacturers (OEMs). Badr has also played a key advisory role in the strategic development of Nibras Al Ain Aerospace Park, a joint initiative between Mubadala and Abu Dhabi Airports Company (ADAC), which aims to establish a sustainable aerospace ecosystem in Abu Dhabi and the United Arab Emirates. Badr is also Executive Director with the UAE Investments platform at Mubadala.

Nominated as a Young Global Leader for the Middle East and North Africa region by the World Economic Forum, Badr heads the organizing committee for the world's first Global Manufacturing and

Industrialisation Summit (GMIS), a joint initiative between the UAE Government and the United Nations Industrial Development Organization (UNIDO), which aims to transform and shape the future of manufacturing.

Earliest Memories

I grew up in Dubai, just off al Wasl road. It was a very small house with me and my three brothers. Some of my best memories were in that house. We were very close as a family. I used to play football in our small garden with one of my brothers, Sharif, who is now Under-Secretary of the Ministry of Energy. When it rained it was our first swimming pool!

We then moved to Jumeirah 1, and I remember bicycling in the neighbourhood, going to Safa park and skateboarding in the Jumeirah beach park. Of course, that's now the Four Seasons Jumeirah, and here we are sitting in the Mandarin Oriental!

Journey

I was at the same school as my brothers - Al Ittihad Private School. However, when I hit Grade 7 my mother wanted to take me to Choueifat. Not many UAE nationals went there as it was co-ed in Sharjah. It was a long drive, it was a French/Lebanese curriculum school. I think my mum saw me as a bit of an experiment. The transition wasn't easy, but it was part of my journey. I graduated saying I wanted to be a lawyer. However, to be a lawyer in the UAE then, I needed to choose a civil law jurisdiction, so I decided to go to the UAE University in Al Ain. It was a wake-up call as everything was in Arabic. I had grown up thinking and learning in English, so I had to reformat myself to be able to write and think in Arabic. I was there for 4 years.

I then began work at Habib al Mulla law firm, currently known as Baker & McKenzie Habib Al-Mulla. I was always traveling across the 7 Emirates. It was hard work but a solid foundation. I then got admitted to Harvard Law School to do my Masters, sponsored by the Executive Office. I focused on corporate governance and commercial law. As I was graduating, I got an opportunity with Mubadala which was beginning to grow and that changed my career direction.

One of my main interviews was with Waleed Al Mokarrab Al Muhairi, another Harvard graduate. He said, "we don't want you to be a lawyer, we are going to train you in finance, we want you to work on a project, then lead that project, then we'll bring you back to work on other projects, and you'll be on the board of the first company you work on." This was the interview, and that was exactly my career path. He sold it to me. I needed that direction. I was 25 years old.

I also remember working on the early days of Masdar with Dr Sultan al Jaber, who at the time was with Mubadala. Given my legal background, I was looking at the mechanics of setting it up as a Freezone. I completed my CFA and then began working with Homaid Al Shemmari, who was looking at setting up the Aerospace division as part of Abu Dhabi's Economic Vision 2030. Ross Bradley, ex-BAE, had been recruited to support us with establishing Strata Manufacturing, which was Mubadala Aerospace's advanced composite aerostructures manufacturing facility based in Al Ain. Ross wanted a successor so in April 2011 I became his Deputy CEO. I then took over a year later as CEO at the age of 32. I can't think of anywhere other than the UAE where leadership is willing to bet on youth. During my time at Strata, I negotiated a number of big deals, including the carbon-fibre pre-preg manufacturing facility, where we became one of only 4 aerospace suppliers globally for Boeing.

In 2015, I was fascinated with the future of manufacturing, and I was part of a WEF group which was created to discuss this. We decided the world needed a forum on the future of manufacturing in Abu Dhabi, and this became GMIS. In April 2017, we held the first event, with support from the UN Secretary General. The Russian government, under the direction of their government, also got in touch and asked to host the same event in 2019. In 2021 we have just held the event at Expo with a few Presidents and Prime Ministers participating, including John Kerry – the US Presidential Envoy for Climate. It is growing as an initiative. It is now more than just an event.

I have now taken over the UAE Clusters mandate for Mubadala, with Healthcare, ICT and Aerospace. This includes HUB 71. Mubadala has supported me throughout my journey. I have been able to be entrepreneurial within the confines of a large corporate environment.

HH Sheikh Zayed

Sheikh Zayed to me stands for "Sacrifice". He dedicated his life doing what was best for the Nation. It was 2004 when he passed away, and I was 24 years old, still at Harvard. I remember we had exams the next day and we were all devastated. During the exam, Professor

Andrew Kaufman, who was a legend at Harvard Law School, came to me and whispered "I head your president passed away. I'm sorry for your loss. I heard he was a great man." It was a testament of Sheikh Zayed that he was recognized globally by people that had never met him, never been to the UAE.

Exponential Growth

I look at the UAE exponential growth in two segments. Segment 1 was the early 2000s in Dubai where there was extraordinary cultural and business transformation with everyone coming and setting up new 100% foreign owned businesses in the freezones. Segment two was Post-2006/7 in Abu Dhabi. This was triggered with the formal publication of the Economic Vision 2030. A new generation of people were coming in and initiating ambitious projects. The government sector reformed completely. Both segments signified change with the engagement of the young generation. We all knew each other and we worked well together as a team.

The growth for me was obvious when I compare my two trips to Las Vegas. I first went in 1997. I was 17. I was amazed by the Bellagio and the Venetian. I went to Vegas again in 2017, 20 years later. It felt dated. The UAE has completely outpaced it. No one in 1997 could have expected that!

Secret of Success

Diversity and inclusion. These were the factors that allowed the country to prosper in the way that it has. We have multiple views and perspectives. My friends at school were Russian, Lebanese and Indian. I learned that there are many different ways of doing things better and faster.

Challenges

2020 we were in crisis mode dealing with covid, but it enabled us to pivot into a new direction. Any new direction comes with more challenges. We have unlimited opportunities, but limited resources and talent, so it's trying to get the best combination. We have to prioritise. We also have to balance between focus and not getting distracted.

Opportunities

Philosophically, I think the UAE can be a beacon of hope for the rest of the world. We have shown that different nationalities can all live together in a harmonious way.

From an economic perspective, I think there is a bigger opportunity for us to be a dynamic, innovative hotspot, where applications can be rapidly tested and deployed faster than anywhere else. We have an entrepreneurial culture. We can make things happen. We managed to 3D print an interior component for a Boeing 777 aircraft through a collaboration with EOS and Siemens (two German companies) and Etihad and Strata in the UAE. We got it certified by the General Civil Aviation Authority in record time, and through this project Etihad can now 3D print many of its aircraft interior thermoplastic components.

Expo

I didn't know much about what it meant before it opened, but the first real experience was visiting the Italian pavilion. I understood how Italy had contributed to the world. It is an amazing opportunity to see how different parts of the world contributed to humanity and prosperity. You get inspired when you see what others have done.

Future

For the first 50 years of the UAE, it was all about "catch-up", where we benchmarked ourselves against countries which had been around for 100s of years. We put in the infrastructure, the roads, networks, schools, and created businesses like ADIA, ADNOC, Mubadala, Strata – we developed all the necessary clusters. Now, for the next 50, we have no excuse why the UAE can't be better than any other nation. We have everything we need to excel. The next 50 will be about outperforming. That is the opportunity.

37. INVESTING IN INNOVATION

Dr Tariq bin Hendi

"We want to accelerate economic progress not just in the UAE but further afield"

Born to an Emirati father and an American mother, Dr. Tariq Bin Hendi was raised on two continents amid an extended family of multiple cultures and ethnicities. His education and professional experience across Europe, the United States and the UAE has allowed him to appreciate further the drivers in human behavior, commercial strategies, and value systems across cultures and business. He holds a PhD in Economics from the Imperial College of Science, Technology and Medicine, and has MBAs from Columbia Business School and London Business School.

Our interview with Dr. Tariq Bin Hendi was conducted when he was Director General of the Abu Dhabi Investment Office (ADIO), a post he held up until the end of 2021. Under his leadership, ADIO launched international offices around the world. Devoting his career to progress, bold ideas and teamwork, Dr Tariq positioned ADIO to always seek new ideas and challenges in order to promote Abu Dhabi globally. Prior to joining ADIO, Dr Tariq held leadership roles at various institutions, including Emirates NBD, Mubadala, and Citibank. He also sits on a number of boards, including AXA and Emirates Post Group. Dr Tariq earned his stripes in professional finance at Citi Bank in London.

rliest Memories

One of the clearest memories to me was how everyone, both nationals and expatriates, created and enjoyed such a cohesive community, albeit at a much smaller scale. As a child, we had friends from so many various countries, both at school and in the communities we lived in, that it created a unified culture between everyone. This is especially true today as the UAE population closes in on 10 million people in the UAE, with citizens from over 200 countries, and how that cohesiveness, forward-thinking, and mutual respect continues to create a community that welcomes all. The scale is much larger today, but that sense of community continues to thrive.

Journey

My professional journey has involved multiple countries and different sectors. I have experienced the various business ethics and styles in the US, UK, Europe and UAE through my career and have taken valuable insights from each role. Whether it be a call center agent role connecting Asian and North American clients to one another or finance roles in London and New York, they have all added to my knowledge and exposure.

I have seen first-hand the growth and development in Abu Dhabi over the past decades. All these have led me to the most fulfilling role of my career at ADIO. ADIO plays a key role in empowering innovative companies and enabling them to achieve their vision in the Emirate, thus developing the private sector and supporting the UAE's diversification strategy. Every day, I have the opportunity to spread Abu Dhabi's message of innovation to the world and support businesses looking to expand in the emirate.

HH Sheikh Zayed

I began every presentation at ADIO with a quote from the late Sheikh Zayed bin Sultan Al Nahyan: "I dreamt of our land keeping pace with the growth of the modern world." To me, this encapsulates his forward-looking vision for our nation. His aspirations are as relevant now as they were during his leadership. They have placed us at the forefront of innovation and, to this day, motivate the vision of the country we are trying to build.

Our leadership continues to build on his legacy and the pillars he established not only in the UAE, but across the world in different countries.

Exponential Growth

For me, the UAE's evolution from building our own successes to building the region's success symbolises our growth story. In our early years, we were focused on nation-building and laying the foundation for the future. We prioritised education and attracting skilled workers as the basis of a competitive workforce; we developed our hard infrastructure with cutting-edge technologies and advanced infrastructure; and we created a knowledge-based economy supported by an integrated innovation ecosystem. All these cemented Abu Dhabi's position as a leading innovation hub.

Having reached that point, Abu Dhabi expanded our long-term focus. We want to create solutions and technology that are locally relevant and globally exportable. To do this, we are supporting innovation in all sectors, including agriculture, finance, ICT and tourism. Our objective is for the cutting-edge solutions here to be applied to other markets and benefit those in the region and beyond.

Secret of Success

There are different standards that address success, but by all measures, what we have accomplished in the UAE is nothing short of a major success. We have grown exponentially, we have diversified, we have welcomed the world to the UAE, and we continue to push the boundaries of business and technology. I believe that this is the key factor in our success: we take calculated risks and embrace change. We operate in unison to ensure that all aspects are covered, and we also excel at resolving challenges. Our leadership provides us with the platform to keep pushing forward.

Challenges

The UAE's population size is disproportionate to the outsized impact we have made in the international arena. Despite our small citizenship base, we are proud of the thriving city we have built out of the desert. Much of this can be attributed to our competitive workforce and talent base. Locally, the UAE's established world-class universities foster knowledge development among youth, while the Emiratisation policy helps boost the capabilities of citizens. We continue to attract world-class talent through immigration processes that make it easy for skilled workers and those with higher education qualifications to obtain work permits. Furthermore, the 'Thrive in Abu Dhabi' programme encourages talented professionals, students and investors to set down roots by highlighting the long-term visas and paths to citizenship.

Opportunities

Innovation has always been a key focus for Abu Dhabi and is the underlying theme for all the initiatives that we are pursuing. We have created a welcoming and supportive environment for innovative businesses to thrive. Companies in the UAE can access advantages including a favourable tax regime, established infrastructure and financial and political stability. The government has also established numerous business enablement entities to support companies at every step of their journey.

There are many business opportunities in Abu Dhabi. The emirate can serve as a base to carry out R&D and innovation, a hub for collaboration, or a launchpad to the wider Middle East region. The amount of innovation being created here is tremendous and set to grow.

Lessons

A fundamental aspect of the UAE's success is the interplay between the public and private sector. Ensuring that the two pillars work complementarily, rather than in opposition or in silos, has been instrumental in our continued progress. The government plays a key role in establishing the overarching vision, as well as ensuring mechanisms to achieve its goals are in place. In Abu Dhabi, the leadership has been clear on its vision for the emirate from Day 1, and has institutionalised infrastructure and support to mobilise private sector involvement. The impetus then falls on businesses to take the reins in driving progress in line with the government's vision.

The key to achieving the right balance is continued engagement between the public and private sectors. This will allow the government to provide the right type and amount of support to businesses to boost the country's economic growth.

Expo

Expo 2020 can be said to be a microcosm of the UAE. In the same way that Expo has gathered almost 200 participating nations in a showcase of culture and innovation, the UAE is home to 200 nationalities working and learning together every day. Expo provides a platform to bring together the best ideas from around the world and innovate for the future. This is aligned with the message of unity and collaboration that the UAE has been sending to the world for many years. Expo gives us a chance to amplify that on the global stage.

Future

The UAE leadership's vision combined with the ambition of the people in the last 50 years has accelerated achievements on a scale never seen before. We are excited about the innovation that is being created here in Abu Dhabi, in sectors such as AgTech, healthcare, ICT and more. These advancements are the outcome of the government's investments towards supporting companies as they develop locally relevant technology, such as agriculture solutions for desert and arid climates, or educational online content for Arab youth. Going forward, our yardstick will be our ability to export cutting-edge solutions and technology that can benefit the region. We want to accelerate economic progress not just in the UAE but further afield.

38. SMART THINKING

HE Wesam Lootah, CEO, Smart Dubai Government Establishment, Digital Dubai

"*We are always trailblazing*"

Wesam Lootah is a digital transformation leader with more than 20 years of strategic leadership that drastically shaped Dubai into the Smart city it is today, he built his extensive leadership portfolio and experience through various executive roles in institutions affiliated with the Dubai Government, the Dubai World Trade Center and Emaar Group.

As CEO of the Smart Dubai Government Establishment, the technology arm Digital Dubai; the government entity entrusted with Dubai's city-wide digital transformation envisioned by HH Sheikh Mohammed. He also serves as the Chairman of Executive Committee of Dubai Cooperative Society and acts as an advisory council member of Dubai Chamber of Digital Economy. Since becoming CEO in 2015, in record time Wesam has managed to transform technology from being the backbone of the Digital Dubai initiative to become a true enabler of digital transformation, with a focus on humanizing technology to influence life's experiences. He pioneered the Digital Dubai strategy and plans related to Artificial Intelligence, and has the distinction of launching the first AI Lab in the Middle East and North Africa region, in addition to launching hundreds of initiatives and numerous smart services.

Lootah holds a Master's degree in Computer Science and Engineering from Pennsylvania State University, USA and a Bachelor's degree from Ohio State University. Wesam is also an author with published research in the field of Computer Security and is a renowned speaker on smart cities and digital transformation at top events.

Earliest Memories

I was born in 1974. One of my earliest memories was when I was at elementary school, I remember we were celebrating National Day and they got us to plant trees. It was symbolic: the tie with the land, that early on we had, and with the environment. Trees are a symbol of growth for our country.

My other early memories are of visiting family, whether in Dubai, Abu Dhabi, Al Ain, or playing with the kids from our wider family. We've always been a community, with family members across all the emirates: one big family.

Journey

I graduated from public school and I did my bachelors in the US in Computer Science. I then came back to the UAE and worked in The Rulers Court in the IT Department. I remember a couple of years into my career, we were faced by the prospect of the "Millennium Bug" in 1999. I was responsible for creating the first government platform where all the government entities had to update us on the status of their digital security, how was their preparation, making sure the airports and all the port systems were working fine.

Just after this, in the year 2000 His Highness launched Dubai eGovernment. He believed in taking the government to the next stage, from the traditional government where you have to go to a government entity, stand in line, wait, apply, wait for the answer. If you compare that with what we have today… We have an application called 'Dubai Now' this is what people expect: they expect their services now. This is the amazing journey of the UAE, the digital transformation. I am blessed to have been part of this journey. I was part of the initial team, which implemented the Government Resource Planning platform which is an application that runs 95% of the government's business today. It is used by 70 government entities, 70,000 employees, it helps the government manage its financial resources, human resources, procurement activities and more. It's been a regional example. People from all around the region come to see how Dubai has done it. That is another example of leadership that Dubai shows.

I left the government in 2004 and went and did my Masters in Computer Science and moved to the private sector, worked for Emaar for a few years, and then for Dubai World Trade Centre, and finally came back to the government in 2011. I've been with Digital Dubai for the last 10 years.

I've worked 2/3 of my career within the government and 1/3 in the private sector. My work has always been an intersection between technology and the public sector: the business side of what government does.

HH Sheikh Zayed

I didn't have the privilege of meeting him personally. I remember when he passed away, I was studying abroad. It was like you've lost your grandfather, everyone was mourning his passing, the entire country. That's because of his spirit. Right from the beginning, bringing together all of the emirates, being the father of this country, all of the achievements the UAE has been able to achieve is because of the courageous steps that he has taken in his leadership leading the country where it is today.

Exponential Growth

When I joined Digital Dubai, we had a few shared government applications that were being used. One of the ideas was to allow people to make very fast payments for the government, paying for your Salik, for your DEWA bill. The collection on the system was about 8 million dirhams at that time. What we are doing now is 1.7 billion dirhams in just a span of 10 years, it really has been exponentially growing. We've seen double-digit growth every year on the take up of electronic services.

Another huge achievement was marked on 12 December 2021 with the announcement that Dubai is the first government to be completely paperless. That initial idea was approved by HH Sheikh Hamdan in 2018 and at that time Dubai Government was using over 300 million pieces of paper annually. In our daily life it is very hard to comprehend what 300 million pieces of paper actually look like! If you were to stack these 300 million pieces of paper on top of each other, how high do you think it will be? We calculated it was 30 times the height of Burj Khalifa, that is how much paper was being used by the government on an annual basis. On average 14 million hours saved annually, can you imagine what Dubai can do with another 14 million hours of productivity!

Secret of Success

I think strong Leadership and collaboration. It's not a one-man show. It's the government, the academia, the entrepreneurs, the large companies, each individual. It takes everyone to realise the vision.

Diversity for me is very important part of the secret sauce of the UAE and Dubai. We are very diverse and tolerant as a nation, and everyone has a verse in this story.

Challenges

In any transformation, there are always challenges. Dubai is always transforming. It's very important to have a clear vision. Because in a complex environment like a city or a country, there are always going to be competing priorities. Every individual stakeholder is a piece of the puzzle that has their own priorities that they are trying to optimize for. It's critical in any transformation programme, that everyone has the same vision, and that they are aligned on the vision. I think this is where a lot of places around the world see transformation programmes that fail or take much longer than expected, because the vision is not clear, the leadership is not strong and maybe people don't believe in the vision. Ensuring that people believe in the vision and are aligned is very critical, and I think His Highness is the master of this. He sets the goals, is very ambitious, and everyone is aligned towards these big audacious goals. Once you have that alignment, it's making sure you are collaborative, that everyone gets the credit, gets to be part of the story. We compete together but we also collaborate.

With the Dubai Government Excellence Awards, individual government entities compete to be recognized as the best entity. At the same time, we have to collaborate. So being able to constantly challenge ourselves by competing, and also working together, is not an easy thing.

We need to be more responsive to customer needs as a government, and it's one of the biggest challenges that the public and private sectors face. We're in the era of social media and immediate responses, and expectations have been set by Internet giants like Apple, Google or Amazon. They've led the private sector in terms of customer experience. This is what Digital Dubai has been focusing on for the last three or four years. In the past, people were happy if they ordered a book online and it arrived two weeks later. Now, you expect it to come immediately with services like Amazon, where you download a digital copy instead. Expectations have grown year after year.

Opportunities

I think the UAE, specifically Dubai, has always been a future looking city. We've always tried to lead from the front. In some countries and some companies, they are happy to wait and see. They see a new trend, a new tech, and say they will wait. In Dubai, we don't have that option. We are always trailblazing. I remember in 2016 when we launched the Dubai Blockchain Strategy. At the time people were not sure what blockchain would do. Dubai took the lead and said it would use blockchain in the government to increase efficiency. That announcement was an invitation to the small startups and SMEs that were just starting to work with blockchain and creating new products, to come here, to come to Dubai, and we said "we're here, we believe in what you are doing; we want to help you grow and we want to grow with you". That has always been the case, whether it's Blockchain, AI, Agrotech, Fintech, all across the board. I don't think there's one industry that I'd say Dubai is not a good place for. Whatever it is that you are working in, I think Dubai is the right place to call home for your business and also as a launching pad and access to the entire MENA region. I think 4 billion people live within a 3-hour flight from Dubai. We are the most connected city with the busiest airport in the world.

Lessons

I've always thought, as a digital leader, what is my role, and what am I trying to do? For me, it is using technology to improve something.

If you take that question a bit deeper, what is the role of the government? I came up with my own theory, of what the role of government is, which I can summarise around 3 major things:

One is about giving us something to belong to – as human beings we gather, we create tribes, we create villages, we need to belong to a community, and that's what the government defines. It defines the state, the nation. Eventually we belong to this nation. I think the UAE and Dubai are very good examples of this, because it creates a boundary that welcomes everyone. We have 200 nationalities that all call this country home. That is a very critical role of government: defining this community that we have built, that we belong to.

The second role is providing our safety, security, and protection. You live here in the UAE, in Dubai, and many times I leave the keys in the car, the car is unlocked, and the front gate is always unlocked. We have that sense of safety and security. You make a booking for dinner with your wife, you go to a restaurant, and you don't worry about food poisoning. The Dubai municipality is making sure your food has been cooked properly, has been stored properly, from the source, from where it's been shipped from all the way through the ports to the warehousing, all the way to your plate. The government plays a very important role in regulating different industries within the city. By doing this regulation, we ensure that the right people are driving, what the RTA does with licensing, the Dubai Economic Department ensures that the right people are getting the trade license to conduct business. A lot of government entities have this role of regulation and protection.

The third critical role that the government plays is to ensure that everyone has an opportunity to prosper. This is the leadership of His Highness. We are open for business, we welcome people to come here, we've always been known as a country and a city of trade, right from the beginning with His Highness Sheikh Rashid investing in digging the creek further to make it deeper for more ships to be able to come in, to creating the Jebel Ali port, when it was a complete desert. That vision of creating a future where people can come here and call this home and create economic opportunity, is a very critical role of the government.

Around all of this, the priority, are the citizens, residents and visitors. We hear this all the time from HH Sheikh Mohammed. The happiness, the wellbeing of the people, this is what the government aims for.

I remember this one tweet saying, "I've never been so happy to pay a fine". In some places in the world you have to go physically to pay the fine, and they really punish you and make it hard to pay the fine. The process is punishment and the fine is punishment. In Dubai we make it easy. Just go into the DubaiNow app, one single application has all the services in one place. Our vision is for anyone who interacts with the government to see the government as one. It doesn't matter if you try to build a house, or open a restaurant; you're dealing with one entity, which is Dubai. Dubai is serving you. You don't need to know each individual entity. Dubai is the one that is here to help you and to serve and provide the value add.

Expo

I've seen Expo right from the time it was still a plan on paper, going through the different phases. It's an entire city that's been built within Dubai, with the theme connecting minds creating the future. It's an amazing theme.

I believe this has been the best world Expo that's ever been, and will be for the foreseeable future. It's just the diversity and the focus on sustainability.

I've worked closely with the team that was responsible for the digital experience within Expo. There's an amazing partnership there with Siemens, Cisco, Etisalat, and others that created world class structures for Expo so they were able to welcome everyone. But I think the story of Expo, also ties to a very important thing, the fact that Expo opened at the beginning of October 2021, is a testament to how Dubai has managed the pandemic. How Dubai has been able to manage through a global crisis. It took the world by surprise, but we were prepared. The investment that the UAE has done in the infrastructure, and technology, allowed us to navigate through this with the least amount of harm. There was an amazing balance between ensuring the safety security and health of people and also making sure the economy continues to operate properly. We were one of the first cities to implement the national sanitisation programme, and have a lockdown, but we were also one of the first cities to open up, in a very calculated way. This was done through data and machine learning and being able to predict what the different policies would affect the number of infections. We had a Dubai COVID 19 Command and Control Centre, the team from Digital Dubai was represented, and the information that was collected from all the different data points, whether it was the labs, the hospitals, information about the number of beds, infections and so on, were collected, and based on this information, using sophisticated algorithms to predict the trend, the leadership was able to make decisions, and now we are able to open up for the entire world to come and to see this amazing thing we've built here.

Future

People who make predictions about the future always get caught out! We've always aspired to be the best country in the world, that's a national vision for the country, and I think that will continue to be our vision to make the UAE the best destination for anyone to live. We want

to create cities that people love to be in. Whether you call it hom
do business here, you have fun as well. That's the charm, the attract
of being here.

39. GLOBAL VENTURES

Noor Sweid, General Partner, Global Ventures

"The UAE's journey of growth thus far and its innovative approach to the future continues to inspire many and serves as a blueprint for success for countries in the region and beyond."

Noor Sweid is General Partner of Global Ventures and passionate about enabling disruptive technology companies and their emerging market founders to solve real problems while changing the world with measurable impact. Noor is a founder, investor, and operator. Identified by Forbes magazine as one of the "World's Top 50 Women in Tech", Noor's previous roles include CIO at The Dubai Future Foundation, and founder of ZenYoga studio chain (acquired by Cedarbridge). Furthermore, Noor was the first Arab woman to scale, IPO and operate a public company in the MENA region, listing Depa on the NASDAQ Dubai and the London Stock Exchange (DEPA:DU) for US$1.1. billion in April 2008.

In addition to board roles on Global Ventures' portfolio companies, Noor is Chairperson of the Middle East Venture Capital Association and Director for MIT Sloan and TechWadi. Noor is also the independent Chairperson of the board for Clue Health.

Noor holds a Bachelors' degrees in Finance and Economics from Boston College, an MBA from MIT Sloan, and began her career as a Biotechnology and pharmaceutical strategy consultant in the US. She is a Fellow of the inaugural class of the Finance Leaders Fellowship and a member of the Aspen Global Leadership Network and is recognized as a Young Global Leader by the World Economic Forum.

Earliest Memories

My father first came here in the 90s. At the time, the city of Dubai was on its way to building and completing the world's first 7-star hotel. This accomplishment would put the city on the radar of travelers and city-dwellers seeking the highest possible levels of luxury. An architect by design, my father was inspired to move Dubai because he wanted to be part of that new chapter for the city... and he was! His company, Depa, was selected to work on fitting out the interiors of the hotel. 5 years later, the hotel was complete. 22 years later, my father still speaks fondly of that story as one of his and Depa's greatest accomplishments. For me, whenever I look at the Burj Al Arab, I am reminded of how early the UAE's ambitions to be a global hub began. What we see today is not a result of the past 5 to 10 years, but a product of the past 20.

Journey

I started my career in the US as a biotechnology consultant before returning to the UAE in 2005 with Booz Allen. I quickly changed my career path and joined Depa, a company my father had started. At the time, the company was in six markets, had about 1000 employees and was making $60 million in revenues. It was growing fast, taking on new deals in Dubai's booming hospitality and real estate industry. Being part of Depa's growth story was thrilling… but stressful! For that reason and due to the absence of yoga studios anywhere in the city, I founded Zen Yoga, which grew to become the largest chain of wellness studios in the UAE.

Leading Depa's public listing was a moment of pride for me. By 2008, the company was generating $600 million in revenues, and was operational in 22 markets. It was the largest interior contractor globally. I led the process with Morgan Stanley and UBS in April 2008, just before the financial crisis. It was a dual listing on the LSE and the NASDAQ Dubai. It was a great success story for the region because it was a Dubai-based company that had become a global success story and truly reinvented the market.

As the founder of Zen Yoga, I realised how challenging it was to start and scale a business. While paramount to growth, capital was scarce in the region. I was also an angel investor at the time, and was working closely with a group of stellar regional founders who were building truly unique products. At that point, I found my purpose: to expand access to capital and enable founders to build impactful businesses that have a positive impact on their communities and the world. Global Ventures was born!

HH Sheikh Zayed

Earlier, I spoke about Burj Al Arab and how the UAE's global ambitions began in the 1990s. As a matter of fact, those ambitions began much earlier in the country's history, and more specifically, with HH Sheikh Zayed's vision which he began to realise in 1966. At the time, the UAE had just started exporting oil, marking a new era for the country's development. HH Sheikh Zayed built governance structures, roads, public services such as healthcare, education and public housing. In the spirit of collaboration, he actively involved local and foreign communities in this development process. 50 years later, it is no surprise that we are still witnessing co-existence between both communities.

HH Sheikh Zayed was building bridges at all levels: between different communities, between all seven emirates and between countries. Sheikh Zayed was a leading force in the foundation of the Gulf Cooperation Council. Today, the UAE still acts as the essential bridge between East, West, North and South, making it a sought-after home for work and life for business people, families and individuals from all walks of life.

Exponential Growth

The UAE's extraordinary and continuous growth story is transforming the country into a global and regional hub for tech and innovation, making it an attractive destination for entrepreneurs, global tech giants and investors (both regional and international). The UAE is enabling of business, whether it is its strategic location between Asia, Africa and Europe, its connection to these markets, the ease of setting up businesses or its strong macroeconomic fundamentals including high GDP per capita, record smartphone and internet penetration rates and a sizable youth population.

The UAE government is continuously investing in the ecosystem's development; its exponential growth will continue into the next decade and beyond.

Secret of Success

There are a number of factors that have led to the UAE's exponential growth and success. First, the government is proactive about advancing key regulations and building the necessary infrastructure for individuals to start and grow businesses, to build a family and a home and to attract tourists from all over the globe.

When it comes to business particularly: The UAE ranks 16th on the World Bank's ease of doing business list, and is taking active steps to rank even higher. From free zones allowing 100% foreign ownership to attractive tax programs, the ease of setting up businesses is another factor that makes the UAE a destination for tech start-ups and big tech companies. As immigration policies relax with the introduction of golden and remote working visas, SMEs will benefit from a global talent pool. New immigration laws are also encouraging for current and prospective residents of the UAE who are now considering the country a permanent and secure home. By 2026, Dubai aims to train 100,000 programmers and coders, create 1,000 digital companies and increase government support for start-ups from AED 1.5 billion to AED 4 billion. These types of initiatives are poised to boost the country's tech sector, and reinforce the UAE's position as a regional and global tech hub.

The UAE is located between Asia, Africa and Europe. Importantly, it is also seamlessly and richly connected to these markets, with a large majority of them being a mere 6-hour flight away. That said, it is possible for start-ups to do local, regional and international business simultaneously in and from the UAE. This connectivity also means that the UAE is an easy to reach destination for tourists, but also an attractive place for expats to settle while still being close to their homeland.

The UAE's success is also a result of strong macroeconomic fundamentals, boasting high GDP per capita, translating into a high tendency for spending. Its 10 million residents also have a high affinity for technology and propensity for digital adoption, due to their diverse and cosmopolitan nature. This population is also largely young, and smartphone and internet penetration rates are among the highest in the world, at 99% as of January 2021.

In terms of my professional career, I would say that the secret is to keep the eyes and heart open to opportunities, and seizing the ones that come your way, irrespective of what they are. My career has been anything but linear and traditional: I started in biotechnology then interior contracting, followed by wellness and now, I'm a venture capitalist. I accepted early on that I will never know everything, but that that should never stop me from pursuing an opportunity deeply and meaningfully. Quite the opposite, it drove my curiosity to know and learn more, to become the best that I can be.

Challenges

While working at the family business (Depa), I also founded my own company, ZenYoga, which ultimately became the largest chain of wellness studios in the UAE. But the journey up until Zenyoga reached that point was a challenge. It was during the early years of being an entrepreneur that I realised it is more difficult to grow a company from scratch, than to scale a company from $6 million in revenues to $60 million. It was also then that I noticed the significant funding and capital gap in the market for aspiring entrepreneurs to build their businesses successfully. There was a lack of support for entrepreneurship and as a first-time founder, it was challenging to grow my business.

That challenge then became an opportunity, and ultimately, it became my purpose. I founded Global Ventures from a deep desire to bridge the capital gap between founders in emerging markets and regional/international investors.

Opportunities

For investors and founders, the next 5 to 10 years will focus on addressing post-COVID challenges, starting with healthcare, education, as well as food and water security. They will also usher in a new era for financial technology, the future of work and e-commerce.

Fintech and e-commerce have consistently ranked highest in terms of funding and deals in the UAE. I expect this trend to continue into 2022 and beyond, and greater investment flow into digital health solutions, especially those in the telemedicine or at-home care verticals.

The future of the UAE's tech space will also be underpinned by a common understanding that technology companies are not only fruitful investments with positive prospects of financial returns, but also a vehicle for social change and impact. We will see more investors interested in allocating capital in private companies that are making positive contributions in their communities, in areas such as financial, healthcare and education inclusion, as well as gender equality and job creation. The future of business and technology lies with companies that do well and do good.

Lessons

The UAE has been highly proactive in developing policies, building out infrastructure and setting objectives, but what truly sets the country apart is effective delivery and implementation. The UAE thrives on a culture of innovation that permeates sectors and drives economic growth, particularly in trade, transport and technology which sit at the core of its strategy. Through the development of highly robust infrastructure, the UAE has not only established itself as an international trade and transport hub, but has also created an attractive tourism and business environment for international visitors.

Though relatively small when compared with other countries in its region, the UAE's forward-thinking goals like achieving a top rank in the global food security index by 2051 and emission free public transport by 2050 coupled with its strong leadership continue to position it near the top of every economic performance index.

The UAE's journey of growth thus far and its innovative approach to the future continue to inspire many, and serves as a blueprint for success for countries in the region and beyond.

Expo

Expo 2020 celebrates innovation across a spectrum of sectors in fields of art, science and business. Held for the first time in the Arab world, the values that Expo 2020 embodies – creativity, exploration, and the reimagination of traditional thought – are synonymous with the UAE's vision for the future. The fair showcases innovative technologies that are capable of revolutionizing our daily lives - I would hope that the takeaway for each visitor would be to recognize that Expo 2020 serves as a microcosm of the UAE as a whole – a hub for growth, innovation and the future.

Future

The forward-thinking mindset of the UAE's leadership is evident in UAE Centennial 2071, which lays out the country's vision for the next 5 decades. The plan focuses on investment in future generations, developing skills, knowledge, reputation and soft power to position the UAE as the best country in the world. Innovations across the country's knowledge economy, its society, quality of education and a future focused government are all key pillars that underpin economic productivity and the success of generations to come. With policies, programmes and infrastructure already in place across each of these focus areas, I have no doubt that the UAE will achieve these goals by 2071, firmly solidifying the country's reputation as a global hub.

40. HEALTH IS WEALTH

HE Sheikh Abdulla bin Mohammed Al Hamed, Chairman of Department of Health, Abu Dhabi

"For the UAE, the pandemic served as a catalyst for our healthcare system and I'm proud to say that our country rose to the challenge."

HE Sheikh Abdulla Bin Mohamed Bin Butti Al Hamed was born in the emirate of Abu Dhabi-United Arab Emirates in 1973. He completed his Bachelor of Science in Business Administration at Marylhurst College, Marylhurst, Oregon, U.S.A. in December 1996 and in May of 2007 H.E obtained his Master's Degree in Business Administration from New York Institute of Technology, Abu Dhabi branch.

HE is currently serving as the Chairman of the Department of Health in the Emirate of Abu Dhabi. He is also a member of Abu Dhabi's Executive Council. He has played a critical part in Abu Dhabi and the UAE's response to COVID-19.

Earliest Memories

If there is one thing that I am sure of, it is that my country, the UAE has been through an incredible transformation, thanks to the wise leadership we have. The discovery of oil and establishment of the union in 1971 were significant milestones in the development and prosperity of the UAE. It wasn't long before the country started to evolve bit by bit into one of the most significant financial and economic centers in the region. This transformation was founded on the vision of our late founding father, Sheikh Zayed Bin Sultan Al Nahyan, who was a firm believer that the country and its people had the potential to accomplish advancements across industries, including healthcare, education, science and tech, oil and gas and more. Our late founding father was committed to making use of all of the resources available in the service of the nation and the people living in the UAE. Today our wise leadership follows in our founding fathers' footsteps ensuring that all citizens and residents are instrumental to the nation's collective success.

Journey

I am grateful and fortunate for having the chance to contribute to the growth and prosperity of my country. Regardless of my capacity, and throughout my professional journey, I have always wanted to pay back to my country and to play a part in its growth and prosperity. Prior to serving as Chairman of the Department of Health – Abu Dhabi, I held several positions as Chairman of Abu Dhabi Energy Authority and Chairman of Regulation and Supervision Bureau, Chairman of Abu Dhabi Water & Electricity Authority – 2015-2016. Undersecretary of Ministry of Foreign Affairs – 2012 to 2014. I was also the Managing Director of the European Affairs Department at the Ministry of Foreign Affairs – 2011 to 2012. Chairman of the Western Region Development Council – 2004 to 2011 & Undersecretary of the Ruler's Representative at Al Gharbia Region – 2001 to 2010. And I also worked in Abu Dhabi Investment Authority back in 1996.

HH Sheikh Zayed

Sheikh Zayed is a founding father and political and humanitarian figure who continues to be honoured and remembered both in the UAE and throughout the world. He was a man of great vision and profound wisdom and morals. He taught us that the impossible is possible. He taught us resilience, patience, determination and self-respect. Over the years, he lived life modestly and had an open heart and mind, but above all he was genuine and inclusive towards all people, regardless of culture or background. He continued to work hard to improve the lives of everyone around him and has in turn earned the love and respect of all the people who lived in this country. He is who I aspire to be, a person who remains at the heart of everything the UAE does, a person who serves as a great example to the community and for generations to come.

Exponential Growth

It is undeniable that the UAE's story of progress since the unity of its Emirates has been an impressive story of success. Over a period of

50 years, the UAE has achieved many important milestones in the medical, educational, technological and social arenas. It also witnessed impressive economic and urban revolutions, crowning the UAE as one of the leading touristic destinations and investment hubs, both regionally and internationally. On behalf of the healthcare sector, I could say that we are fully committed to building a strong and dynamic society and for ensuring the health, safety and wellbeing of all those who call Abu Dhabi Emirate home.

Secret of Success

The secret behind the UAE's success is the strong foundation that our late founding father established. Sheikh Zayed Al Nahyan rose to become a national and world leader, who gained the respect of citizens in the UAE and around the world. He taught us that for the nation to succeed, we need to achieve excellence across all sectors. And because of his efforts, the UAE has become a leading country and it is undeniable that the UAE has built an impressive story of success. In the healthcare sector, Abu Dhabi has evolved exponentially over the years. It transitioned from traditional to more innovative healthcare practices that have enhanced the quality of the healthcare system in the Emirate.

Challenges

The biggest challenge that not only the UAE but the whole world had to overcome is the road to recovery from the worst pandemic in human history. We strongly believe that no one can overcome this crisis alone and that we, as individuals and as organisations, need to work together and give the strongest support to those who are fighting the pandemic. But despite the challenges that were imposed on us, it is no surprise that the UAE was ranked as one of the best and safest countries during the pandemic. Abu Dhabi was ranked number 1 city globally in responding to Covid-19 by Deep Knowledge group This was only achieved because of the support and guidance of our wise leadership, the bold measures we took, the dedicated resources and the leading strategic initiatives in place. Today we continue to work with all entities and members of the society to ensure the safety and wellbeing of the community and business continuity.

Opportunities

The healthcare industry serves as a beacon for individuals from nearby countries due to more affordable healthcare options in the UAE and there is a considerably rapid development in our healthcare sector that attracts major international companies to the market. The UAE's goal is to be a global destination for both domestic and foreign patients and to be the place for medical tourists around the world with the country's high quality and cost-effective treatments and procedures. Another exciting opportunity is that Abu Dhabi is stimulating foreign direct investments opportunities in the healthcare sector, granting ownership up to 100% and this is a significant step forward for DoH. We also invite research, innovation and technology companies to join us as we continue to position the Emirate as a research and innovation hub in the region.

Lessons

The UAE knows how to set visions, plan for the future and attract the best talent and capital while also upskilling and investing in its own human capital. The country has collaborated and partnered with international organisations, private and public entities, to further provide solutions for the world's biggest and most challenging problems.

The COVID-19 pandemic brought the world to a halt and put large amounts of pressure on healthcare systems across the world, in terms of infrastructure, mode of delivery, financing and much more. For the UAE, the pandemic served as a catalyst for our healthcare system and I'm proud to say that our country rose to the challenge. Our priority has always been to safeguard the health and safety of all who call Abu Dhabi home. Our Covid-19 efforts included continuous and transparent updates and public education, free-of-cost vaccines, drive-through testing healthcare facilities, innovative monitoring system for COVID-19 patients in home isolation and ambitious awareness programmes across all emirates.

These efforts are a testament to the country's proactive approach to achieving a sustainable pandemic recovery and being able to achieve one of the highest vaccination levels in the world while staying open for business and tourism. Moreover, the UAE is building its reputation as a leading medical tourism destination, ranking first globally in terms of the number of accredited healthcare facilities, destination environment and patient experience. It also launched digital platforms that provide UAE visitors with access to diverse medical offerings and healthcare facilities available throughout their visit. The country strives to provide care that is accessible by all, anywhere and at any point in time.

Expo

The UAE is the country of dreams and Expo will be unlocking thousands of opportunities. It will allow us to meet the people worldwide who are transforming dreams and aspirations into the realities of tomorrow. It will be a place to be empowered to shape the future by unlocking the potential within yourself, a place that will prove to you that your smallest actions can make a big impact. It will be your gateway into new markets and new revenue streams. The UAE is the place to be inspired to live smart, think smart and feel smart.

Future

We envision a future that belongs to the youth, a future that inspires the next generation of doctors, astronauts, data scientists, cyber security specialists, technology specialists and more. The UAE is already focusing on developing centres of excellence with most, if not all, sectors proactively planning and building a forward-thinking community that is built for the youth. In the next 50 years, UAE will have the best and most established government in the world that aims to achieve happiness in society and will develop a mechanism for monitoring long-term variables in various sectors.

The country will also be offering excellent quality of education with advanced science and technology, space science, engineering, innovation and health sciences. The future will be made of a diversified knowledge economy and most importantly, an ethical and cohesive society that embraces happiness and a positive lifestyle, and a high quality of life. In the healthcare sector, we aim to develop a system for citizens and residents that continuously delivers good quality healthcare to international standards and improves access to healthcare through e-health and smart health and making the UAE a top destination for medical tourism. The UAE has embraced digital health, artificial intelligence and telemedicine to build a future-ready healthcare system for the country. The Department of Health – Abu Dhabi, is investing in cutting-edge projects which will undoubtedly revolutionise the future of healthcare in the Emirate.

41. READING BETWEEN THE LINES

Isobel Abulhoul OBE

"This is the land of opportunity."

Isobel Abulhoul is Festival Director of the Emirates Airline Festival of Literature and CEO of the Emirates Literature Foundation. Isobel was born and educated in Cambridge and came to Dubai in 1968 where she has worked throughout her career to promote education, reading and writing in the UAE. Co-founder of Magrudy's bookshop chain, Isobel has also been awarded the Order of the British Empire (OBE) by Her Majesty Queen Elizabeth II in 2011 in recognition of her years of service to education and British literature in the UAE.

Earliest Memories

I grew up in Cambridge, which is where I first met my future husband. He was studying English with HH Sheikh Mohammed bin Rashid and a number of other Emiratis, and he invited me to meet his family in Dubai. I arrived in Dec 1968 on a BOAC plane. We stopped 3 times on the way and it was a 12 hour flight. When we landed, and the door opened, all I could see was a few lights, but I felt the sand on my feet. It felt magical. This was before the UAE was formed. Many people had not even heard of Dubai or the Trucial States. I had to get a No Objection Certificate from the UK Home Office to come. It was such an adventure. Dubai has been home ever since and in a strange way, I felt I had come home when I first arrived.

Journey

My first job in the UAE was as a teacher at the Dubai Infants

School. I noticed there wasn't a habit of reading bedtime stories amongst my Emirati friends. There were limited numbers of children's books in English or even in Arabic. All my own books had to come from the UK by sea. I then co-founded the Al Ittihad Private School in the early 1970s to provide a new model of education.

In 1975, I decided to set up a shop where one could buy educational toys. It was called Magrudy's, and was on the Dubai – Sharjah road. As I had no prior experience of retail, I included children's books in the mix. Listening to customers I then added more and more books, all brought by sea.

I used to phone the commercial section of the British Embassy for new addresses of suppliers. I wrote letters and kept carbon copies. I ended up with two 40-foot containers that arrived at the port in the days before it was set up as a container terminal. They were tough days but hugely rewarding.

I also founded a publishing house and then pulled everything together when I established the Emirates Airline Festival of Literature. The idea just came about from a lunch where I was asked whether Dubai had a literature festival. I responded that it didn't, but that planted the seed!

HH Sheikh Zayed

I actually met HH Sheikh Zayed in the UK. I had gone to an Arab racing event in Kempton Park and HH Sheikh Zayed and HH Sheikh Mohammed were there. My husband and son Mansoor went up to them and they had a long conversation. They were very approachable and making jokes.

As well as being a wonderful warm and humane person, HH Sheikh Zayed planted many trees and understood the importance of greenery. He was a dedicated conservationist. Nothing was wasted. You couldn't afford to waste water and food.

I love a story I heard where HH Sheikh Zayed went to a café in Geneva, and he started feeding the birds. When he got the bill, he asked the café owner to continue to feed the birds and left funds to do so. This for me was just a tiny example of the humanity of this great leader.

Exponential Growth

You can come to the UAE penniless with an idea but see it blossom and grow. This is a country where dreams really can come true. It is the same story for so many people who have made the UAE their home. You are able to dream, work hard and achieve that dream. There is no red tape for good ideas.

Secret of Success

People are valued and trusted for who they are. Deals are done on a handshake. If someone says let's do it, you have to deliver.

Before I came to Dubai, one of my mother's friends was a professor who had once stopped off in Dubai on the way to India. He had simply said "it's a wonderful place, you'll be fine". This comforted my mother and he also gave me a copy of Arabian Sands. The book gives you a great insight into the Bedouin mentality. Honour, dignity and trust are deeply embedded in the culture. This is a secret of the UAE's success.

Challenges

I don't think there are any challenges that I haven't overcome! I'm an opportunist by nature. However, if you're a perfectionist, you won't flourish here. You just have to get on with it.

I was a bit of a novelty in those early days and ladies from the neighbourhood would come and visit me in the afternoons. Learning Arabic was a great opportunity, and I was immersed in the language living in the community. I don't know but I think had the situation been reversed with an Emirati lady marrying an Englishman and living in the UK, I'm not sure they would have had the same warm reception I did. It might have been considered a challenge, but I saw the opportunity.

Opportunities

It's the land of opportunity. I think it's impossible not to succeed here. It's certainly not the hardship posting that it used to be. I remember eating my first mango that a relative had brought from Egypt – now we can get them everywhere…

I remember coming from Cambridge where I was surrounded by books and realizing that books were the only thing I missed here: This is something that I knew would enrich society. I believe many people can come from their own countries and see similar opportunities. Diversity is a key strength of the UAE.

Lessons

Do not judge others by your standards. Be open. There are so many different cultures and nationalities living side by side in the Emirates. It is a chance for us all to open our eyes and learn.

Expo

I cried when I visited Expo. Who could have expected to see this mirage rising out of the desert. No one can see that except the true visionaries. They made it possible.

Future

I think there will be a real focus on making the UAE as sustainable as possible. I see more cycle tracks, more solar power, sustainable communities. I think the UAE will return back to its natural roots, but always be a land of opportunity.

42. UNLOCKING GENIUS

Dino Varkey, CEO of GEMS Education

"If you are willing to work hard, you're going to get rewarded here. You're going to meet a lot of likeminded people who share a similar outlook: success breeds success."

Dino Varkey currently serves as the Chief Executive Officer of GEMS Education, responsible for providing vision, insight and strategy across the organisation. Dino Varkey represents the third generation of an education family, driven by providing access to quality education for almost 60 years. His grandparents first came to Dubai in 1959 as English teachers and set up a small school in a villa. Now, GEMS Education runs 44 schools in the UAE and GCC, educating over 155,000 students, as well as schools in Europe, Africa, India, Southeast Asia and North America. Over 400,000 students have been taught at GEMS schools.

Dino is a frequent speaker and moderator at global conferences and gatherings. He is a member of the World Economic Forum's Global Future Council on Education, Gender and Work (2016 – 2018). He was also a Founding Board Member of the YPO Dubai Chapter.

Earliest Memories

When you get families that are multi-generational, especially when you've had very bold and courageous elders that have emigrated from their home county in order to make a better life for themselves and their community, almost their first memories of Dubai become your own, because it is so etched in how you are raised. I grew up with their stories of what life was like here. I think it's generational, and it's deeply embedded.

When HH Sheikh Rashid became Ruler of Dubai in 1958, he began to diversify the economy, and started to attract foreign investment and people. I think there was a very clear recognition that their people, their society would need to be educated, and at that point, there were people already in Dubai from India that supported the Ruler and the story goes that HH Sheikh Rashid said "I need somebody to teach my people English", and they said they knew a great educator, and that educator was my grandfather. So, he came out to Dubai in 1959, and my grandmother joined him in 1961. She travelled by ship was dropped off at the creek and she waded onto the shores of Dubai two years after to follow her husband. For them it was an important journey to make. We were educated but we were from a lower middle-class family in the South of India in the 1950s and there was really no opportunity there. They wanted to make a better life for themselves, and their children who they left behind at that time - my father was sent to boarding school at the age of 3 or 4.

They just started tutoring adults and children, so effectively think of them as the first educators of the community, that were recognized as the 'wise people', they would teach adults and children English and Maths. It was that simple. These are the two foundations you need. My grandmother used to teach the girls and they taught some of the very prominent families of Dubai, their children, people that are in positions of influence and power today. They had a real hand in helping them groom and develop and giving them the power of education. They were tutoring kids at people's homes, and then in 1968, they founded the very first school which still exists today: "Our Own English High School". Today the school has over 10,000 students in it, predominantly girls. The original school was in the Bastakiya.

My grandparents believed in the power of education and its ability to transform the lives of individuals, families and communities. They were Educators. They weren't necessarily business people. It was my father who saw the opportunity that the power of education has the power to transform nations and ultimately transform the world. Their underlying belief was entirely consistent – that has survived 3 to 4 generations, which I am incredibly proud of. It's not easy to retain or maintain purpose.

Journey

I was born and brought up here in Dubai. I went to prep school here in our schools and I left for boarding school in the UK just before I turned 11. Then on to Winchester College, to University, and I came back and started working in February 2003. For me the decision to join the business was a decision that frankly didn't take very long. I wanted to join a social enterprise and the nature of the work we do is – if we do our jobs right, we ensure we are giving our students not just qualifications but character as well. That is a big part of it for me. We'll be an incredibly powerful catalyst to improve the state of our world.

If you look at those that have passed through a GEMS school, we've reached over 400,000 students. That's an incredibly powerful community. I would hope those young people in whatever sphere of life they are going to be successful, they will do well for themselves, for their families, for their communities, for their country.

Founding Fathers

With HH Sheikh Zayed and HH Sheikh Rashid, and HH Sheikh Mohammed and the whole leadership, for me they epitomize the adage that "impossible is nothing". I see it from my father, and the most prominent leaders, the CEOs of this nation, because they've taken a cue from them, that everything is possible. I think the leadership of our nation has been remarkable. They genuinely love their people and their nation and wanted to create the very best environment and ecosystem for that to thrive. We are blessed with benevolent leadership that really cares about its people, that's few and far between today. That's the advantage we have.

Exponential Growth

For me, the exponential growth of the UAE is most evident when I compare it with my Grandparents hometown in India. I have just returned from a visit there, and it's been 18 years since I last went, and it's amazing to me how little has changed. It's still very sleepy, nothing has happened. Which is why you have this exodus of Indians that have come here and come to other parts of the world. For the 41 years I've been alive nothing has changed, period. And in comparison, to the last 40-50 years of what's happened in the UAE it's staggering.

We literally came from nothing. If you'd seen the home that my maternal grandparents lived in, these were quite basic conditions. It's staggering we've been given this opportunity. All we had was passion, ambition and humility. If you are willing to work hard, you're going to get rewarded here. You're going to meet a lot of likeminded people who share a similar outlook: success breeds success.

We've gone from one school to many schools, one student to 155,000 students in the UAE, and over 200,000 globally. When I look at the work of the Varkey Foundation, we've also impacted the lives of tens of millions of students. It's also given us as a family an opportunity to be able to scale impact beyond our own core business. From a philanthropy perspective, whether it's the Global Teachers Prize or the initiatives we've worked on with the foundation, it's impacted tens of millions of students.

As a family, we could have emigrated to the UK or the US, while we would have been in education, I'm not sure we would have been given the opportunity to have quite the same opportunity for scale and for this scale of impact, just because those markets are different. We just happened to come to a place where it was a city and a nation that was being built from the ground up and when you are part of the journey from the start, you suddenly find the opportunity to effectively build, alongside many others, the education infrastructure. If you just looked at the private schools, we're amongst the top 10 nations in the world. You're talking about a city that has built a world leading education infrastructure from effectively nothing. We're a big part of it but it's not just us. There are very few markets that compete as effectively in terms of education.

The UAE today is still the largest market in the world for private international schools, which is staggering. It's bigger than China! [The International Schools Market in the Mena Region 2021 Report, produced by ISC Research, found that the UAE has a total of 696,600 pupils in International Private Schools, with China in second place behind the UAE, with 419,000 children.] We are the largest operator in the UAE, which is why we can claim to be the biggest globally.

Secret of Success

For me it's that belief that "anything is possible" from the leadership, that impacts the business leaders and everyone living in the UAE. I used to have to help orient staff or senior leaders who joined the organization, and I said 'Look there will be moments where you think the parameters set by the Chairman are completely unrealistic or unfeasible, let's understand why he structures it that way, it's because by setting what you think is an impossible goal we will get further than perhaps we imagined we ever could." And that is a consistent theme, you hear HH Sheikh Mohammed do it. That's the cue. Set an audacious goal. It's our Leadership that truly, truly care about their people and their nation, and wanted to create the most amazing ecosystem and environment for their people to thrive. That's a big part of it. That has permeated the general culture of the nation. It doesn't matter if you are Emirati or not. There is this very clear culture and identity that the nation has developed across an incredibly diverse population group.

The UAE has created a culture of enterprise and innovation, hard work and passion, and rewards those things. It celebrates diversity, it always has because of its position, because it was a trading hub. These are all things that culturally, form the identity of the nation, whether you are an expatriate or an Emirati, they really ring true.

I think this is what the US must have felt like in the nineteenth century: Incredible diversity coming together because they believe in the same set of principles and the nation was conceived on these ideals that everybody believed no matter where they were from. There is an interesting analogy here: think about what the US was able to do in the next 100 years, almost galvanized by those ideals. Galvanized by those common beliefs no matter where they were from. You had a country that the world looked to for a very long period of time, and I think this bodes very well for the UAE for the future.

Challenges

I think the UAE's challenge is how do you sustain the economic momentum that still gives us the resources to be able to ensure societal success?

There are always challenges around being isolated – we're such a small nation. What I explain to investors, is if you look at Dubai and the UAE on the map, it's around what has historically been a "hot zone". However, I think we've been able to manage our place within that. I do think the geopolitics has changed. I think that's a big part of that.

I do think there is still an incredible amount of disbelief, and a perception issue in and around the UAE and how Dubai in particular is perceived. Mainstream media often portray the country with caricatures. This is a challenge – people don't get a sense about what this place is. I think for everyone, whether you're a teacher or a nurse, somebody who drives a taxi, for what you earn, you can actually have a really good quality of life, you can educate your children, you can access healthcare, you still have income to be able to support family members back home. It is amazing to me, no matter what strata you come from, there is choice. There is a good quality of life.

Opportunities

We're a pretty diversified economy and that diversification fundamentally leads to opportunity no matter which sector you're in. I think where it becomes interesting for companies is this becomes the most suitable geographic economic hub, given what's going on in the rest of the world, for companies and people who want to tap into economic or trade opportunities, whether it's with the East or West. The conditions and the environment that we've been given are only going to mature.

I think the regulatory environment and the economic environment is only going to mature, and that will enable the UAE to become such a compelling place that you can do anything you can conceive of.

The UAE also still wants to attract people that are really focused on exponential technologies. The ambition is there, the aspiration is there. The government has made it possible for us to develop that kind of ecosystem that is incredibly future-focused. It's only a matter of time. It's still relatively new in my opinion - food security, renewable energy for example. These are all things that the country is focused on. It will still take some time to mature but the direction of travel is positive.

Lessons

I believe some of the issues we see around the world are symptomatic of inadequate education provision. I think a lot of the challenges we see globally in and around political systems failings, democracy being challenged, is a function of people not being educated enough to recognize or realize that they are being manipulated, that policies are not necessarily serving them. So for me, the work that we do was always going to be a really powerful catalyst to change the world for the better.

I think in the UAE we don't have the same constraints in and around what other countries have in terms of bureaucracies or legacy systems that frankly don't enable things to get done or to get done efficiently. Here we have real accountability for delivery. For example, HH Sheikh Mohammed has run Dubai as close to a private enterprise as you can imagine. He absolutely holds people accountable. It's why they call him the CEO Sheikh. I don't see that accountability in other political systems around the world.

If I take a specific school example, we take it for granted that our kids have been effectively going back to school for a year and a half, when the rest of the world is suffering from the effects of Covid, where there is huge economic impact of learning loss, of kids being out of school or in school sporadically. I read that the impact is $17trillion in lifetime earnings. For the vast majority of the world, kids have gone backwards. Meanwhile, our kids in the UAE have been learning, and have continued to make progress. We've had two years of record-breaking results when the rest of the world declined. In other parts of the world they are still arguing about whether kids should wear masks or not, whether teachers should wear masks or not. Just getting kids back into school has become a political issue, and it's shocking. It's really sad to see. The nature of dialogue, speed of response, during Covid, I think the UAE did a remarkable job. All of the key stakeholders were actually talking and listening and designing the best fit. When the rest of the world has faced significant learning blocks, our kids continued to progress and we got record-breaking results.

Expo

Frankly this is the most important Expo that's ever happened. Taking place during a Global pandemic, it has genuinely been an opportunity to connect the world again. Through what is perhaps the most significant unnatural economic and social dislocation of our lifetimes. I think the real intrinsic opportunity to genuinely bring people together again and connect the world again, post this dislocation, makes it the most meaningful Expo ever.

Future

I can only see a scenario where the UAE continues to strengthen its position globally. It's going to be a place that has real meaning and influence, on a global scale. It's hopefully a nation that people will genuinely start looking to.

The future is difficult to forecast, but I think the UAE is still going to be a place of significant influence. I think the nature of the impact the UAE is going to have outside of the country is where it's going to be in 50 years.

I still think there's so much disbelief about what the UAE has achieved, and I think because of the perception issue people discount the achievements and accomplishments of the UAE. I think it's an interesting thing, when people actually come here and their eyes are opened. The impact the UAE can have for the world as a model for what is possible is where I think the real mark of the UAE will be. That I do believe. The way we make diversity work, the way we are able to collaborate, the way that you're trying to ensure that no matter who you are, you can live a happy life, you can pursue your opportunities. If you work hard you know you can be rewarded without fear of the system taking advantage of you. There's safety, security, you can practice your faith without fear of discrimination. It's amazing, you apply that to many parts of the world, and you don't have that opportunity. I genuinely believe that that opportunity exists here. It's not going to be handed to you on a platter, you need to be able to work for it. But if you do, I think there's real opportunity for reward and the ability to be able to live a happy and fulfilling life.

43. INVESTING IN TALENT

Homaid al Shimmari, Deputy Group CEO and Chief Corporate & Human Capital Officer of Mubadala

"For me, the future is not just about excelling within our borders but contributing positively to communities all over the world. We're a global player now; we'll be even more global in the future. The main driver is human capital, so our focus on people growth must continue as a priority."

Homaid is the Deputy Group CEO and Chief Corporate & Human Capital Officer of Mubadala Investment Company. He has oversight of Mubadala's Business Services, Enterprise Technology Services, Government Affairs, Construction Management Service, Employee Career Growth, Talent Acquisition, Learning and Development, Performance Management and Emiratization.

Prior to the merger of Mubadala Development Company and International Petroleum Investment Company (IPIC), Homaid was the CEO of the Aerospace and Engineering Services platform in Mubadala. His main focus was driving forward the strategic vision and plans for developing technologically advanced industries within Abu Dhabi and the UAE, in addition to ensuring Mubadala is well positioned to become a key global aerospace, ICT and Defence player.

Earliest Memories

One of my earliest memories is from kindergarten, when I first started going to school, the infrastructure wasn't really there. I remember running around the make-shift classrooms and that there was only one cold water cooler in the whole school. I would often skip class to go for cold water (not that I was thirsty) and I remember getting shouted at and told to go back to class.

This memory has always stuck with me and reminds me that the UAE came from very humble beginnings. When the first McDonald's opened in 1955 in the United States, the UAE didn't exist. When I was growing up, we had basic education, basic healthcare, basic infrastructure. We were given our first Government house in 1978, and it was a year before it had electricity and took two years, before we had the infrastructure of a road outside the front.

Here we are, 50 years later. In a short space of time, the UAE is one of the biggest economies in the region, our name is renowned for its advancements and as a center of innovation. We're known globally for helping to lift other countries up and we are influential in our own right. Tell me another nation that has achieved so much in only 50 years?

That, to me, is the essence of the UAE. I have watched its development and growth across education, healthcare, infrastructure, and the very landscape of Abu Dhabi. Alongside this, I have also witnessed how attitudes and values have expanded into a nation that is always giving.

That is the journey I have seen during my lifetime.

This is also the challenge I see today. How do we get our youngest generation to realize and understand that whatever luxury they are living in today, it hasn't come at the touch of a button? How do we get them not to forget that our way of life today isn't how it has always been so as not to take it all for granted? We need the leaders of tomorrow to understand and appreciate how we got here. We cannot afford to get lazy; it is important for the nation for us to champion the pace of change and growth.

We have to keep reminding everyone of what it was like in the 1960s and 70s, and the journey we have been on to get to where we are today. This will keep us grounded, keep us honest, and fighting for the nation's future.

We must continue to excel and grow and impress the world with our inspirational UAE story.

Journey

When I started my career in aerospace, engineering services and defense, I quickly developed a passion for building capabilities and competencies. This desire to help people reach their potential has always been with me, particularly during my time as a Lieutenant Colonel in the United Arab Emirates (UAE) Armed Forces.

I remember my father telling me, when I joined the military: "You are no-longer just my son, now you are the son of the nation, and you will always serve your country". This continues to stay with me, and throughout my career and my life, my belief has been to always serve the UAE and do what I can to help the nation grow and to achieve. Serving my country in the military instilled in me qualities, such as strategic thinking, planning, communication, accountability and responsibility for the chain of command that serves me to this day.

Now I serve my country by developing talent across Mubadala and setting a foundation for the future leaders of the UAE. This is something special for me – I am committed to inspiring and encouraging today's youth that will elevate our nation's growth and further progress our global story. This is what drives me and makes me most proud.

It gives me a great sense of purpose when you see people develop professionally and personally to reach new heights of accomplishment, and I see them serving their country and helping to build our future.

HH Sheikh Zayed

I never actually met His Highness but there are two stories about the late Sheikh Zayed bin Sultan Al Nahyan, that I always reflect on. First is one my father would often tell me. It was early in the nation's development, when my father went to His Highness to ask for a job and a house. He took my father's right hand in his own and said, "God created this earth in six days, when he could have created it in one second. He created it in six days to teach humanity patience, and you my son, should learn to be patient".

This really resonated with me, and still does today. I believe that one of our biggest flaws is impatience and some of the younger generations, more so than others, suffer from wanting everything immediately.

I also remember when a journalist said to Sheikh Zayed, "You give UAE nationals everything. Free education, free health, free housing. They are going to grow up and be dependent on you". He replied to the journalist "do you have children? Do you pay for their food, their clothes and their education?" His Highness went on to explain that there was no difference between him being a father to the UAE nation and the journalist being a father to his children. "These are my children; and this is how I look after them."

These are the stories that have shaped my view of Sheikh Zayed. He is this nation's father, and that is why we call him, 'Sheikh Zayed father of the nation.'

As our father, he symbolizes our history and our limitless future. He spoke to the older generation and those ahead. He was a visionary father figure to us all and he inspired me to push beyond the ordinary and do something meaningful. He motivated me to live my life in a way that helped me overcome individual pursuits to focus on other people and contribute to society for the benefit of us all.

Exponential Growth

In 50 years, the UAE has made significant leaps and bounds, allowing us to stand on the world stage as a peer and an equal. This has occurred for multiple reasons, ranging from our accelerated economic development to our technological transformation and commitment to become a knowledge-based economy and from our smart and agile government infrastructure to our religious, social and cultural heritage and values - such as tolerance, inclusivity and respect - which have drawn people from all over the world to come and call the UAE their home.

What has been achieved is nothing short of phenomenal and it is difficult to select one or two things that signify the UAE's exponential growth story. However, one of the accomplishments for me that epitomizes the UAE's unwavering spirit of ambition and growth is The Cleveland Clinic Abu Dhabi. Before Cleveland Clinic, the people of Abu Dhabi would have to travel overseas for complex medical care, but once His Highness Sheikh Mohamed bin Zayed Al Nahyan had the vision and drive to secure the Cleveland Clinic here, it was a game changer. Now not only do we have a world-class healthcare system, but one that attracts medical tourism from across the region.

Additionally, space science was unimagined for the Arab world a decade ago. The UAE changed that by rewriting history and bringing in the dawn of the interplanetary exploration age, as the Hope Probe reached Mars, marking the UAE as only the fifth country in history to reach the red planet and a first for the Middle East. I know His Highness Sheikh Zayed would be proud, for it underscored his unshakeable belief that nothing is impossible.

Secret of Success

The key ingredient in the success of the UAE is its Leadership. We have been blessed in this country with leadership that is a shining example for the region. There are many nations that have similar advantages and similar challenges as us – they have oil, are of a similar age, they have similar climates and deserts. But our leaders are visionary in their wisdom and their paternal view of this nation, and its people. This has also shaped my career and my success. I realized early on that I am a soldier in the Army of this nation. As the lesson my father taught me, my job is to serve the people and help and enhance this country. I have always put the benefits of the UAE ahead of any personal interests and that has helped to drive my career and the growth of the nation.

Challenges

The biggest challenge that we have overcome is attracting talent to support our ambition and growth. We are under no illusion here in the UAE. We are where we are because of exceptional people, who have contributed to our success.

We recognized early that talent attraction, development and growth are vital to Mubadala and to the UAE's key sectors. The establishment of programs including government accelerator programs, free zones, incentive systems, ease of doing business measures, golden visas and ecosystems, such as Hub71, Abu Dhabi's tech ecosystem, have all helped bring in new talent and provide opportunities to nurture existing talent and support ancillary businesses.

Opportunities

The focus on innovation and the undying quest for excellence in everything we do means that the business and people opportunities in the UAE are vast. While we have strong traditional sectors and champions of industry, the UAE is also a hub for disruptive startups that are challenging the status quo and reinventing the way in which we do things. This underlines the huge opportunities presented to us – whether you are an established company looking to expand in the Middle East or a startup that is seeking growth opportunities; whether you are a career professional rising through the ranks or an entrepreneur creating the next unicorn – the UAE is a place where ambitions can become reality.

With Covid-19, the digitization of industries accelerated rapidly and we saw a lot of overdue disruption across multiple sectors and companies. I'm seeing the huge potential in this disruption, particularly around everything tech be it healthtech, fintech, legaltech or proptech. Every day, new propositions are being introduced to the market, creating exciting opportunities for companies.

At Mubadala we've seen innovation and disruption across our assets, as they harness their adaptability to react to a changing environment. Strata for example, our leading UAE aerospace manufacturer, reacted to the Covid-19 pandemic and pivoted to producing high quality, N95, facemasks. Emirates Global Aluminum also recently delivered a world-first when they began using the power of the sun – something in abundance here in the UAE – to produce aluminum. These are both examples of the innovation and adaptable mindset of the nation, and more entrepreneurs and companies are coming here to tap into this vital resource.

This in turn creates huge opportunities for people, whether in established industry or in the innovative startup scene. In terms of Mubadala, we have several initiatives in place to foster, nurture and develop talent such as a Train For Work program for young Emiratis, mentorships and workshops in partnership with other entities and an Emiratization program. For instance, over 1,500 young Emiratis have been trained by us since 2019 and are now in work.

Separately, due to our focus on encouraging female talent as part of our youth outreach program, we saw a 13 percent increase in female joiners between 2019 and 2021. Young people – irrespective of age, experience or gender – have an opportunity to make their mark in whatever they choose to do.

Lessons

I think partnership is something we can all benefit from. As we were developing our 2030 Strategy, we looked to other countries to learn from them and build their experiences into our own local plans and vision. We have looked to countries like Singapore, the UK and South Korea and took their lessons to build our own future.

Our vision has driven us to succeed, but nothing would have been possible without hard working and talented people, who each in their own way contributed to our growth story. There's a big lesson in setting long-term visions and breaking that down into more manageable annual plans. Our Founding Father had a vision to unite the seven Emirates. The UAE's leadership today, has a vision to become a destination for both work and leisure which is supporting economic diversification.

Along this journey, what has helped is speed and agility. When things need to get done, we don't let bureaucracy get in our way; we make informed decisions quickly; and, if things need changing, we adapt and change accordingly.

Expo

Expo 2020 has an abundance of opportunities for all those attending to build relationships and understanding, facilitate trade and business, and create collaborative initiatives that are going to help solve tomorrow's challenges. Visiting the different pavilions, the eclectic nature of the world is striking. What we have essentially is all the world gathering in one space to discover together, develop awareness and forge new relationships. It's a melting pot of ideas and I'm confident that it will give birth to a host of new possibilities.

While there is of course a business angle to Expo 2020, we are encouraging businesses from around the world to also come and discover the expansion opportunities that exist in the UAE. For me, Expo transcends financial and economic motivations. I would be proud if anyone visiting the UAE for the first time sees the UAE as not only a land of opportunity but also appreciates our Emirati culture, values and heritage. We are hosting and showing our hospitality to the world and in doing so we are displaying our humanity, tolerance, peace, and generosity.

The UAE has always welcomed people from other nations, and many have been instrumental in helping to build the country throughout our history. Recently, a street in Abu Dhabi was named in honour of the late Egyptian engineer Abdul Rahman Makhlouf, who helped to design the capital city, and the landscape many of us call home today.

We are also a nation that is looking to make a difference in society at large, be it through efforts for a more sustainable environment, our social infrastructure of diversity and inclusion and our commitment to lead by example with integrity which are core elements of our Emirati identity and a source of pride.

Future

It is hard to predict what the UAE will be in the next 50 years, but as a nation that continues to evolve and grow at an accelerated pace, I predict we will pave the way for innovation, dynamism and development at every level. Aligned with our Founding Father's vision, we are looking ahead to the next 50 years determined to grow in influence, further contributing not only to our prosperity but the success of the world. With this in mind, the UAE recently made a clear statement of intent with the Principles of the 50 and Projects of the 50, which charted the strategic roadmap for the next five decades. We are resolute in building the best, most dynamic and sustainable economy, pushing the boundaries in our sectors, and creating global leadership in digital, technology and science, the disciplines that will help shape tomorrow. This will need greater levels of efficiencies, with a more entrenched role for Big Data, AI and robotics in our lives, and in helping to solve global challenges.

For me, the future is not just about excelling within our borders but contributing positively to communities all over the world. We're a global player now; we'll be even more global in the future. The main driver is human capital, so our focus on people growth must continue as a priority. As part of this, our continued focus on human fraternity, humanitarian aid and support for our fellow human beings will continue to be driven by our global friendship and in the spirit of peace and harmony.

44. FUTURE FOUNDATIONS

HE Khalfan Belhoul, CEO of Dubai Future Foundation

"The fast pace comes from the founding fathers, and they set the pace for everyone and its now in our DNA."

Khalfan Belhoul was appointed as the Chief Executive Officer of the Dubai Future Foundation (DFF) in February 2018. DFF was launched by HH Sheikh Mohammed bin Rashid, to play a pivotal role in shaping the future of Dubai. Prior to his current role, Belhoul was a Vice President of Strategy at Dubai Holding, where he was responsible for formulating Dubai Holding's strategic direction and enhance its investments and its role in the diversification of Dubai's non-oil economy. Before joining Dubai Holding, Belhoul played a key role in setting up the Belhoul Investment Office, responsible for rolling-out a sophisticated asset allocation strategy spanning private equity, alternative investments, real estate and conventional assets. Khalfan holds a BSc in Finance, M.I.S. and a Masters in Ecommerce, all from Boston University.

Earliest Memories

My earliest memory is kicking a football against the wall of our family home in Al Hamriya. My parents would be really upset as I'd leave dusty football marks! I think it was a 1982 World Cup ball, about 5 years old. I lived there until 1990, just after Italia '90. You can tell I have always liked football!

I studied at Al Ittihad school, close to our home, until 5th grade, then Rashid School for Boys in Nad al Sheba. It was founded in 1986 and funded by the Royal Family of Dubai. There was an amazing, diverse mix of students. Many of the current government leaders are all products of that school, and we have all known each other since then. A group of us are all part of the board now and trying to keep that beautiful mix of students and instill the same leadership attributes.

Journey

I went to Boston University, came back and then worked for my dad for 13 years, setting up our family office, investing primarily in healthcare and education. My involvement with the Government was completely unplanned. It took one conversation with the Vice-Chairman of Dubai Holding at the time in 2013, who wanted me to come and join him. He wanted me to do essentially the same thing that I had done for my family, but with Dubai Holding on a much larger scale. I asked my dad and he said "when your government calls you must go" and I said "am I fired"?! Seriously though he said it was a great opportunity and I just signed the contract straight away.

I was introduced to the Dubai Future Foundation (DFF) at its birth in 2016, when I helped set up and subsequently ran the Dubai Future Accelerator programme. There were lots of synergies with Dubai Holding and DFF and I ultimately transitioned to DFF.

DFF is an entity, or as I like to call it, an engine and incubator that is mandated to enable every facet of Dubai's society and economy, be it the public or private to preemptively embrace emerging opportunities, be skilled for future economic sectors, and be above the curve when it comes to technological and non-technological disruptions and future trends. Sheikh Mohammed once said, "The future is not built on possibilities and numbers but on clarity of vision, planning, action, and implementation." DFF was established to play a pivotal role in shaping the future of Dubai through our three main pillars: Imagine, Design, and Execute. Our role is to two-fold, catalysing sustainable progressive change, and being Dubai's flag-bearer for societal, technological and economic innovation, be it through our own direct activities or those which the foundation incubates and transfers to the optimal future owners.

We inspire others through our proprietary foresight and research activities and draw together local and global thinkers, visionaries, practitioners, and special interests' groups to ideate opportunities that propel Dubai and the world towards the future. One of the ways we do this is through the production of visions of the future, such as the Future

Opportunities Report, issued annually, which leverages the insights of industry pioneers across geopolitical, technological, environmental, and human behavior trends, to identify the most pressing and significant opportunities to be considered by governmental and private sector decision-makers in the next fifty years. Most of the opportunities are geographically agnostic, however, often the foundation takes the lead to design Dubai's strategic response, incubate and execute relevant initiatives and programs.

The world today as we see it is witnessing rapid changes across all sectors and industries, the future can be lived and foreseen right here in our present. With the legacy of our forefathers, and in line with the vision of our leadership, Dubai has long realized the significance of keeping pace with the future and making the best of technological, societal and regulatory innovation to shape a better future.

This is the core of what Dubai Future Foundation represents; the tangible outcome of this vision to define the future in the present.

With this mandate, the Foundation has within a short period of time established a robust view of the future, through our extensive internal foresight activities and knowledge networks, which have created world-class innovation platforms for ideas to take shape, established strategic partnerships both locally and globally and has managed to foster an environment that encourages and recognizes creative minds from around the globe.

Guided by a strategic roadmap, and through collectively imagining, inspiring and designing Dubai's future, the Foundation, in collaboration with the government and private entities, seeks to position Dubai as leading city of the future.

With a focus on the most pressing opportunities and challenges for Dubai and the world, through its activities spanning research and foresight, incubating projects which challenge local and global norms, showcasing the future (through the Museum of the Future), investments in early stage disruptive ventures, and its own applied R&D lab, Dubai Future Foundation continuously works towards achieving its vision and goals of placing Dubai and the UAE as the world's platform of for understanding and creating the future.

HH Sheikh Zayed

HH Sheikh Zayed's wisdom, communication and the way that he

treated people comes to mind. HH Sheikh Zayed and HH Sheikh Rashid also thought like entrepreneurs. If you look at the country, they made big bets. They had a star they wanted to reach to.

Exponential Growth

In 1970 an airport was commissioned with a sand runway, and in around 60 years, this airport became the world's busiest. In 1961, a full decade before the UAE was formed, Khor Dubai, or the Dubai Creek, was dredged to allow larger vessels in to welcome the world. In 1979 a gateway hub and a global trade link of the world is born in Dubai: Jebel Ali Port became the largest man-made port in the world, connecting global markets and facilitating trade.

The fast pace comes from the founding fathers, and they set the pace for everyone and its now in our DNA. This is now enshrined in the Dubai Future Foundation. Dubai 10X is an example of facilitating exponential growth, which has been designed to positively challenge every government entity to think outside of the box, disrupt their existing processes, and design a better future within their sector. Our vision is that Dubai achieves today what other world cities will implement in 10 years. In just 365 days, 36 entities made more than 160 propositions, of which 26 have been approved. For example, one of the 36 participating entities is KHDA, which is disrupting the schooling and education sector through a system in which a student is no longer confined to a physical space in a school. KHDA has now launched a pilot project called "Rahhal," which was founded on the idea that the world is one big classroom. It is a customizable platform that aims to turn any organization into a learning provider, and to turn people into lifelong learners.

Secret of Success

The entrepreneurial mindset. Big bets, gutsy decisions and belief in the people. Taking well-studied risks. For me personally, I'm fortunate to be in a diverse culture throughout my whole journey. I think this has really helped my communication and understanding of all different sorts of people. You can be the smartest person, but if you can't communicate or get your point across, it is lost.

Challenges

One of the biggest challenges is our neighbourhood – it's tough. We are a small country, but we have humungous ambition! This challenge is even more important going forward. The Fourth Industrial

Revolution also accelerates some challenges, as well of course providing opportunities.

Opportunities

We need to always grow our ecosystem, so the country will always look to attract more people and companies. We want to create an enabling platform for businesses to thrive. In particular, the need to enable new business activities based on agile regulations emerged to accelerate innovation and its application throughout all sectors. In January 2019, we launched the regulation lab (RegLab), a revolutionary approach on behalf of the UAE in the legislation and application of emerging technologies. The lab works closely with regulators, the private sector, innovators, and business leaders to co-create legislation that is in step with innovation speed. Regulations passed too early may stifle new innovations, while those that come too late may have already negatively impacted people and markets. That is why RegLab works in the regulation space to align regulation speed with innovation speed. RegLab was launched as part of the UAE's pathway to becoming a global innovation incubator and a testing ground for future technologies and their applications shaping human life and activity in the future, such as mobility, health, 3D printing, AI, and more.

Lessons

I think the strong message of collaboration is an example for the World. Our intent is peace and collaboration. We want to put our people and their health and well-being as our priority.

EXPO

EXPO is a small example of what the UAE is all about. The UAE naturally has all the nationalities represented by the country pavilions at EXPO. It is all about unity and collaboration. There were a few doubters out there that thought EXPO would not succeed, but it has. We have silenced the doubters.

Future

You need to go to the Museum of the Future! There are two variables: the further you look into the future (i) the more unknowns there are, and (ii) the bigger the unknowns can be. That said, we try and shape what the UAE and the World will be like in 2071 through our own Area2071, a physical and digital ecosystem that supports public and private sector disruptive collaborations and experiments. Area2071 is strategically linked to the UAE's Centennial Vision 2071. It aims to solve challenges for the next billion people by producing system-level, disruptive questions, and experiments. The solutions to these questions are co-created through collaborations with a wide ecosystem of public and private x-labs, startups, accelerators, incubators, venture capital, and academia.

45. FUTURE FORESIGHT

Dr Noah Raford, Futurist-in-Chief & Chief of Global Affairs at the Dubai Future Foundation

"The magic of the UAE is at its finest when improbable connections come together to create something incredible, in exactly the way you always dreamed of but never could have predicted."

Dr Noah is responsible for identifying emerging opportunities, strategic projects and future initiatives, as well as leading the Dubai Future Foundation's thought leadership and global partnership activities.

Earliest Memories

My first memories of the UAE began, appropriately enough, in the Rib Room at Emirates Towers. I was a baby strategy consultant, fresh off the plane from London, about to pitch my first project to the UAE Prime Minister's Office. I didn't realise at the time, but this building would become my home, my family and much of my world for the next 12 years (and counting).

Everyone you needed to see, every conversation you needed to have, and everything you needed to do was contained in Emirates Towers. Celebrities mixed with politicians, inventors with investors, citizens with expats and friends with executives; all coming together in that vertical village to haggle, laugh, brainstorm and create the future.

There were days back then when I couldn't even make it to my desk. From the parking lot to the elevator, a chance meeting at Starbucks (now Flow) would lead, time and again, to a ground-breaking new project, soon to be launched by His Highness Sheikh Mohammed, often in the blink of an eye. Whether it was testing the UAE's first drones in the parking lot (surrounded by peacocks) or the construction of the world's first 3D printed building (and now, the creation of the Museum of the Future), Emirates Towers was where it was at.

Like Dubai, the building and its grounds have changed quite a bit since then, but the spirit of those 12 years lives on. The kitchen of the Rib Room is gone, making way for a pedestrian bridge to the Museum of the Future. The Persian carpet shops, cigar stores and luxury antique shops have given way to Area 2071, the Dubai Future Accelerators, and dozens of start-ups. Hakkasan transformed into an Avengers-like robotics facility for the Dubai Future Labs and is now home to the UAE Minister of State for Artificial Intelligence and the National Program for AI.

Despite these changes, Emirates Towers still represents a rare and special blend of political possibility, entrepreneurial spirit and human warmth - a blend which embodies the spirit of the UAE to me. Like the UAE as a whole, it's not only a place where magic happens and dreams come true, but it's a place where friendships are formed, relationships grown, and lives are lived, together - all with a sense of comradery, humanity and smiles.

It's not always easy, and not all of these relationships stood the test of time, but I've been lucky to call Emirates Towers home for all these years. During that time I've had the privilege of working on dozens of extraordinary projects and initiatives, but it's the friendships I've formed and the relationships I've had that stick in my memory the most. These, more than anything, are the real magic of Dubai.

Journey

I started as a strategy consultant in both Abu Dhabi and Dubai in 2010, but joined the UAE Prime Minister's Office as a full time advisor in 2011. I've been privileged to work under His Excellency Mohamed Al Gergawi for that entire time, first at the PMO (with Her Excellency Ohood Al Roomi), briefly under The Executive Office and then helping to establish the Dubai Future Foundation, where I currently serve as Chief of Global Affairs and "Futurist in Chief".

Dubai has always been a city of the future, but the period from

2010 to 2020 is considered to be the decade when Dubai formalized its relationship to the future and institutionalized the spirit that drove its growth. I've been lucky to play a small role in some of the initiatives that helped shape this time, from the very first Museum of the Future exhibit at the World Government Summit in 2014, to the world's first blockchain strategy, the first 3D printed building, the most successful government accelerator and now, the iconic permanent Museum of the Future at Emirates Towers.

The thing I'm most proud of, aside from the tiny role I've played in helping deliver His Highness Sheikh Mohammed's vision for Dubai, are the many deep and long-lasting friendships I've developed here. Dozens of friends and former colleagues are now Ministers, CEO's or Chairpeople, in dozens of industries and sectors, throughout the UAE. From sharing coffee and brainstorming PowerPoints together to seeing them on stage at Davos or launching global initiatives, this has truly been one of the most fulfilling parts of my time in the UAE.

HH Sheikh Zayed

When I first started to get to know the UAE, what struck me was the connection with the original vision of the Founding Fathers in the United States. Indeed, the idea of a federation of colleagues, voluntarily bound together to create a common destiny, was a key part of His Highness Sheikh Zayed's vision.

The UAE isn't just a political union, however. It is also an idea that expresses Emirati and traditional culture in a profound way. The American values of individuality and self-determination gave that union its own unique character, but Sheikh Zayed's values of tolerance, respect, and care for family, tribe and community have shaped the UAE in a very different way.

Instead of shaping a nation based solely on the idea of individual success (often at the expense of community), the UAE's vision recognizes our fundamental interconnectedness, our obligations and debts to our ancestors, to our families and to future generations. It is fundamentally an Arab view, connected to the land and culture of the region, which has always been a deep tapestry of relationships, cultures and points of view.

From opening up his treasury when Sheikh Zayed was made

Ruler of Abu Dhabi to the UAE's historic welcoming of talent and opportunity, the Founding Fathers of the UAE have demonstrated a commitment to taking care of people, on a personal level, in a relationship driven, multi-generational way. That character, combined with a sense of daring, ambition, and willingness to try new things is what set the tone for the UAE's development.

In the long run, the idea of a political institution based on relationships, interconnectedness and shared destiny may be one of the Sheikh Zayed's lasting contributions to the world. He reminds us that there is more to life than just profit and that, in the words of His Highness Sheikh Mohammed bin Rashid, "nothing is impossible." No matter who you are, where you are from, or where you began, a better future is possible for us all, but only if we work together.

Exponential Growth

The story of the Museum of the Future is what represents the UAE's exponential potential to me. Exponential growth is when something that starts very small multiplies and becomes something huge in the blink of an eye.

As many people know, the Museum started in 2014 as a tiny experiment inside the World Government Summit. It was a test, an experiment, a risk; a new way of doing things that had never been done before, (not just in Dubai, but ever, in the entire world). Leadership took a shot at trying something fresh and brought in the best teams and resources to make it happen. Thankfully, it was a big success, so next year they doubled it in size. Not just a small improvement, but literally doubled the size. Then we doubled the next year and took over an entire small island at Madinat Jumeirah conference centre.

From there, His Highness had the idea to turn the approach into a permanent institution, so he created the Dubai Future Foundation (originally called the "Dubai Museum of the Future Foundation") to realise this vision. It was intended to be a home for labs, incubators, accelerators, think tanks and training facilities, as well as experiences of the future.

While we were planning the building, we started testing out the activities that would go inside it. Each of these started small, then doubled in size again and again until they became institutions in their own right. We launched the Dubai Future Accelerators, the Dubai Future Academy, One Million Arab Coders, 10X and so much more. The Foundation actually grew faster than the Museum itself, launching dozens of historic initiatives and projects. Meanwhile, the Museum of the Future is now a gleaming, iconic building on the side of Sheikh Zayed Road just in front of Emirates Towers.

None of this could happen so quickly in most other countries. It shows how the UAE's leadership is willing to take chances on small experiments with big potential, test them, scale them, then scale them again. This is the spirit that drove the growth of Dubai and helped position the UAE as one of the most successful countries of the 21st Century.

Secret of Success

The magic of the UAE is at its finest when improbable connections come together to create something incredible, in exactly the way you always dreamed of but never could have predicted.

There are a hundred examples I could share about this, but one that stands out for me is when we were building the very first Museum of the Future at the World Government Summit. One of the exhibits required a "Pepper's Ghost" hologram technique that needed specialized screens which were unavailable in the UAE. It was still very hard to find people who knew how to use this technology at the time, as well. We commissioned a firm in Italy to produce it for us, but with only weeks to go to the opening, they were unable to finish and pulled out.

In a panic I started asking everyone I knew if they knew anyone who could help. Someone recommended someone, who recommended someone else, but it was a long shot and they only lived in Dubai part time. I hastily called them and luckily they were in Dubai at that time. 48 hours later, I was sitting in the Burj Khalifa, overlooking the Fountains, waiting for this man to arrive. Not only did he know about the technology, it turns out, but he was also one of its original inventors!

I couldn't believe our luck, but of course it wasn't just luck. There are very few places in the world where you can test new ideas and ambitious concepts at such a scale. If you're passionate about your work, you want to be where you can test them out. This is especially true for emerging technologies and new ways of doing things. The UAE has always been that kind of place – a place which attracts idealists, innovators and passionate inventors looking to make it big. This, in turn, increases the odds of such serendipitous events.

With a handshake and a proposal, in less than two weeks, we had our new system design, all the right technology and were building our experience just in time for the opening. That dream of being the first, of attracting talent, and for creating the environment which connects dreamers and doers is, to me, one of the secrets behind the UAE's success. Leadership creates the vision and conditions, which attracts the people who want to make it happen, and the rest, as they say, is history (or the future!).

"Dream no small dreams," said Goethe, "for they have not the power to stir men's souls."

Challenges

I'm not in a position to describe the extraordinary challenges which the Emirates has overcome in its past, but I have often experienced challenges related to international stereotypes about the UAE. Most people don't know the UAE's history or what it is really like here. All they know comes from the media, which is why they are often surprised and delighted when they actually come visit.

I experienced the limited effects of these stereotypes directly for the first time years ago. I was presenting the details of Dubai's 3D printed "Office of the Future" at an international architectural conference and, after my talk, the CEO of a large 3D printing company came up to me. I thought he wanted to discuss the project but instead, he said, "I don't believe a word you just said." This was shocking, so I asked him what he meant. I had literally just given a 30 minutes presentation on how it was built, with pictures, videos and floor plans and everything. "I know," he replied, "but I think you're lying." This kind of closed mindedness was stunning, but it also made me realise how the idea of a futuristic, successful, visionary Arab state can be challenging for some.

My bosses taught me that these misconceptions can become an advantage, however. His Highness Sheikh Mohammed always says to never compare yourself to others. Focus on what is possible and work hard to take advantage of your opportunities. Underestimating what the UAE is capable of serves to filter out those who don't believe in the future, while selecting those who are willing to try new things. This leads to a higher than usual concentration of dedicated people who are willing to aim for the stars which, in turn, leads to a greater chance of achieving extraordinary things.

In the end, these stereotypes and this approach end up working to the UAE's advantage. Instead of trying to argue why they are wrong, it has proven a winning formula to actually just do great things instead. Actions speak louder than words.

Opportunities

The UAE serves a global market but most of its trade is regional.

While the UAE may be high tech and futuristic, many of our trading partners in the region are still grappling with basic needs. Half of the world lacks access to basic healthcare, over 600 million people lack adequate housing and 40% of those living in Asia lack regular access to clean water. Food and water security are a major issue and basic services like electricity, sewage and public safety are often inadequate. While there is still tremendous opportunity for serving the global luxury market in and from the UAE, the real opportunities lie in addressing these classic development problems but with a 21st century approach.

How will this be done? The world often looks to companies like Amazon or Apple as examples of 21st century innovation. Before COVID, however, e-commerce only represented less than 10% of total retail sales in the US. After COVID, that rose to around 14%, but retail only represents about half of all consumer spending. There are trillions of dollars in consumer spending which hasn't even been touched by digitization, virtualization or roboticization in any meaningful way, especially in emerging markets.

This represents a historic opportunity for value creation. Climate change, inflation, state failure and market collapse will only enhance this opportunity. Tomorrow's successful companies will be those which make a meaningful dent in basic human needs but do so in digital, automated or distributed ways. Whether in housing, energy, commerce or transport, there are still vast fortunes to be made providing better services which improve people's lives around the world.

The catch is that most of this must take place in regulated sectors. If you're growing a business like this, you have to have regulatory support. That is why the UAE is such an attractive place. It offers a testbed for 21st century solutions with flexible regulations, accommodative governance and visionary leadership. The technology may be invented and developed elsewhere (for now, although this is increasing rapidly in the UAE as well), but there are very few places that can compete with the level of leadership support, market access and quality of life that the UAE has to offer.

That is why the future is full of opportunity for businesses focusing on these goals; improving people's lives in regulated sectors using 21st Century tools, techniques and approaches.

Lessons

The major lesson of the UAE is that anything is possible. The second, more subtle lesson comes from how to achieve this. Of course it all comes down to leadership first. The UAE's leaders have a management style that is unlike anywhere else I've ever worked. They don't just plan for the future and set inspiring, ambitious targets; they also create the conditions to achieve them.

This sounds easy but it's actually quite hard for governments to do. When I first moved to Dubai I couldn't figure out how things worked. Why were there several teams working on the same goal, often in competition with each other? Why not just streamline things and have one office or team per project? Why invest in all projects which didn't seem to succeed? How could a seemingly chance meeting end up in a major new project or strategic approach?

Over time, I realised that this is part of the UAE's genius. It is an extremely sophisticated response to fast moving change. It's not based on predicting the future, committing all your resources to one plan and then hoping things don't change. Instead, it's a strategy developed over time for dealing with lots of uncertainty, rapidly changing conditions and fast moving competition. At its heart, it is a strategy which is forward looking but tactically opportunistic. It is based on sensing change, identifying opportunities in real time, and then taking advantage of them to actually *create* the future you want.

This may actually be the only way to succeed in a fast and rapidly changing world. While some experiments fail, it is far more efficient to focus on identifying opportunities through action-oriented experiments that teach you what will really work, then leveraging these experiences as fast as possible to gain competitive advantage. Instead of studying every aspect of a problem and waiting until you understand it before acting, it is far more intelligent to take many, small actions and learn directly from experience. You learn about a problem faster, and in more detail, than any analytical exercise could provide. And the best way to do that is by running many small, often competing, experiments at once.

This is how design works and it's also how the most successful venture capitalists work. Most governments are culturally unable to operate this way, unfortunately. The UAE excels at this because it balances flexibility and entrepreneurship with stability and responsibility for the public. While it may seem wasteful when you look at it from the outside, it is actually the only intelligent approach to investment when everything is changing all at once.

The results speak for themselves. As the rest of the world begins to grapple with the effects of exponential change, governments will need to relearn how to operate on this model. Thankfully, there are many lessons from the UAE which can help.

Expo

The biggest takeaway from Expo is what it represents for the changing world order. It's remarkable that Expo is being hosted in an Arab country for the first time. What the Expo team pulled off, in the face of COVID-19 and a global recession, is truly extraordinary. But the real take away for me is the fact that it is the first ever Expo, in the history of the world, where every participating country has its own pavilion.

This may seem like a small thing, but is actually huge. It demonstrates two things; first, the UAE's understanding of and appreciation for emerging economies, the Global South, and the developing world. Second, the overall shift to a multipolar, multicultural and multiracial world and how we might live in.

We all know 85% of the world's population lives outside of Europe and North America. Yet these two regions still dominate global attention. Beneath this, however, the world is changing at an ever faster rate. The fastest growing populations are in Asia and Africa and most of fastest growing cities in the world are within an 8 hour flight of the UAE. These markets represent where the future is heading. They look different, think different and have different needs.

By celebrating this fact, Expo2020 has positioned itself as the first truly global Expo. The UAE not only supported and celebrated the many players of tomorrow's world, but also *paid for* many of these pavilions, as well. This demonstrated a profound understanding of the way the world has shifted and a deep respect for the global community. It embodies the UAE's approach to building partnerships and creating opportunity for everyone, regardless of their religion, nationality, or skin colour. Yes, it is an expression of Emirati hospitality, but more deeply, it also expresses the UAE's view that we all share this world and must learn to live together. That, I believe, is far more significant than it may seem on the surface.

Future

Let me start with the global picture first. Climate change is accelerating rapidly and will be worse than anyone wants to admit. This will cause unprecedented levels of stress to every aspect of society, infrastructure, government and the economy. At the same time, the world has printed more money in the last few years than in the entire history of the world. As of 2021, there are over $300 trillion dollars of debt outstanding. This will lead to inflation, currency devaluation and financial crises over the next 5 to 10 years. The combination of historic levels of stress and what will become many government's inability to pay for adaptation will produce additional crises, resulting in large scale migration and possible armed conflicts towards the middle of the century. Finally, during all of this, digitisation and virtualisation will continue its exponential march through every sector, resulting in large chunks of the economy either evaporating, moving to virtual worlds, or transforming dramatically.

We are already at the beginning of this period and the opening act will last anywhere from 10 to 20 years. The effects of climate change will continue to be felt well into the 22nd Century, but the combined stresses of climate, finance and technology will be felt much sooner. While scary, they will also open up new opportunities for growth.

Different countries and regions will respond in different ways. Countries such as the UAE, who have a flexible and change-oriented approach coupled with good governance, modern infrastructure and sustainable natural resources will be able to absorb these challenges and convert them into opportunities. Others which lack the ability to change, have greater infrastructure and other forms of debt and fewer sources of income, will have a much harder time.

The UAE is well positioned to succeed in this world. It has the vision, resources, talent and drive to do what is necessary to navigate the transition. As a result, it will likely emerge as an even stronger global leader, not just by pioneering solutions to its own challenges, but by creating and scaling solutions which help the entire world. As we move beyond the "transition decades" of the mid-21st Century, the UAE has everything it needs to achieve its goals for the next 50 years, then to play a major role in the stabilization and reconstruction of a better future for us all.

46. ENGINEERING THE FUTURE

HE Sara al Amiri, Minister of State for Advanced Technology and Chairwoman of the UAE Space Agency

"We are relentless in the pursuit of our ambitions to shape a competitive national economy based on knowledge, innovation and future technologies, which merge physical, digital and biological spheres"

HE Sarah bint Yousef Al Amiri is the UAE Minister of State for Advanced Technology and Chairwoman of the UAE Space Agency. In her role as Minister of State for Advanced Technology, her Excellency spearheads the UAE Ministry of Industry and Advanced Technology's efforts to empower the adoption of Fourth Industrial Revolution technologies and promote research and development in the advanced science and technology sector, to create new industries that drive the shift towards a knowledge-based economy. This, in turn, contributes to the overall mandate of the Ministry to strengthen the UAE's industrial base, ensure in-country value, and raise the competitiveness of local industries.

As Chairwoman of the UAE Space Agency, Her Excellency is responsible to oversee the Agency's mandate of pioneering the space sector, ensuring its contribution to the national economy and to the UAE's sustainable development. Her Excellency is also the Chairwoman of the Emirates Scientists Council.

Prior to her Ministerial role, Her Excellency was the Director of Research and Development at MBRSC, where she established the Centre's Knowledge and Research Department and put in place product assurance and functionality systems. She was also involved in DubaiSat-1 and DubaiSat-2, and the project development for KhalifaSat. She was also the Deputy Project Manager and Science Lead of the Emirates Mars Mission prior to her appointment as the Chairwomen of the UAE Space Agency.

In 2014, Her Excellency was tasked with and led the establishment of the Advanced Aerial Systems Program, where she championed development efforts on a prototype High Altitude Pseudo-Satellite. The project resulted in a successful 24-hour flight of the unmanned vehicle, which recorded the highest altitude of any unmanned aircraft over UAE airspace.

In 2015, the World Economic Forum honored Her Excellency as one of its 50 Young Scientists for her contributions to science, technology, and engineering. In 2019, she was selected as one of the World Economic Forum's Young Global Leaders.

She has been named in Time magazine's 2021 Next 100 Most Influential People in the World, as well as receiving in 2022 a TIME100 Impact Award: a recognition of leaders who, through sustained effort, have done extraordinary work to shape the future of their industries and the world at large. She also appeared on the BBC 100 Women list in 2020.

Earliest Memories

The "Volcano Fountain" in Abu Dhabi on the corniche. It was a fond meeting place. Now it has been replaced with greenery, but it reminded me of simpler times. I used to go there with my father and brother, and race him to see who could get to the top first.

Journey

I moved to Sharjah when I was 17 to study at the American University there. When I was there, I got a slightly obscure email from the Emirates Institution for Advanced Science and Technology asking for computer engineers. Unbeknownst to me, it was the Space Programme, and that entity was to become the Mohammed bin Rashid Space Centre. I began working there in 2009, two months after graduating, as a software engineer. When I first started working there, Dubai Sat 1 was done as far as production, but we were awaiting a launch date, which happened in July that year. I worked there for a number of years on various satellite projects.

A few days after the UAE won the right to host Expo, We got a call from the Prime Minister's Office to look at the feasibility of sending a probe to Mars. This project became the Hope Mars Mission, the first uncrewed, interplanetary satellite spearheaded by the UAE, and the first planetary science mission led by an Arab-Islamic country. The UAE purposely set lofty goals for the project, which was designed in part to mark the country's 50th anniversary. The Hope spacecraft launched successfully on July 20, 2020 aboard a Japanese rocket and arrived successfully in orbit around Mars on Feb. 9, 2021. We have made discoveries that have made real contributions to the scientific community.

It was a really tough project, and now I talk about there being "Life after Hope!"

HH Sheikh Zayed

I remember seeing him from afar when he returned from surgery in the US in 2002. There was a huge "welcome back" bouquet. He was truly a fatherly figure. He was nurturing and aspirational. It's actually more than "hope". Hope can imply an element of luck. He symbolized a realization of dreams.

Exponential Growth

Growing up with stories about how life was in the 1950s and 1960s, it was just such a stark difference. It's just such a complete transformation in one generation. To build the country as we have, would have seemed unrealizable and unobtainable, but we did it. Imagine telling someone in 1971 what we would have done in 2021. Roads, hospitals, schools. The Hope project is a symbol of everything that we did. It was a series of daring projects and programmes. Very risky at several points. We couldn't fake it: it was either going to work or not.

In 2021, the UAE launched the 'Operation 300bn' strategy to position the country as a global industrial hub by 2031. It sets out to increase the industrial sector's contribution to the local gross domestic product (GDP) from the current Dh133bn to Dh300bn – that's trying to double it in the next 10 years.

Secret of Success

The secret is genuinely leadership. The world might look at this form of government as different from what they know, but the more I work with the leadership, I realise that the more daring programmes are decisions from the top. The leadership has often ignited some of the big projects, including the Mars Mission. This was not even on our radar of something that was possible or probable. The leadership had had a retreat and they decided that going to Mars in our Golden Jubilee year will mark the start of our next 50 years. The rest is history!

Challenges

Personally, delivering the Mars Mission was a huge mission. The method we did it was different from how missions have been done. However, we had a highly collaborative team, and a great program director that brought us all together to achieve the goal of getting Hope to Mars.

More generally, in the MoIAT, we work together to define our challenges and find solutions to them. Only through doing so can we build the UAE's credibility as a pioneer of innovative solutions, expand its digital infrastructure and create the opportunities that will make our future a prosperous and inclusive one.

Opportunities

There are too many to list!

To continue moving in the right direction, the MoIAT is encouraging businesses in the UAE to adopt cutting-edge technologies, align with best international practices and accelerate the transition to clean and sustainable industries. We have incentive programmes and access to capital. The priority areas are Oil & Gas, plastics, metal, pharmaceuticals, food production systems, healthcare, space and biotech.

Our next stage of growth requires seizing new opportunities. We must design and action plans that can further enhance collaboration among all government entities.

Lessons

I'd say there are so many components to the UAE that they are hard to convey and replicate. For me the one takeaway is that there is no one blueprint for success. You can see how something was done, and learn from the decision-making process, the pitfalls and challenges.

Expo

I go to Expo a lot for meetings but it was only a few weeks ago that I realized the massive impact that Expo will have, and that's when I took my children. My son is almost 12 and my daughter is 5. Seeing two young Emirati kids, going through Expo, at their ages, and seeing how much they learned in just 5 hours, how much they're talking about it 2 weeks later. That's when I realized how it will impact even just the children in the UAE. It is so unifying. It's such a transformative experience that our country will go through.

Future

Our trailblazing team at the Ministry of Industry and Advanced Technology is moving into the future with agility, confidence and clarity of purpose. We intuitively understand the correlation between investing in an advanced R&D ecosystem and further enhancing our national capacities with future-focused skills. As such, we are pushing the envelope of scientific discovery. Raising the bar of advanced technology adoption. And equipping future generations with the tools to take on tomorrow's world. We believe that doing this will significantly boost the UAE's global competitiveness. It will generate new levels of in-country value. Enable pioneering industrial development across the value chain. Forge new economic sectors. Fortify our supply chains. And reaffirm our status as a global leader in industries of the future.

Through our work, MoIAT is shaping future-focused sectors by leveraging Fourth Industrial Revolution (4IR) solutions, making the UAE a regional vanguard of the digital era. To further accelerate our efforts to lead the pack, we established a national plan to ensure greater cooperation and support for our partners and stakeholders in the industrial sector. Together, we will ignite innovation in our thriving industrial landscape and energize our commercial production capabilities.

We are working tirelessly to enhance the UAE's position as a global 4IR leader. We are relentless in the pursuit of our ambitions to shape a competitive national economy based on knowledge, innovation and future technologies, which merge physical, digital and biological spheres. And, through it all, we are aligned with the UAE's Strategy for the 4IR which seeks to establish the nation as a global paragon of proactively preparing for future challenges through the adoption of Industry 4.0 technologies and tools to better serve society as a whole.

We have set out on this bold journey of discovery by supporting national applied research endeavors and building frameworks and systems to advance the industrial sector. Our goal is to realize the vision of our leadership: to position the UAE as a global industry leader and boost its competitiveness. In 2071, I see us being a truly Global country.

47. MOONSHOTS

HE Salem AlMarri, DG of the Mohammed bin Rashid Space Centre (MBRSC)

"The UAE leadership is dedicated to big objectives and achieving them in record time, often in a way that hasn't been done before."

His Excellency Salem AlMarri is the Director General of the MBRSC and is responsible for ensuring the success of various initiatives within the UAE National Space Programme, including Mars 2117, Emirates Lunar Mission, UAE Astronaut Programme, and the UAE Satellite Programme. AlMarri also oversees the expansion of the MBRSC into new scientific and technical fields alongside ensuring continuing developments in the space sector.

With over fifteen years of experience, AlMarri has been an integral part of the teams that set up both the Emirates Institution for Advanced Science and Technology (EIAST) in 2006, which then merged under the umbrella of the Mohammed bin Rashid Space Centre (MBRSC) in 2015. He was one of the first engineers to form the core of the Knowledge Transfer Programme based on an agreement with South Korea's Satrec Initiative.

AlMarri received the UAE Pioneers Award in 2014 for being the first project manager of the UAE satellite projects Dubaisat-1 and Dubaisat-2. He has represented the UAE and the MBRSC in over 50 international conferences worldwide and has been a returning member of the delegation to the United Nations Committee on Peaceful Uses of Outer Space (UNCOPOUS).

AlMarri was the head of the bidding team that won the rights to host the International Astronautical Congress (IAC) in Dubai. He chaired the local organising committee (LOC) for this global event that was held for the first time ever in an Arab country.

Earliest Memories

I'm 39 going on 40. I grew up in Dubai and it was a much smaller city in the late 80's. I grew up as it was transforming into a global city. Fridays were extremely quiet. Five dirhams in those days for a taxi would take you anywhere!

Journey

I loved doing things with my hands: gardening and doing woodwork with my dad who used to do carpentry at home. We used to take things apart and then build things. When we had our first computer, we did the same, which got me wanting to be an engineer. In terms of space, "I'm a Trekkie!" I watched ***Star Trek*** and ***Star Wars*** growing up and loved Captain Kirk. When I graduated, I worked in telecoms on a satellite programme that eventually became Dubai Sat 1 under what was then called the Emirates Institute for Advanced Science and Technology that morphed into the Mohammed bin Rashid Space Centre, so it wasn't clear cut from day one that we were going to be headed for Mars! The second I heard "satellites and space" being mentioned together, I was in, and went to South Korea for about five years to learn how they did it. Now as DG, I have a big responsibility to drive the MBRSC forward. What we have achieved at both the MBRSC and as a country in such a short period of time puts a lot of pressure on us moving forward towards the next 5 years!

HH Sheikh Zayed

From a personal perspective, when I think of HH Sheikh Zayed, I think of his kindness and generosity.

From a space perspective, I have been wanting to achieve Sheikh Zayed's ambitions for space. If we did, that's something I would be proud of. The fascination for space in the UAE dates back to when the country was first formed, which incidentally coincided with the space race. Just a few years after the first lunar landing, the Apollo 17 mission's American explorers met with Sheikh Zayed and presented him with a piece of Moon rock. A popular Time magazine photograph shows Gene Cernan, Ronald Evans and Harrison Schmitt explaining the details of the shuttle and the mission to Sheikh Zayed while he listened intently to them. That meeting laid the foundation for what the UAE as a spacefaring country has achieved today.

Exponential Growth

From pearl diving to the discovery of oil and gas to exploring space, the UAE has emerged as a progressive country and a leader among nations with all that it has achieved, and what it is still trying to accomplish. For the MBRSC, we started with modest beginnings 17 years ago. We began with Earth observation projects and then moved to space observation, then human space flight, which are all huge steps forward. Now we will be landing a rover on the surface of the Moon that is designed and built here in the UAE.

Secret of Success

For me the secret is having a very strong vision and direction, and a "can-do" attitude. The UAE leadership is dedicated to big objectives and achieving them in record time, often in a way that hasn't been done before.

Another element is hard work and dedication. Everyone here works overtime and all the time! That wasn't necessarily the case 20 years ago. People are challenged and inspired.

The exemplary vision of the nation's forefathers has been carried forward by its citizens, enabling the country to excel in many domains, and catapulting the UAE into a lofty position on par with progressive nations today. As the country marches towards its Golden Jubilee this year, celebrating the past 50 years, it also looks towards a vision of growth, prosperity and unity for 'the next 50.'

Challenges

Space has many challenges! We learned from other countries' challenges and mistakes. This enabled us to grow quickly. We didn't want to reinvent the wheel.

Opportunities

The UAE has had one of the most efficient responses to the pandemic. From nationwide testing to the sterilisation drives and being one of the most vaccinated nations in the world, the country has not only helped curb the spread of COVID, but also allowed the Emirates to become a healthier nation that has become a sterling example for the world in effectively facilitating a return to normalcy - from trade, tourism, events and day to day life. This has created a platform for people to come and seek better opportunities. The way that we do things provides a lot of opportunities.

In the space sector, we have many projects in multiple fields, transforming the UAE into global a space hub. Anyone that wants to do anything in space is welcome here to speak with us and work with us. There are a lot of joint opportunities. I see the sector, doubling, tripling even in the next 5 years.

Lessons

The main lesson is that the UAE is very welcoming. We attract and invite great minds to come and connect. We have a global village in one country. As the UAE matures as a nation, we can hopefully export our model and ideas to the region and the world.

Expo

I loved the Expo. I go there every week with my kids. On a personal level, my kids are learning, finding out about the countries they have never heard of before, trying new food, new experiences. On a business note, we at the MBRSC have benefited immensely as astronauts and delegations from different parts of the world came to visit.

It is only fitting that world class events like the Expo 2020 Dubai and the 72nd International Astronautical Congress have found their home here. Both events were held on Middle East soil for the first time ever. While the Expo 2020 Dubai is a reflection of the cosmopolitan, multi-national city that Dubai has transformed into, the hosting of the world's premier space event speaks volumes about the extraordinary achievements that the UAE has achieved over its young history in the sector.

Future

In 50 years, I'd like to see more cities in the Arab world progressing based on the UAE's experience.

In terms of space, I'd like to see more growth. The UAE is currently in the process of building the first Arab rover to land on the Moon, aptly named the Rashid Rover, after the builder of the modern renaissance of Dubai. The Emirates Lunar Mission is an ambitious national project, which hopes to reinvigorate Arab scientific renaissance in the region and consolidate the gains made by the UAE in the space sector over the past decade.

Other strategic programmes in the field of space for the coming decade include sourcing new and unique scientific data from the Hope Probe that will be accessible to more than 200 academic and scientific research institutions around the world. The UAE is also home to the Mars 2117 Programme, which will utilise the latest human knowledge to explore space, while the satellite development programme will help increase the efficiency of the satellite network and locally developed advanced space technologies.

So back on to the Moon and Mars!

48. GIANT LEAPS

Hazzaa Al Mansoori, UAE's First Astronaut

"I applied for the program because I had a dream as a boy and our leaders encourage us to achieve our dreams."

Hazzaa Al Mansoori made history as the first Emirati to be deployed on a space mission to the International Space Station (ISS) on 25th September 2019 aboard the Soyuz MS-15 spacecraft. During his mission aboard the ISS, he conducted 16 scientific experiments. Six of these experiments were conducted in microgravity to study the reaction of vital indicators of the human body aboard the space station, Brain DTI, Osteology, motor control, time perception in microgravity, fluidics (fluid dynamics in space), and DNAm-Age. The scientific mission included experiments involving universities in the UAE as part of the Science in Space initiative of the Mohammed bin Rashid Space Centre (MBRSC). His Highness Sheikh Mohammed bin Rashid Al Maktoum, Vice President, Prime Minister and Ruler of Dubai, said "Hazzaa Al Mansoori's entry to space sends a message to the Arab youth that we can march forward and keep pace with the rest of the world." HH Sheikh Mohamed bin Zayed Al Nahyan, Crown Prince of Abu Dhabi and Deputy Supreme Commander of the UAE Armed Forces, said on the day, "Today, we celebrate the historic flight of the first Emirati astronaut to the International Space Station. An Emirati achievement we take pride in and dedicate to Muslim and Arab nations."

Hazzaa was born on 13th December 1983 and graduated from Khalifa University. His combined passion for astronomy and his country led him to join the UAE Armed Forces. He became an outstanding military pilot, the youngest to fly the UAE Air Force's F-16B60, one of the world's most advanced aircraft. He has more than 14 years of experience in military aviation, participating in the 2017 National Day air show and the 2018 50th Anniversary of the UAE Armed Forces celebrations. He also took part in Exercise Red Flag, in which the best pilots from the USA, NATO and allied countries perform realistic air combat exercises.

Earliest Memories

I'm from Liwa, right in the middle of the desert, in the Rub al Khali, the Empty Quarter. I thought I was maybe less fortunate growing up away from the city, as it was a quiet, simple life, like many of my ancestors before. We had a farm with a lot of camels. I spent my time sitting around the campfire, looking at the stars. Our ancestors used the stars as a navigational tool and that influenced my interest in astronomy. I saw a lot of cartoons and sci-fi movies as a kid. I really wanted to be an astronaut, but everyone said it was impossible. I was told many times to stop dreaming.

Journey

Growing up in Liwa, I also saw fighter jets flying overhead, and I spent my time trying to catch them on bicycles. I didn't think I'd be able to go to space, so I decided to become a fighter pilot. I got my degree in aviation science.

Until 2017, I was just focused on being the best father and fighter pilot I could be, then I heard a rumour that the UAE was going to run an astronaut programme. I always spoke about space and that year I went to the Dubai Airshow and went up to the booth of the Mohammed bin Rashid Space Centre to find out more. On 7 December 2017, HH Sheikh Mohammed bin Rashid al Maktoum tweeted, "Our ambitious goals are fueled by dedicated people, who support us until, without hesitation or skepticisms, we succeed. I invite young Emiratis to register for the UAE Astronaut Programme through the Mohammed bin Rashid Space Centre."

"Wow!", I thought, "It's happening." Without any hesitation I applied and sent my resume through the website. We went through a screening test – there were over 4000 applicants! The main thing was that I had to get permission from my wife and my mother!

In September 2018, HH Mohammed bin Rashid Al Maktoum tweeted that I and Sultan Al Neyadi had both been selected. I went to

Moscow, to Star City, where the first cosmonauts trained. They were speaking Russian and we had an interpreter. We trained for one year. Our objective was not just to travel to space but to participate in different space experiments. After training we flew to Kazakhstan, two weeks prior to launch. We were in quarantine for two weeks. Launch was 25 September 2019.

On the day of the flight, I just kept my focus on all the instruments. Three of us together looking at all the levers. As I heard the countdown, I recalled the picture of HH Sheikh Zayed, the tweets, the journey, the pride in my kids and the whole nation.

Once we were in space, I was just looking at Earth 200km below and I saw the curve, the glow, the atmosphere. I just thought "Wow! We're floating!". I just felt amazing appreciation for my parents and our leaders for the opportunity to reach this important milestone, in my career and in my life.

My first call from the ISS was with HH Sheikh Mohammed. He said, "Impossible is not in our dictionary. Yes, you are the first. After you, there will be a lot of people following in your footsteps." I spent eight days onboard in total.

HH Sheikh Zayed

HH Sheikh Zayed planted the seed of space travel when he invited NASA astronauts to the UAE. They came in 1974 and 1976 and they spoke to him about space. They took a UAE flag to space and they gave him some moon rock. Two years ago, I spoke to one of the astronauts from that visit. He told me that of all the world leaders he'd met, HH Sheikh Zayed asked the most questions. Sheikh Zayed had a vision and interest in the space sector, and maybe a dream that the UAE will have astronauts, and that dream has come true.

Exponential Growth

When I was a kid, I was always talking about space, I thought it was impossible. At flight school I gave a presentation about space shuttles in 2003. Everyone laughed. I didn't let it go. No one is laughing now!

Secret of Success

Our leadership looks ahead to the future. The secret of our space programme's success is the leadership and the people. Our people are very ambitious. We always want to explore and travel. It's in our genes as Bedouins. We are a young country and very ambitious.

HH Sheikh Mohammed bin Zayed was the first to welcome me at the Abu Dhabi airport. He was there with a lot of kids. They all said, "Thank you Hazzaa for making our dreams possible." We called it "Mission Possible". We have since visited a lot of schools to hopefully inspired young people. The UAE provides a stimulating environment for young people to make achievements in all areas, thanks to our leaders.

Challenges

One of the biggest challenges was to show people we were serious. Now they know we are.

Opportunities

Last year we hosted the International Astronautical Congress, which is proof for everyone how the UAE has now become a leading nation in the global space sector. We did a lot of collaboration and agreements, for example the Artemis Accords.

This has been like the Apollo flight for the Arab world. There was a human element after the flight, it was different than just a mere probe. We had the eyes of the kids on us. We now have two of our astronauts training at NASA. By focusing on the space sector there will be a waterfall effect on other aspects of the economy. It directly helps us further our knowledge and innovation. This will help focus on the jobs for the future. I think the space sector is giving us new opportunities in different fields.

Lessons

The UAE is an example for other countries in the Arab world in terms of setting objectives and collaboration. What I realized in space was that there are no borders between countries. We achieved this amazing feat aboard the ISS laboratory by working together: astronauts from Russia, the USA and the UAE. We had one goal, to explore. When I reflect, our leadership always promotes tolerance and partnership. By working together, we can do amazing things.

Expo

We held Space Week at the Expo 2020 Dubai, where we had a lot of astronauts and cosmonauts from Japan and from other countries around the world. They were amazed at how we managed to convene everyone.

Future

Our badge said number one, and that means there are many more missions to come. In the near term, the Moon Rover is launching later this year. In 50 years, we're going to be even more focused on space, and our leadership is giving us the tools and the opportunities in this sector. In 100 years we're going to send people to Mars!

49. CREATING THE FUTURE

HE Reem al Hashimy, Minister of State for International Cooperation and **Director General of Expo 2020 Dubai**

"The seeds have been sown for a beautiful garden. We are not complacent about how much effort it will take to make the garden grow, but we are all driven by the vision of the beauty that is to come."

Her Excellency Reem Al Hashimy was sworn in as Minister of State for International Cooperation in the UAE's Ministry of Foreign Affairs and International Cooperation in 2016. Since her first ministerial appointment in February 2008, Al Hashimy has managed the Office for Political Affairs of the HH Sheikh Mohammed bin Rashid Al Maktoum. She is also the Chairperson of Dubai Cares, a philanthropic organisation launched in 2007 and dedicated to improving access to quality education in developing countries.

As Director General of Expo 2020 Dubai, she led the UAE's successful bid to become the first nation in the Middle East, Africa and South Asia region, to host a World Exposition. She currently serves as the Managing Director for the Expo 2020 Dubai Bureau and is a member of the Higher Committee of Expo 2020 Dubai, under the chairmanship of His Highness Sheikh Ahmed bin Saeed al Maktoum.

Earliest Memories

My earliest memories are of home. It's such a stark contrast now with when I grew up. Our home in Jumeirah was so far off the highway that we'd have to take a dirt track. We'd be in my mum's car, wobbling away with no paved road to our little plot.

The pace of change from a physical infrastructure perspective is probably the memory that sticks out the most. That image of the Trade Centre on Sheikh Zayed Road, the 'Lone Hero' on its own, without anything else around it, you'd be looking at this white rectangle in awe and wonder. Now it's dwarfed by everything around it.

I remember National Days being a big deal. We always used to find red, green, white and black hair clips, bracelets and clothes at home to wear on 2nd December each year. I remember distinctly each anniversary of National Day and how our neighbourhood would change over time. Each summer we'd come back from holidays, and even having been away only a short time, we'd notice the changes: a new road, a new building, a new park.

Journey

I earned a BA in International Relations and French from Tufts University and later graduated with a Masters from Harvard University and a PhD from Tsinghua University. On returning to the UAE, I was initially appointed to work in HH Sheikh Mohammed bin Rashid's office. My task was to look at ways in which the city could be more competitive and resilient, to attract the best talent and ensure that we are always striving for excellence. At that time, we didn't have the DIFC or some of the other landmark projects in the city that you would recognise today.

Afterwards I was appointed as a diplomat to Washington DC and became Deputy Chief of Mission. I was still in my twenties and I was looking at how the UAE would negotiate a free-trade agreement with the USA. I then moved from the Ministry of Economy to the Ministry of Foreign Affairs in Washington and looked at different policy areas beyond trade. I was appointed a Minister in 2008, initially a Minister of State without portfolio, and that's when I worked on IRENA and Ministry of Energy portfolio, before 2016 when I was appointed Minister of State for International Cooperation.

My Expo journey began with a single phone call from HH Mohammed bin Rashid in 2011. It was late one evening and I remember it very clearly. He said "we would like to bid for Expo." I said "how can I help?" He said "well, you're going to lead it!" And now, a decade later, because of His vision and leadership, here we are sitting in a new city.

HH Sheikh Zayed

Sheikh Zayed is everyone's father, and the symbol of the values of this nation: of compassion and tolerance, of kindness and inclusivity, of strength and solidarity, determination and ambition. First and foremost, he recognised that investing in people's welfare, knowledge, and capabilities produces the greatest dividends for individuals, families, and society as a whole. This vision underpins our work both at home and abroad.

His principles also drive our relationships all around the world: Sheikh Zayed understood the value of reaching out across cultures and continents to embrace those who could be friends and partners. He sought nations developing in parallel to ours, those with similar experiences that might inform a brighter shared future. And as he conceived our nation, he extended a hand of kinship to many countries represented here at Expo today.

Every one of us remembers where we were when Sheikh Zayed passed. I was in Washington DC. Sheikh Zayed was so central to everything we were striving for that we couldn't believe he was gone. Yet his legacy inspires and informs us every day: we work to the values and principles he set out to create the very best future that we can, today.

Exponential Growth

In the UAE we constantly strive for "exponential everything". You can see this by looking at everything we have done in just one generation, achieving massive leaps in government services and empowering government employees with the skills to accelerate progress. It means we all embrace technology and future foresight, placing agility, risk-taking and the ability to embrace change at the centre of our thinking.

For example, we have our Government Accelerator Programme in Emirates Towers, and HH Sheikh Hamdan bin Mohammed bin Rashid Al Maktoum, Crown Prince of Dubai, has instigated the Dubai 10X programme. From the UAE Economic Vision 2030, to the Emirates Science, Technology and Innovation Higher Policy, which launched 100 initiatives with major investments in education, health, energy, transport, space and water, to Dubai's 3D Printing and Autonomous Transport Strategies, to the National Innovation Strategy and most recently the UAE Net Zero by 2050 Strategic Initiative, all of these and more are helping to create the perfect environment for the exploration and application of new technologies and solutions, the adoption of which is accelerated by our world-class infrastructure and fast-moving transition to a digital-focused, knowledge economy.

Secret of Success

There is no secret. We have clarity of vision. Holistic, fully engaged stakeholders and government teams working together. Hard work, and a lot of grit. It's constantly uphill and that's where two of our national attributes are particularly useful: courage and ambition. We lead by example, push new boundaries, and explore new frontiers.

I think people from all over the world recognise this, and it's part of what draws them here. We offer everyone the chance to be the best they can possibly be, and we offer this country as an incubator and accelerator of new ideas and innovations, a testing ground for scalable solutions that will get us to where we need to get to in terms of our relationship with each other, and with this planet.

We have done this for 50 years: offering a place where people can come and work through the changes and advancements that will unlock new opportunities globally. And we're doing it again now, supporting those who come here, offering a place to work and play and grow, whether that's through responsive and adaptable government legislation, or world-class infrastructure, or a standard of living conducive to personal growth and mental wellbeing.

Challenges

Given our geo-strategic position and the confluence of ideologies in the region, we have had to navigate a careful path to ensure stability, security and sustainable growth. It hasn't been easy, and with wealth comes great responsibility, not just to provide for the people, but to provide for causes according to our firmly-held values and principles. That's why we get engaged with the likes of IRENA and COP: so that we can make a contribution to the pursuit of solutions to global challenges, issues that no single nation can solve, but which will require sophisticated and impactful international cooperation.

Of course, in recent times we have faced a more immediately obvious challenge with the onset of the pandemic. At Expo, and in the wider UAE, our priority was always the health of all citizens, residents and visitors, while at the same time finding a way to move forward safely and responsibly. The challenge was to rally large and complex teams around a common cause in a fluid and changing environment. Yet that dynamism is a part of who we are and what we have been doing for the last 50 years. I think the international community recognised this and rallied around this idea, ambition and expectation.

We are flying the flag for the Arab world. This is the first time in the 175-year history of World Expositions that an Expo is being held in the region and we feel that responsibility. We can't just have a great event, our children would never forgive us. Because Expo isn't just about putting on a show: we're also asking people to think about the kind of world they want to live in.

This is the first global mega-event of the COVID era, and as a consequence the eyes of the world are upon us: people want to know that they can still come together safely, and celebrate, and have fun as well as learn new things about and from one another. And they want to know how they can be active participants in the making of a cleaner, safer and healthier future for people and the planet.

This is what we do every day here in the UAE, which is to chart a path forward for human development: scientifically, socially, and in so very many ways. And so at Expo we are representing not just ourselves, or our families, but this nation and the spirit of this nation.

Opportunities

New technologies are rapidly transforming all aspects of societies, sectors and markets across the world, and the UAE is very well positioned and equipped to create new value in this sphere. I'd emphasise also that the opportunities for the UAE are not just within the parameters of our borders. The UAE is a platform for a much larger region: situated within an eight-hour flight of two-thirds of the world's population, it's a cross-continental gateway perfectly positioned to access new opportunities at a time at which the global economic landscape is being reimagined to meet the rigours of a pandemic world.

Established industries, and centres of industry, are being disrupted and displaced by those bold enough to push boundaries and embrace systemic, generational change. And we are uniquely positioned to reconnect the business world and present exciting avenues for growth in both new and established markets.

Lessons

You can't underestimate the value of trusting your leadership. There is a deep trust between the government and its people, as reflected most recently in the Edelman Trust Barometer 2022 which ranked citizens' trust in their government as the highest globally.

Expo

There was the foresight 10 years ago to say, "when we turn 50, let it be with the whole world present." And yet this is not our first opportunity to welcome the world; far from it. Dubai is already a city of more than 200 nationalities, and over the course of the last half-century the UAE has fulfilled an invaluable global role as a convener of different cultures, a link between vast and diverse continents, a dynamic and energetic hub enabling the free and fruitful exchange of centuries of ideas and innovations. As such, our Expo theme of 'Connecting Minds, Creating the Future', is something we have been doing for far longer than we have been planning this event.

This thought inspires me in my hope that Expo will continue to live in the collective consciousness of the people of this country and region. If it lives on, it's because it reinforced the values of the UAE, chief among them the pursuit of human dignity and progress for all. This goes to the heart of how we view the world around us: not rich and poor, developed and developing, but human, and welcome.

Future

At Expo we have always said that we are building the city of the future, one that just happens to be hosting a World Expo for the first six months of its life. And this is what we have done: invested in the Dubai 2040 Urban Master Plan, the UAE *Centennial* 2071, and beyond. Expo is a milestone in the history of the UAE, but this is not a new era. Rather, it is the continuation of a trajectory that was set more than 50 years ago: one of responsible and sustainable growth and development. The seeds have been sown for a beautiful garden. We are not complacent about how much effort it will take to make the garden grow, but we are all driven by the vision of the beauty that is to come.

50. AN ACCELERATING FUTURE

HE Mohammed Al Gergawi

"We want to build something beautiful in a mad crazy old world"

HE Mohammed Abdullah Al Gergawi became the Minister of Cabinet Affairs of the United Arab Emirates in 2006. He oversees the development of the federal government strategy, supervising its implementation, aligning efforts to achieve the objectives of the UAE National Agenda, as well as ensuring the highest level of government performance and efficiency across all sectors.

He is the Chairman of the Executive Office of HH Sheikh Mohammed bin Rashid Al Maktoum, Vice President and Prime Minister of the UAE and Ruler of Dubai; the strategic think-tank focused on the development of Dubai and the delivery of His Highness' strategies and initiatives. Al Gergawi is also the Deputy Chairman of the Ministerial Development Council (MDC) and the Deputy Chairman of the Emirates Investment Authority (EIA). In his capacity as Chairman of the Emirates Competitiveness Council (ECC), Al Gergawi oversees advancing the UAE's position on the global competitiveness indices across all sectors.

Al Gergawi formerly held the position of the Secretary General of The Executive Council of Dubai, which leads the strategic planning and implementation of Dubai's economic and social development. He is also Founding Chairman of the Young Arab Leaders (YAL) and the Secretary-General of the Mohammed bin Rashid Global Initiatives (MBRGI), a philanthropic foundation that combines under its umbrella over 30 humanitarian and developmental initiatives and entities. He managed the inception of strategic projects in Dubai such as Dubai

Future Foundation (DFF), Dubai International Financial Centre (DIFC), Dubai Internet City (DIC), Dubai Media City (DMC), and the Dubai Media Inc (DMI).

At the regional and international levels, HE chairs the Board of Trustees of the Arab Government Excellence Award. He is also the Co-Chairman of the Global Future Councils launched in collaboration between the UAE government and the World Economic Forum (WEF). Al Gergawi was chosen as a member of the High-Level Panel on Digital Cooperation, a panel of independent experts advising the United Nations' Secretary-General on technological developments and technology-related issues.

Earliest Memories

I was born in 1963 and grew up in the Deira area of Dubai. My father was a merchant, born in the souk. I know every alley in Deira! I was always embedded with the merchants and businessmen. My first school was there on the beach. In winter the shamal wind whipped the sea up to the school door. Life was simple but beautiful. Beyond our houses, we could see the white sand dunes.

After the Union in 1971, I remember carrying the flag on the visit of Jaafar Nimeiri of Sudan. Our whole School was there to receive him, we waved the flags enthusiastically, and it was the first time that I remember our flag, the symbol of unity. After that I played volleyball for the National team and wore the flag with pride on my chest.

One of my first memories was driving from Dubai to Abu Dhabi then Al Ain in 1969. It was a week's trip! We had two open-topped land rovers. There was basically no road. We went from that, to uniting the Emirates, and 50 years later we went to Mars! This is the real human journey that we have undergone. We went from no road to the furthest place humanity can reach. This shows the ability of human beings, the story of Humanity, of progress.

With the right leadership and environment, humanity can thrive. We now live in the most globalised place on earth. It doesn't matter about nationality, race or religion, it is about what you are adding to life. We have shown that with tolerance for each other, people can live together harmoniously.

Journey

After secondary school, I went to study Business Studies in the USA. I came back in 1987, where my career started when I joined the United Nations Development Office in Dubai Municipality where I worked for a number of years. In 1993, I joined Dubai's Department of Economic Development as Director of the Department of Finance and Administration.

I led the launch of the Dubai Quality Award in 1994. I was still young at 31. In 1996, I oversaw the launch and management of the Dubai Shopping Festival and the Dubai Summer Surprises, aiming to boost the tourism and retail sectors during the low summer season.

I became director of business registration at DED at that time. I was thinking of leaving to go to the private sector a year or so later and I suddenly received a letter from HH Sheikh Mohammed saying I was promoted to the second in command in DED. This was totally out of the blue, and of course I then wanted to stay. In our culture, the proper thing to do was to go to Sheikh Mohammed's majlis to say thank you, but I was nervous to do so and kept pushing it back but my mother kept insisting I should go.

I waited another month as I still wasn't sure but my mother said I must go, so I went to the old majlis in Zabeel. I didn't know the formality. A man I recognised ushered me over and said to come and sit with him. Each person sat next to Sheikh Mohammed to take their turn to speak. When the next man finished, my friend pushed me forward and I sat next to Sheikh Mohammed. Although I had been around him in the past, I didn't know him. I had prepared what I was going to say: I said simply something along the lines of "thank you, and I promise to deliver for you" and then I got up to leave but Sheikh Mohammed grabbed me by the arm and pulled me back. This surprised everyone in the majlis. Sheikh Mohammed drew me close and said "Mohammed I know everything about you. I've been following your progress!" I was shocked. The next thing I knew was that he sent for a man called Me'dad. Me'dad took his time to come to the majlis. When he arrived, he stood in front of the whole majlis. HH Sheikh Mohammed said "tell us the story about when you met Mohammed al Gergawi"

Now, When I began as Director of registrations, I had potentially a lot of power in the business community. Early on in my new role, an elderly man walked to my office who I didn't know and he said: "I knew your late father Abdullah al Gergawi. My son, the chair that you're sitting on, is like a barber's chair, there'll be a lot of people sitting there". His point was that I shouldn't let this go to my head. I felt like it was like a message from my father. I can't even remember the man's face but his message resonated and for me it was very important that I didn't change as a human being in my new role.

When I had been setting up the Dubai Quality Award, I had studied closely the Japanese Quality Model. I liked the way they approached things and symbolic for them was always that you should meet people on the same level. I removed my desk and replaced it with a small round meeting table, so that I'm equal to the person I'm sitting with. Also, I started spending more time on the operations floor. I was there greeting people, enhancing processes, just sitting there making sure that people got their licenses issued. Me'dad had been a "mystery shopper" and had seen this and went straight to Sheikh Mohammed and, unbeknownst to me at the time, said "I have found you a Minister".

Sheikh Mohammed that day gave me a small project that I completed the next day and I went back, then he gave me a slightly bigger project that I completed and went back, then slightly bigger and so on - it's been 25 years!

HH Sheikh Zayed

When I think of Sheikh Zayed I think of his wisdom. Arabia has always been a home for philosophers and wise men, and this is personified in our Founding Fathers. The UAE was established because of visionary men who wanted more than anything to provide a decent life for the people of that land. It is with this value and this vision that the UAE continued this journey, and continued to achieve everything that it has achieved today.

Exponential Growth

I think the extraordinary growth that we have seen can be witnessed in the improved government processes over the years, and the culture for change. Sheikh Mohammed every year announces the top-rated government entities... and the worst. I got all the blame from those ones selected as they thought it was me choosing them! We saw an administration revolution. No one wanted to be in the bottom category. This drives growth for the whole country.

Secret of Success

The secret of success is very hard work. You balance this with your heart: with good intentions. You don't just work for yourself; you work for a higher cause. You need to also be courageous, and agile.

Challenges

The challenges make us what we are. They are tough but can give you the ability to fly. We live in a tough neighbourhood: being part of a region is a daily challenge. We want to be a beacon of hope for the region. We believe that we in the UAE and in Dubai have a mission. This region needs a puller from its misery. There is tremendous conflict. There is a lot of hatred, sectarian war, religious war, ethnic cleanses, refugees. We see the story. Then you come to Dubai. We want to make heaven on earth: to create a beautiful place, where life is good.

Opportunities

We are in the business of building a nation. When you are building a nation you can give people their calling in life. We want to enhance life and be a model. Our job is to help people and elevate them. We want to build confidence.

Lessons

In today's world, governments cannot create the future on their own; it is important to involve everyone including the private sector, the youth, international partners and others in creating policies.

We're not perfect and will never be perfect but always we'll seek perfection. This is our philosophy and what we strive for.

Expo

Fifty years ago we looked at the world, now the world looks at us. They see the creativity here. We are holding the World Government Summit at Expo. The missions of WGS and Expo 2020 Dubai are seamlessly aligned. We seek to enhance the participation of countries around the world to shape a future of shared prosperity and opportunity. We are seeking to build better governmental, economic, social and technological structures that support our global ambitions. We are connecting the world's greatest minds to create the future we all want.

Future

We can glimpse the future through the Museum of the Future which reflects the philosophy of Sheikh Mohammed and embodies concepts we have championed over the years.

Allow me to summarize this reflection in seven points: First reflection: The Museum reflects His Highness' passion for the future. Sheikh Mohammed taught us that understanding the future and envisioning it before others, generates the greatest opportunities and impels nations towards development. His Highness envisioned Dubai as a centre for tourism, culture, trade and opportunity. He saw the future of this city as bright and beautiful. Today, this passion for the future will be reflected in our icon for the future, a global platform for defining new opportunities for all of humanity.

Second reflection: It lies in one of the main ideas His Highness enunciates, that nothing is impossible and ambition has no limits. There is no greater challenge that the human mind, with all its potential, energy and determination, cannot overcome.

When building Burj Khalifa, Sheikh Mohammed requested it be the tallest building in the world. When building the Palm Island, His Highness requested it to be the largest man-made island in history. When we wanted to launch a new space mission, Sheikh Mohammed asked the team to reach Mars. Sheikh Mohammed promised the world that Expo 2020 Dubai would be the best in the history of international exhibitions, and once again His Highness has fulfilled his promise. This building resembles His Highness' belief that nothing is impossible.

The third reflection: Sheikh Mohammed believes in the power of ideas in creating the future, changing lives and driving human development. The Museum of the Future reflects the philosophy of His Highness, as it will be a factory for futuristic ideas.

Fourth reflection: This new civilized edifice will play a pivotal role in applying one of the main values established by His Highness during his 50 years of leadership. His Highness believes that the UAE is destined to be a model and play a positive role in this region. His Highness believes in our important role in reigniting the civilization of this region, which has been leading the world scientifically, cognitively and culturally for more than ten centuries.

The fifth reflection: This is the most beautiful building on earth.

It is beautiful because of its design, it is beautiful because of its message and it is beautiful because of its purpose. Sheikh Mohammed says that the beauty around us is reflected on us, and that the beauty inside us will be seen in our projects. That is why this Museum resembles the philosophy and vision of His Highness.

The sixth reflection: This Museum is a "living Museum", with constantly changing contents and exhibits. It will be a center of many live discussions, specialized forums and futuristic seminars. In this, it reflects Sheikh Mohammed's philosophy of life.

The seventh reflection: It is about the bet on technology. When the world was hesitatingly dealing with the Internet revolution, Sheikh Mohammed was confident about it, making Dubai its capital. The Museum will continuously search for the latest technologies the future holds for us. It will be the largest laboratory for the technologies of the cities of the future, the communities of the future and the governments of the future.

The façade of this Museum holds one of the inspirational quotes of H.H Sheikh Mohammed bin Rashid Al Maktoum: "We may not live for hundreds of years, but the products of our creativity can leave a legacy long after we are gone."

We want to be the best nation in the world. We want to build the best community, have the best economy and the quality of life. We want to build a big family. We want to build something beautiful in a mad crazy old world.

CONCLUSION

"If I have seen further, it is by standing on the shoulders of giants."
Sir Isaac Newton

I am deeply indebted to all 50 giants who have kindly agreed to be interviewed. In the same way that Sir Wilfred Thesiger's "Arabian Sands" gave us a snapshot of the region in 1946, I believe that this book serves as a unique insight into the shifting sands of time, 75 years later, just at the moment that the world has come to visit the UAE for Expo, marking the Golden Jubilee of the UAE.

I have learned many things, not just about the UAE, but lessons that can be applied personally and professionally and which have profoundly altered my own outlook. How does one conclude? What does the Emirates stand for? What is the secret of success? What are the lessons? You will be pleased to know that I won't repeat everything. However, I do think that a few themes stand out that I have summarized and grouped. Yes, there has been extraordinary, exponential growth, but more than that, I think the EMIRATES can stand for:

E: Exponential Vision & Execution
M: Mindset & Motivation
I: Investment & Innovation
R: Responsibility & Respect
A: Adaptability & Agility
T: Tolerance & Talent
E: Environment & Ecosystems
S: Safety & Stability

Exponential Vision & Execution

"We are like those who had climbed a mountain and reached the top. When we looked down, we still wanted to go higher to realise our goals. Despite all the achievements, we still have an ambition for more. That is my way of looking at things" - HH Sheikh Zayed.

"Vision" has of course been a common theme, but it is not just any old vacuous vision that appears on so many corporate websites. The vision of the UAE can truly be described as "Exponential Vision". A reporter once famously asked HH Sheikh Mohammed bin Rashid, Ruler of Dubai, how much of his vision he had completed. He responded saying 10%. A few years later, the same reporter, seeing the visible change, asked the same question, expecting the vision to be near complete. HH Sheikh Mohammed responded that he had only accomplished 5% of his vision. Despite the huge achievements, the goal posts had moved. As he is well-known for saying: "The race for excellence has no finish line." Another of his famous analogies is the following: "With each new day in Africa, a gazelle wakes up knowing he must outrun the fastest lion or perish. At the same time, a lion stirs and stretches, knowing he must outrun the fastest gazelle or starve. It is no different for the human race. Whether you consider yourself a gazelle or a lion, you simply have to run faster than others to survive."

This for me perfectly sums up the "Infinite Game" as articulated by Simon Sinek in his book of the same name, where he identifies, whether in business or in politics or in life itself, the players come and go, the rules are changeable, and there is no defined endpoint. There are no winners or losers in an infinite game, there is only ahead and behind. If one wants to understand the UAE, one has to understand that the guiding principle is that the nation is united by seeing a future in 50 years in which the UAE is racing ahead of everyone else across every metric. As the world's progress accelerates, so does the vision.

However, as Thomas Edison has been quoted on previous pages, "vision without execution is hallucination." As the UAE pavilion at Expo points out, not only was this "all just a dream" but this is a country of "Dreamers that Do". You need the vision, but you also need to execute on that vision.

Mindset & Motivation

"The evidence of our material development that you see all around you did not emerge from nothing. It is the result of hard work, perseverance and commitment" - HH Sheikh Zayed.

There is a work ethic and a growth mindset that underpins everything. HE Sara al Amiri, discussing how the UAE achieved the Mars Mission, said "for us, it was monumental shift in mindset, especially with regards to the appetite for risk. And this is what societally having a space programme does - it increases your appetite for risk because the bigger the programmes are, the chances of success are lower and therefore your appetite for getting into endeavours that are riskier becomes higher."

The UAE attracts people who want to make things happen. They can "chew the dynamism in the air," as Sir Maurice Flanagan describes it. As Mohammed Omran said, "We want people to come here and win!" This is the land of opportunity. There is an optimistic outlook, and a positive perspective that pervades.

Investment & Innovation

"We must not rely on oil alone as the main source of our national income. We have to diversify the sources of our revenue and construct economic projects that will ensure a free, stable and dignified life for the people" - HH Sheikh Zayed

This diversification and investment in infrastructure and innovation is key to the Emirates' success. As HH Sheikh Rashid's famously said, "My grandfather rode a camel, my father rode a camel, I drive a Mercedes, my son drives a Land Rover, his son will drive a Land Rover, but his son will ride a camel", pointing out that if Dubai didn't diversify from oil, it would all be over in a few generations.

Similarly, HH Sheikh Mohammed bin Zayed said, "In 50 years, when we might have the last barrel of oil, the question is: when it is shipped abroad, will we be sad? If we are investing today in the right sectors, I can tell you we will celebrate at that moment." At the launch of Shams 1 solar field in 2013, he said "The future, with its needs and challenges, calls upon us to embark on a perpetual quest for alternative sources of energy. This can only be done through the support of relevant scientific research." "Our reliance upon knowledge and scientific thinking to achieve total development is the only way to bring our nation ahead to the stage of qualitative, non-oil production, a lesson learnt from nations with little or no natural resources."

Hub 71 and Area 2071 are classic examples where the leadership is proactively creating platforms for government entities in particular to disrupt themselves, and be a conduit for investment and innovation and set the stage for the next 50 years.

On the wall of the Museum of the Future are inscribed the words of HH Sheikh Mohammed bin Rashid "The secret to the renewal of life, the evolution of civilizations and the development of humanity is simple: innovation." This is also etched into the foundations of the UAE.

Responsibility & Respect

"Our experiment in federation, in the first instance, arose from a desire to increase the ties that bind us, as well as from the conviction of everyone that they were a part of one family, and they must gather under one leadership.... This could not, however, have been achieved without deep devotion to the service of the country and its citizens, over and above any other consideration, and without there being an intimate unity of purpose between the leadership and the people. The ruler, any ruler, is only there to serve his people and secure for them prosperity and progress" - HH Sheikh Zayed.

There is an unquestionable mutual responsibility and respect between the leadership and the people, and it is summed up in the unity of the federation and the nation. The foundations of the federation created a framework of checks and balances that have ensured that each Emirate can thrive and, united, can be bigger than the sum of their parts.

There is a Bedouin trait that one is responsible for guests in one's territory, and one can see that in the relationship between Emirati and Expat. I would call it a form of "Tribal Democracy" where the dynamics of the tribe provide a glue that brings everyone together, and everyone has a say, where the "majlis mentality" allows for discussion and resolution.

Adaptability & Agility

"Future generations will be living in a world that is very different from that to which we are accustomed. It is essential that we prepare ourselves and our children for that new world... Situations change from time to time. A friend may become an enemy and an enemy a friend. Life is inconsistent and ever changing. So are health and weather. We must, therefore, be prepared for the unexpected changes coming our way" - HH Sheikh Zayed.

The global events that surround the Golden Jubilee have shown that these words have never been more true. However, the UAE has always been ready to adapt to change, and to do it quickly. As HE Abdullah bin Touq has said, the UAE has transitioned from "Seaport to Airport and then to Brainport." In more recent times, COVID has shown how fast the UAE can react. There is quick, decisive decision-making.

Tolerance & Talent

"To treat every person, no matter what his creed or race, as a special soul, is a mark of Islam.... Wealth is not money. Wealth lies in men. This is where true power lies, the power we value. This is what has convinced us to direct all our resources to build the individual, and to use the wealth which God has provided us in the service of the nation.... We are pleased to mention, with pride, that which our women have achieved in terms of strengthening the economic and social role that they play in society, in both the public and the private sectors. We re-affirm our commitment to provide all necessary support for our women, such that will ensure that their role in society can be further strengthened, and so that the scope of their participation in the comprehensive development of our country can be widened" - HH Sheikh Zayed.

As has been discussed, "tolerance" goes far beyond merely tolerating others; it is about embracing and celebrating diversity and attracting talent. The UAE is about open skies, open ports, open doors, open minds and open hearts. To have so many different nationalities in one big community is astonishing. Tolerance, in this case, should also not be mistaken for a freedom to do whatever you like; there are clear boundaries, and one has to balance this tolerance with the responsibility and respect of all the cultures which comprise this cosmopolitan community.

"Talent" is not just about attracting international talent; it is also about nurturing local talent. There is "extreme empowerment of youth" where the best are promoted regardless of age. There are "Secret Shopper" programmes in government, where outstanding individuals are identified and fast-tracked. Education is key. Addressing the youth of the UAE, HH Sheikh Mohammed bin Zayed once said "You are the real wealth, not the 3 million barrels of oil. You are the future of this nation's security and safety net. We are in a good condition now but we want to establish the vision for 50 years ahead."

Environment & Ecosystem

"We cherish our environment because it is an integral part of our country, our history and our heritage. On land and in the sea, our forefathers lived and survived in this environment. They were able to do so only because they recognised the need to conserve it, to take from it only what they needed to live, and to preserve it for succeeding generations" - HH Sheikh Zayed

There is a focus on environment and ecosystem in all their manifestations: natural, living and business. The Bedouin used to recycle everything and knew the importance of their natural surroundings. Nowadays, the emphasis is on the happiness of citizens and residents. There is a Minister of Happiness and Wellbeing, and also a Minister of Climate Change & Environment.

Safety & Stability

"We can be proud of what we enjoy in terms of stability, peace and an open society.... My dear citizens, the respect that the UAE enjoys in the international arena is the result of our principled foreign policy. This policy is based upon adherence to the Charter of the United Nations and to international conventions, upon the principles of non-interference in the internal affairs of others, upon respect for territorial integrity and the sovereignty of nations, upon a belief in solving conflict through peaceful means, and on support for the principles of right and justice. Foreign aid and assistance is one of the basic pillars of our foreign policy. For we believe that there is no true benefit for us from the wealth that we have unless it does not also reach those in need, wherever they may be, and regardless of their nationality or beliefs. That is why we have ensured that our brothers and our friends have shared in our wealth" - HH Sheikh Zayed.

At the individual level, this is about being able to walk the street at night and leave your home unlocked in a way that is unthinkable anywhere else in the world. At a national level, it's about surviving in a chaotic region, indeed in a chaotic world. As HH Sheikh Mohammed bin Zayed has said, "The process of building man means, in the final analysis, building the nation and instilling the values of free, promising, stable and secure life."

***

I believe that these "8 Pillars of Wisdom" dovetail with the 10 "Principles of the UAE", and underpin everything that the UAE stands for and strives to be. They are the golden threads that weave together the 50 stories told here that celebrate the Golden Jubilee of the country, and are visible in the fabric of the nation, from generation to generation, and bode well for the Next 50 and beyond.

UNITED ARAB EMIRATES

Principles of the 50

The UAE's 10 Principles for the Next 50 Years

As the United Arab Emirates (UAE) approaches its Golden Jubilee, the country is entering a new phase in its history, a new era of its development path, and a new cycle of economic, political and social growth. This document summarises the new guidance for the UAE in its upcoming historical phase as directed by His Highness Sheikh Khalifa bin Zayed Al Nahyan, President of the UAE, and envisioned by His Highness Sheikh Mohammed bin Rashid Al Maktoum, Vice President and Prime Minister of the UAE and Ruler of Dubai, and His Highness Sheikh Mohamed bin Zayed Al Nahyan, Crown Prince of Abu Dhabi and Deputy Supreme Commander of the UAE Armed Forces.

This document sets forth 10 principles for the UAE, which all government agencies, including the legislative system, the police and security institutions as well as the scientific entities, must adhere to and use as guidelines for all their decisions, and strive to implement through their frameworks and strategies. These principles are as follows:

The First Principle

The major priority shall remain the strengthening of the union, its institutions, legislations, capacities and budgets. The urban, developmental and economic development of all parts of the country is the fastest and most effective way to consolidate the union of the UAE.

The Second Principle

To completely focus, over the upcoming period, on building the best and most dynamic economy in the world. The economic development of the country is the supreme national interest, and all state institutions, of all sectors and across different federal and local levels, shall bear collectively the responsibility of building the best global economic environment and maintaining the gains achieved over the past 50 years.

The Third Principle

The UAE's foreign policy is a tool that aims to serve the higher national goals, the most important of which is the UAE's economic interests. The goal of our political approach is to serve the economy. And the goal of the economy is to provide the best quality of life for the people of the UAE.

The Fourth Principle

The main future driver for growth is human capital. Developing the educational system, attracting talents, retaining specialists and continuously building skills are what shall keep the UAE at the top.

UNITED ARAB EMIRATES

The Fifth Principle

Good-neighbourliness is the basis of stability. The geographical, social and cultural vicinity of the country is the first line of defence for its security, safety and its future development. Developing stable and positive political, economic and social relations with this vicinity is one of the most important priorities of the country's foreign policy.

The Sixth Principle

Cementing the reputation of the UAE globally as one nation is a national mission for all institutions. The UAE is one economic destination, one tourist destination, one industrial destination, one investment destination, and one cultural destination. Our national institutions must combine their efforts, and together benefit from the capabilities, and work to build global enterprises and partnerships across the world.

The Seventh Principle

The digital, technical and scientific excellence of the UAE will define its new development and economic frontiers, and the solidification of its position as a capital for talent, companies and investments in these sectors will make it the capital of the future.

The Eighth Principle

The value system in the UAE shall remain based on openness and tolerance, the preservation of rights, the consolidation of the rule of law, the preservation of human dignity, the respect of cultures, the strengthening of human fraternity, and the respect of national identity. The country will remain supportive, through its foreign policy, of all initiatives, pledges and international organizations that promote peace, openness and human fraternity.

The Ninth Principle

The UAE's foreign humanitarian aid is an essential part of its own vision and moral duty towards less fortunate nations. Our foreign humanitarian aid is not tied to religion, race, colour or culture. Political disagreement with any country should not stop us from providing swift relief for those in need.

The Tenth Principle

Calling for peace, harmony, negotiations and dialogue to resolve all political disputes is the basis of the UAE's foreign policy, and striving with regional partners and global friends to establish regional and global peace and stability is a fundamental driver of our foreign policy.

ABOUT THE AUTHOR

Tom Hudson went to school at Eton College, studied History at the University of Bristol before converting to law and completing his studies at the Oxford Institute of Legal Practice.

Tom trained and qualified as a lawyer with Linklaters, moving to the UAE when they opened an office in 2006. He worked on a number of IPOs, including the IPO of DP World where he ultimately went in-house. In 2016, he left to set up Kestrel, a boutique advisory firm in the DIFC, that advises the world's top companies on their Middle East expansion. In the last 5 years he has worked with more than 50 such companies.

Made in United States
North Haven, CT
28 October 2024

59501533R00193